Marriages & Deaths

from

The

Caucasian

Shreveport
Louisiana

1903–1913

Harry F. Dill

HERITAGE BOOKS
2012

HERITAGE BOOKS
AN IMPRINT OF HERITAGE BOOKS, INC.

Books, CDs, and more—Worldwide

For our listing of thousands of titles see our website
at
www.HeritageBooks.com

Published 2012 by
HERITAGE BOOKS, INC.
Publishing Division
100 Railroad Ave. #104
Westminster, Maryland 21157

Copyright © 2001 Harry F. Dill

Other Heritage Books by the author:

African American Inhabitants of Rapides Parish, Louisiana: 15 June–4 September 1870

Appointments of Postmasters in Louisiana, 12 January 1827–28 December 1892

Louisiana Postmistress and Postmaster Appointments 20 June 1866–17 November 1931

Marriages and Deaths from The Caucasian, *Shreveport, Louisiana, 1903–1913*

Some Slaveholders and Their Slaves, Union Parish, Louisiana, 1839–1865
Harry F. Dill and William Simpson

The Underground Railroad and the Picayune *Connection*

All rights reserved. No part of this book may be reproduced or transmitted in any form or by any means, electronic or mechanical, including photocopying, recording or by any information storage and retrieval system without written permission from the author, except for the inclusion of brief quotations in a review.

International Standard Book Numbers
Paperbound: 978-0-7884-1777-1
Clothbound: 978-0-7884-9120-7

TABLE OF CONTENTS

Preface v
Issues of Jan 1, 1903-June 28, 1903 1
Issues of June 30, 1903-Dec. 31, 1903 11
Issues of Jan. 1, 1904-Dec. 31, 1904 13
Issues of Jan. 1, 1905-June 27, 1905 15
Issues of June 28, 1905-Jan. 2, 1907 27
Issues of Jan. 6, 1907-Dec. 29, 1907 29
Issues of Jan. 1, 1908-Dec. 31, 1908 57
Issues of Jan. 3, 1909-Dec. 28, 1909 59
Issues of Jan. 9, 1910-Oct. 22, 1910 81
Issues of Nov. 14, 1910-Dec. 25, 1910 99
Issues of Jan. 8, 1911-Dec. 31, 1911 101
Issues of Jan. 12, 1912-July 21, 1912 123
Issues of Sept. 1, 1912-Nov. 28, 1912 135
Issues of Dec. 1, 1912-Dec. 29, 1912 137
Issues of Jan. 4, 1913-Dec. 31, 1913 141
Index 163

Preface

Announcements of marriages and deaths in this book were extracted from microfilm of The Caucasian, a tri-weekly newspaper published at Shreveport, Louisiana, from January 1, 1903, to December 31, 1913. The microfilm is on file at Louisiana State University, Alexandria, Louisiana.

These references could be of value to both white and African American genealogists seeking ancestors who lived in Caddo Parish from 1903 to 1913.

The newspaper's stories of marriages and deaths do not identify persons as either white, colored, or black, but it seems likely, because of segregation, that the subjects of these stories were white. The Board of Health's listings of marriages and deaths, however, usually indicate race as either white, colored, or black. (Reports of marriages from July 6, 1913 to December 31, 1913, do not specify any race.)

Shreveport, Louisiana, lies in Caddo Parish, in the extreme northwestern portion of the state. Caddo Parish takes its name from the Caddo Indians who, in 1835, under a treaty with the United States, sold their territory for the sum of $80,000. After the sale, the Caddo Indians moved to Oklahoma.

Incorporated in 1839, Shreveport was named after Henry Miller Shreve, a steamboat builder and inventor. Shreve was engaged by the United States government to open the Red River to navigation and, in 1833, he began clearing the river channel of a massive jam of logs, called "the great raft." Using four steamboats, two of which were of the battering-ram type (his own invention), and 159 men, he removed debris from bank to bank for a distance of 200 miles. The project was not completed until 1836.

Manufacturing, oil- and gas-exploration, and agriculture are the primary industries of Caddo Parish.

Issues of Jan. 1, 1903-
June 28, 1903

Issue of Jan. 1, 1903:

Board of Health Statistics ending Dec. 31, 1902:

MARRIAGES

<u>White</u>: Nathan T Penick and Anne Stephenson; John A Capitan and A D Idens; Charles D Avinger and Mrs. Laura E Underwood; Drew T Ludlom and Vivian E Gamblin; W C Colbert and Zazli Kemper; J B Turner and Mary L Scriber; H Finch and Vashti Neal; G V Evans and E V Oden; E G Beard and Annie Howe.

<u>Colored</u>: Henry Stephens and Annie Hill; Johnnie Rafe and Barbara Scott; Pierce Berry and Lucy Jane York; Evanston Alford and Alice Johnson; Henry Bimmery and Fannie Howell; James Crowell and Nellie Watson.

DEATHS

<u>White</u>: C Bozeman, 12; John J Patton Jr, 18; Henry Wehke, 28; Kate Lysle, 22; G H Houlihan, 30.

Issue of Jan. 4, 1903:

Board of Health Statistics ending Jan. 3, 1903:

MARRIAGES

<u>White</u>: Gordon Mallory and Elenora Perkins; A W Walter and Mrs. Clarra Harris.

<u>Colored</u>: William Vortsey and Jospehine Jones; T Caldwell and Ella Casey; Phillip Marshall and Evie Oden; A Cooper and Caroline Henderson.

DEATHS

Colored: Mary Foster, 24; Kate Gaskins, 80; Fannie Starks, 54; Charles Early, 35; Babe Blackman, 23; Eddra Fullilove, 4.

Issue of Jan. 11, 1903:

Board of Health Statistics ending Jan. 10, 1903:

MARRIAGES

White: E Andrieu and Ida Voight; Joe Adde and Hazel Coulter.
Colored: J Mitchell and Annie Yerger; Joe Collins and Mattie Johnson; H J Lecals and Bettie Parsons; H Lemell and Perl Couston.

DEATHS

White: Dr. J W Kendall, 72; Mrs. J Longsdon, 34; Pat Carey, 38; Flora Brily, 24; J Cooney, 51.
Colored: J L Duncan, 1; Robert Newton, 1; A Hamilton, 70; Harriett Bailey, 75; Sal Hawkins, 20.

Issue of Jan. 14, 1903:

Died in this city January 11, 1903, Willis Rosson Carr, aged 22 years and 19 days.

Issue of Jan. 15, 1903:

Died, date not shown, Josephine LeCalle, 70 (colored)

Issue of Jan. 18, 1903:

Married January 14, C R Jowell and Alma McDonald, by Rev. C L Jones.
Died January 14, Mrs. Julia White Robards.

Died January 16, Adeline, Daughter of C G and Josie Leonard Conway, aged 13 months.

Issue of Jan. 25, 1903:

Married on January 21, W H Bolin and Addie M Fetzer, by Rev. Claude A Jones.
Married January 20, R H Hayes and Camille Giffen, by Rev. J H Spearing, at home of bride's sister, Mrs. J P Flournoy.

Issue of Jan. 29, 1903:

Board of Health Statistics ending Jan. 28, 1903

MARRIAGES

White: H H Thoms and Mrs. R A Browning; R H Hays and Cornelia Griffin; W G Howell and Mrs. E S Alexander; L R Wilson and Mrs. M A Watkins; William H Cohen and Therressa Dabinski.
Colored: W Renfro and Henrietta Johnson; George Adams and Mahala Winston; George Reed and Urma Zeno; Alex White and Eliza Jones.

DEATHS

White: Francis Allioso, 6; Mrs. E D Barnes, 28; Mrs. M P Miller, 29; Mrs. S A Rutherford, 80; Mrs. Otto Paul, 22; S P Graza, 60.
Colored: Harriett Anderson, 70; John Jackson, 23; Sarah Mason, 73; Robert Boores, no age shown; P Moseley, 50.

Issue of Feb. 1, 1903:

Board of Health Statistics ending Jan. 31, 1903

MARRIAGES

White: Paul M Rachal and Gertrude Berlin.
Colored: J Abraham and Hattie Brown; Felix McLaurin and Ivena Robinson; Charles Fisher and Carrie Butler; Preston Hyams and Sarah Johnson.

DEATHS

White: Charles Smith, 36; Jim Patterson, 45; E N Woods, 22; Tracy Rushing, 26; Mrs. S J Mayborn, 68.
Colored: Virginia Jones, 30; Julius Sloane, 8 months; Mrs. A Lewis, 30; Mrs. S Wilson, 48; J F Allen, 36.

Married January 29, Felix McWillie Williams and T Olive Foster, at First Presbyterian Church. A reception was held following the ceremony at Carraghmuir, home of the bride's mother.

Married Thursday afternoon F W Ballauf and L Edith Davis by Rev. Father Scharl. R Ballauf, the groom's father, and his daughter, Mamie Ballauf, of Jefferson, Tex., were among attendants.

Issue of Feb. 8, 1903:

Married February 4, Jefferson C Wilson and Twéattie Busby, daughter of Mr. and Mrs. J L Busby.

Issue of Feb. 15, 1903:

Married February 11, Albert H Van Hook and Mildred Sewall, daughter of Captain John Sewall.

Issue of Feb. 22, 1903:

Board of Health Statistics ending Feb. 21, 1903

MARRIAGES

White: Ed McClary and Mrs. C Fritts; A Smith and Gertrude Varble; W A Stephens and Lulla O McCoy; A H Arnold and Maru L Arnold; D A Minor and Nettie Wheeler.

Colored: James Modkin and Rhoda Brown; J O Betty and Laura V Green; George English and Magnolia Miller; John Smith and Sally Jackson.

DEATHS

White: H Morgan, 32; John Z Archibald, 63; Aron Harris, 68; J G Whiter, 37.

Colored: Child of Lula Jones, 4; Laura Okeith, 45; Lane Linch, 50; Hanna Meredith, 2; Josephine Willis, 38; Jack Sloan, 68; Katey Smith, 15.

Issue of Mar. 22, 1903:

Board of Health Statistics ending Mar. 21, 1903

MARRIAGES

White: A H Shoyd and Amelia Ray; R F Thorne and Julia Walls; F C Ross and Lillian G Pugh.

Colored: J Edwards and Papia F Olds.

DEATHS

White: Gladys Graham, 7; T J Bullok, 55; Charles Dockman, 27; Mrs. Sam Weaver, no age shown; Black R Ross, 24; Harry Ford, 35.

Colored: Eliza Emerson, 19; Carrie Jones, 27; Joe Hawkins, 28.

Issue of Mar. 29, 1903:

Board of Health Statistics ending Mar. 28, 1903

MARRIAGES

White: J R Ward and Mrs. B T Tanner; A Pace and Fannie Carnahan; T L Jones and M Fields; T H Yates and Mattie Woodley; T H Tucker and E Perroncel; T M Yarbrough and Ida Wilson.

Colored: G Paxton and Lucile Bates; C H Wright and Josephine Robinson; L Hughes and Virginia Jones; E Buscom and Penny Lias.

DEATHS

White: John Mahan, 4 months; Mrs. T H Hamilton, 82; M Newman, 66; Mrs. I Hancock, 25; T A Simpson, 38; Mrs. M E Norton, 30; T C Howard, 54.

Colored: Eva Dunbram, 20; Alvie Pennywell, 2; Adline Newton, 75; R Hayden, 32; S Hager, 28; Golden Murphy, 21; W Heart, 7 months; Eliza S Creet, 27; Hy Maples, 30; Rev. T T Mupington, 45.

Issue of Apr. 12, 1903:

Board of Health Statistics ending Apr. 11, 1903

MARRIAGES

White: Osea Watts and Elra Knott; F Hulseman and Bessie Durrum; S B Crawford and Eliza R Crow.

Colored: G Wickers and Sarah Metcalf; F Simms and Lucinda Spillman; A Battle and Lula Bethley; Joe Thomas and Theado Bentfield.

DEATHS

White: Mrs. J W Fray, 20; Nellie Mahon, 4 months; Mrs. M F Manley, 82; Arthur Wildman, 22; Henry Frank, 44.

Colored: A Beasley, 30; F Reese, 2 months; W Williams, 46; Mrs. A Bates, 42; Hattie Jacob, 23; Emma Johnson, 24; Annie Bedford, 23; Dick Fletcher, 23.

Issue of Apr. 23, 1903:

Board of Health Statistics ending Apr. 22, 1903

MARRIAGES

White: J R Blanton and Annie L Kelly; David F Taber and Blanch H Florsheim; R L Curtis and Mrs. C Howard.
Colored: Jeff Horn and Rosanna Hudson; Will Rillar and Mary J Whit.

DEATHS

White: C A Grimes, 28; Effie May Nixon, 10; R L Iler, 51; D H Billiu, 64; J S Finnegan, 24; E H Wilford, 40.
Colored: Julia Hansford, 31; Emma L Bridgman, 14; John Collins, 30; Mezekiah Bannett, 28.

Died April 19, Mrs. Estelle Rumply Sheppard, wife of C F Sheppard, aged 30 years, burial at Greenwood Cemetery.

Issue of Apr. 26, 1903:

Board of Health Statistics ending Apr. 25, 1903

MARRIAGES

White: F O Hudson and Leonard Hudson; J P Blythe and Josephine Bennett; F J Looney and Adeline Leonard; A G Flick and Hattie Jones; C L Hardwick and Carrie W Smith; N T Pickard and Mamie L Pate; Richard Ilke and Mrs. G Keith; R W Dundas and Luin Robert.
Colored: J H Olins and Cora Martin; Ed Burnes and Allie Anderson; E B James and Nettie Brown; A Barret and Mary F Anderson; J R Patterson and Edith Brown; F Miles and Clara Johnson.

DEATHS

White: John Baske, 35; W W Tarleton, 76; T F Hoss, 76; E M Hagen, 76; W H Winfield, 54; Ed Dodd, 39.
Colored: Will Harvey, 2; Mack Fisher, 33; Hattie Jackson, 22; Ema Gray, 38; Jerry Smith, 26.

Issue of May 3, 1903:

Board of Health Statistics ending May 2, 1903

MARRIAGES
White: Robert L Ross and A W Wright; Paul Malekowske and Laura McCabe.
Colored: A Evan and Sauie Brown; A W Gilbert and Ceclia B Clark; George Henderson and Della Parker; A Watson and Willie Harris.

DEATHS
White: L L Evans, 45.
Colored: King Johnson, 24; Dora Collins, 26; Francis Davis, 21; Mattie Stewart, 28; Uncle Jack Cash, 75.

Issue of May 10, 1903:

Board of Health Statistics ending May 9, 1903

MARRIAGES
Colored: A Watson and Willon Harris; Henry Anderson and Eliza York.

DEATHS
White: J B Gilliland, 25; Tom Kane, 18; Ingersoll Furman, 19; Allie M Black, 5 months; Harrel Bell, 4 months; Albert Heasy, 23; S G Williams, 21; Miss E Hidge, 17.
Colored: James Terrell, 21; Robert Thomas, 2 weeks; Mary B Petras, 32; Richard Anderson, 29; A M Turner, 21; Luda

Watson, 6; Elizabeth Miller, 56; J W Miles, 40; Albert LaMothe, 7 days; Sallie Rufus, 31; Lee Ivy, 1; T Rhodes, 39; Antennette Mitchell, 22.

Issue of May 20, 1903:

Married May 17, May Wiley to R M Gillespie in Parkview Baptist Church by Rev. A L Johnson.
Died May 17, Henry Watson Wharton (no age shown), eldest son of Henry S Wharton. His mother was Annie E Watson. A brother, Eugene S Wharton, resides in El Paso, Tex.
Died May 16, in this city, Mrs. Annie R Hutton, 52. She was the wife of T H Hutton, of Company A, Crescent Heavy Artillery, who was engaged during the war in the Naval Service of the South.

Issue of June 11, 1903:

Board of Health Statistics ending June 10, 1903

MARRIAGES
White: J E Doty and Zidia Baird.
Colored: D C Cathrom and Francis Stephens.

DEATHS
White: Bell E Smith, 38; Emmett M Tyman, 8 months; Mrs. Lyle Jones, 17.
Colored: L H Richardson, 40; Sam Jackson, 9 months; Rosetta Wilson, 5 months; Emma Simon, 40; Robert Johnson, 4; John Keziah, 35; Ben Sterling, 61; George Shannon, 23.

Issue of June 14, 1903:

Board of Health Statistics ending June 13, 1903

MARRIAGES

White: R W Eton and Ray Kelso; C H Minge Jr and Theo Vance; C W Osborn and Hattie Raney; J L Heidingsfield and Carrie Lee Kahn.
Colored: A L Blor and Cilla Tatun; Bob Rogers and Ettie Knox.

DEATHS

White: Mrs. E Wolff, 72; H L Willoughby, 30; Mrs. M C Jones, 17.
Colored: E Whitehead, 10 months; Viola Jackson, 23; Amanda Harris, 44; Jane Johnson, 41; Rachel Kirkland, 23.

Issue of June 28, 1903:

Board of Health Statistics ending June 27, 1903

MARRIAGES

White: J T White and Mrs. Della Storrett; D N Valentine and D Lambeth; K C Storey and Blanche Cook; T S Hutchinson and Nina Seay; S J Castle and Jennie Linxwiler; S H Reid and Martha A Mize; J B Jovett and J Doughty; J L Ashborn and Mary E Sober.
Colored: J M Pleisance and N C Clayton; L Holt and Emma L Cain.

DEATHS

White: J W Ford, 43; J M Martin, 58.
Colored: Cordell Dickson, 17; Ellen Gordorf, 90; F Huchens 1; Tim Johnson, 26.

Issues of June 30, 1903-
Dec. 31, 1903

All issues are missing.

Issues of Jan. 1, 1904 -
Dec. 31, 1904

All issues are missing.

Issues of Jan. 1, 1905-
June 27, 1905

Issue of Jan. 1, 1905:

Married December 31, 1904, John Bennett and Helene Wadley, by Rev. Boggs, at Methodist Church. The bride is the daughter of Mrs. W G Wadley.

Issue of Jan. 15, 1905:

Board of Health Statistics ending Jan. 14, 1905

MARRIAGES

<u>White</u>: C T Bailey and Bula V Wever; S C Fullilove and Miss A G Stringfellow; L E Tigner and Leslie Leary.
<u>Colored</u>: Banks McKinney and Annie Jackson; Henry Johnson and Ella Markham; Ben Bradford and Winnie Nelson; F J Lewis and Octavia Wood.

DEATHS

<u>White</u>: J E McAdams (no age shown), B J Costrove, 63.
<u>Colored</u>: Mary Belle Moore, 6 months; Adam Hall, 65; Mike Thomas, 38; Willis Edly, 65; Abe Shelton, 64.

Issue of Jan. 22, 1905:

Married January 18, Mary Etta Metcalf and A O Hendrick by Rev. Charles Jones. The bride is the daughter of V W Metcalf. The groom's father was the late John Hendrick.

Issue of Jan. 29, 1905:

Board of Health Statistics ending Jan. 28, 1905

MARRIAGES

White: Leo Gunning and Miss M E Johnson; Thomas Bradford and M I Bledsal; George E Elens and Myrtle Whitman.

Colored: Eddie White and Mattie Johnson; E A Harding and Ethel Hall; Bob Williams and Annie Boss.

DEATHS

White: Selnine Winter, 7; John Levy, 50; Russell L Smothers, 5 months.

Colored: Arthur Franklin, 22; Mitchell Thomas, 55; Walter Hunt, 13; Elizzie Singler, 31; Harry Robinson, 21; Jefferson Tucker, 66; Allen Lewis, 20; Amanda Jelks, 56; Mandy Washington, 70; Ed Gibson, 50; Tom Smith, 36.

Issue of Feb. 12, 1905:

Board of Health Statistics ending Feb. 11, 1905

MARRIAGES

White: J W Jeters and J E Herndon; Ben A Phelps and J E Cohen; Vincent Gage and Ellen Touby.

Colored: Henry Murrell and Jessie Moss; Will Leonard and P L Waller; Aaron White and Katie Warner.

DEATHS

White: J D Mayer, 68; Mrs. J E Gillian, 73; William Dolan, 50; August Abrahamson, 60; Bertha Garculis, 37; C Dreyfus (no age shown).

Colored: Emma Riley, 30; Jo Anna Wesley, 62; Peter Johnson, 58; Elizabeth Kellan, 57; Robert Mitchell, 1; Hannah Smith, 42; Joseph Hopkins, 1; Amanda Jackson, 30.

Died February 13, J M Farmer. Burial was in Spring Ridge.

Issue of Feb. 16, 1905:

Married on February 15, J B Stoddard and Mattie May Fink, by Father Bertels.

Issue of Feb. 19, 1905:

Died February 18, Mary A Franey, 70, at the home of her son, H Hunsicker. She resided in St. Louis, Mo., and was here on a visit to her son.

Issue of Feb. 21, 1905:

Died February 19, John Batsch, 57, burial in old cemetery. He was a native of Hanover, Germany.

Issue of Feb. 26, 1905:

Board of Health Statistics ending Feb. 25, 1905

MARRIAGES
White: R L Stevens and Blanche Bookout.

DEATHS
White: T C Johnson, 82; R B Patterson, 78; Harry Hunter, 40; John Basch, 57; Ed Callahan, 48; Patrick Deeley, 48.
Colored: Isiah Thomas, 46; Floriada Oats, 51; Mittie Haynes, 28; Talbert Wells, 42.

Issue of Mar. 5, 1905:

Board of Health Statistics ending Mar. 4, 1905

MARRIAGES
White: T E Schermerhorn and Eleanor Frances Lambert;

Peter McGillis and Mary Fitzpatrick; John R Cain and L L Scriber; John R Hebert and Freadia Meltson; Willie Campbell and Lillian Miller; A S Coolidge and Mrs. M E Godfrey.
Colored: Joe Lewis and Lizzie Jones; Andrew Minor and Carrie Chew; Thomas Forsythe and Mittie Harris; Harvey Williams and Lillie Smith.

DEATHS

White: C E Hoover, 38; John Jackson, 82; A L Seastead, 27.
Colored: Annie Stein, 25; Walthie Allen, 7 months; Hester Hampton, 56; Joseph LeWay, 72; Alfred T Robertson, 5 months; Sarah Smith, 42; Annie B Green, 1; Marguerete West, 2; William Jones, 25; Henry Johnson, 71.

Issue of Mar. 16, 1905:

Married March 15, Daniel Herndon and Katherine McAfee, at the home of the bride's mother, Mrs. J M McAfee, by Rev. Doak of Methodist Church.
Died on March 15, Captain Noah Scovell, 75 years, near Sybens, in Lawrence County, Ohio. A brother, Captain M L Scovell, and sisters, Mrs. E McClure, of Shreveport, and Mrs. Rachel Dillon, of Ohio, are nearest relatives, with Captain Dillon of Shreveport, his nephew. He was a steamboatman and saw active service with the Confederacy with his steamboat.

Issue of Mar. 19, 1905:

Board of Health Statistics ending Mar. 18, 1905

MARRIAGES

White: C H Wiley and Pattie Boykin; R C Stockheard and Clara M Pierce; R S Servere and Ora Emery; D R Herndon

and Katie McAfee; Leon B Loeb and Flora Loeb; C C Crooks and Alice Pruitt; S Hockberger and Gussie Abrams.
Colored: Albert Jones and Levina Hamas; James Edwards and Ella Evans; Frank Allen and Mamie Davis; Hylander Peters and Martha Brooks.

DEATHS
White: W H Burnham, 22 days; Marie A Lewis, 22; S C Selig, 28; A H Mays, 62.
Colored: Bertha Morris, 20; Leonard Taylor, 29; Marceline Lewis, 16; Jake Howard, 46; Ollie May Roberson, 13; Buck Taylor, 49, George Brown, 38.

Issue of Mar. 26, 1905:

Board of Health Statistics ending Mar. 25, 1905

MARRIAGES
White: S Piraro and Dannice Cancetta.

DEATHS
White: R I Davis, 47; Gladis Courtney, 5; Mrs. M J Anderson, 56.
Colored: Ida Woods, 41; Ann Brooks, 85; Mary Boykin, 29; Lewis Flick, 29; Eliza Davis, 25; Jim Wells, 35.

Issue of Apr. 2, 1905:

Board of Health Statistics ending Apr. 1, 1905

MARRIAGES
White: L D McGown and A V Locke; R F Pruitt and Annie Ferguson; Oren Reeves and Alma Andrews; Willie Roach and Mable Cafee; L G Walker and Mary C Waxwell; W P Kinkley and Katie Bell Thompson; Charley H Brown and

Daisy O Washington.

DEATHS

<u>White</u>: Mrs. Lilly Alston, 24; Dennis Oats, 72; Larry Richardson, 3; Mrs. E A Wade, 60; James McGrady, 72; James Wright, 24.
<u>Colored</u>: Henry Sherman, 24; John Nichols, 27; Tom Randolph, 50; Silas Gibson, 20; Alfred Patten, 21.

<u>Issue of Apr. 4, 1905</u>:

Died April 3, John Corbett, 84. A native of Canada, he was a resident of Shreveport since the close of the war. He served from the onset of the war in the Seventh Missouri Cavalry. Burial was in Confederate Veterans Rest Cemetery.

<u>Issue of Apr. 9, 1905</u>:

Board of Health Statistics ending Apr. 8, 1905

MARRIAGES

<u>White</u>: Sam Golberg and Fannie Bryant.
<u>Colored</u>: Hampton King and Pearl Stewart.

DEATHS

<u>White</u>: John Corbett, 84; William Avery, 47; C Livengood, 36; Sallie Noyd, 34; Klay Gray, 37.

<u>Issue of Apr. 23, 1905</u>:

Board of Health Statistics ending Apr. 22, 1905

MARRIAGES

<u>White</u>: J E Houston and Myrtle May Wallis.
<u>Colored</u>: John Auchor and Martha Payne; David Ross and

Ella Elias; Jim Silot and Elmira Lambert; Nathaniel McCoy and Rena Young; George Frazier and Pearl Goss.

DEATHS
White: Mrs. Jane Tarkington, 58; J G Giles, 51; Nora Hurt, 37; Wesley Jefferson, 31; Josephine Meix, 40; Virginia Johnson, 21; Amanda George, 31; Laurence Brown, 24; Katy Thomas, 53.

Issue of Apr. 30, 1905:

Board of Health Statistics ending Apr. 29, 1905

MARRIAGES
White: Orlando Gooch and Bridgett M White; H N Rizer and L L Allen; J A Winchester and Ada A Youst; A G Davis and Maud E Bryant; A E Meredith and Adella Godfrey; H C Woodruff and Mary Leopard.
Colored: Root Pugh and Sallie Henderson; Joe Wilson and Emma L Johnson; Jim C Davis and M Johnson; Isaac Dunk and Janie Flynn.

DEATHS
Colored: Charley Thomas, 53; Alice Young, 33; Henry Abel, 20; Joana W Howard, 2 months; P Tell, 23; Sam Johnson, 23; George Kemp, 40; Jo Butler, 21; Howard Humear, 27.

Issue of May 7, 1905:

Board of Health Statistics ending May 6, 1905

MARRIAGES
White: J A Miller and Hallie Williams.
Colored: Thomas Walls and Janie Thomas.

DEATHS

White: Mrs. Hattie C Frisbie, 29; Dasha Racale, 23; J W Cloud, 29; J C Dial, 45.

Colored: Joana Hawkins, 11; Willie Nelson, 20; Mattie Johnson, 31; Sarah Wright, 75; Miles Samuels, 75; W T Gibson, 1.

Issue of May 14, 1905:

Board of Health Statistics ending May 13, 1905

MARRIAGES

White: O J Gutting and Lucy Luchlia; W F Britt and Ida Wappler; G Deneke and Laura Smith; Dr. A S Wither and Mary Ellen Camp.

Colored: M J Bosley and Posey Jones; Noah Morris and Willie Henderson; James Anderson and Anna Brock; Henry Thomas and Rosa Lee Daughtrey.

DEATHS

White: William Lafitte, 19; John Collier, 53.

Colored: Edith Reice, 4 months; A Williams, 15; George Taylor, 19; Will Williams, 20; John Simpson, 46.

Issue of May 21, 1905:

Board of Health Statistics ending May 20, 1905

MARRIAGES

White: Tom T Guy and Susie H Jackson.

Colored: Phillip Smith and Fannie Harton.

DEATHS

White: Mrs. S M Rudy, 20; Mrs. Mary Feldhaus, 60.

Colored: W E Rowe, 28; Leather Brown, 1.

Issue of May 27, 1905:

Board of Health Statistics ending May 26, 1905

MARRIAGES
White: Hugh Goldsberry and Minta Houston.
Colored: John Roberson and Rosa Pouncy; Sam Punch and Pearly George.

DEATHS
White: Allie McAnallan, 3 months; Mrs. M A Collins, 44; L Sullivan, 50.
Colored: Millie Williams, 62; James Roope, 28; James Walker Sr, 54; Henry Anderson, 31; Mary Irvine, 65; Notts Losson, 4 months; Janie S Russell, 26; Monroe Williams, 22; Sam Mims, 41; Joe Maloney, 30.

Issue of June 4, 1905:

Board of Health Statistics ending June 3, 1905

DEATHS
White: D C Wallace, 56; James Hoover, 9 months; Mrs. Dora Notario, 70; Mrs. Kate E Snell, 27; Aline Gaston, 7 months; Lorita Waits, 9 months; Mrs. J A Northern, 55; Cary Hogg, 15; W F Lowry, 65.
Colored: Ethel Smiith, 23; Joe Ela Beaty, 19; Amy Jefferson, 25; Emaline Predo, 57; Theodora Laswah, 7; Birtha Gilmore, 1 month; George Howard, 33; Emaline Durr, 19; Floyd Holmes, 11 months.

Issue of June 18, 1905:

Board of Health Statistics ending June 17, 1905

MARRIAGES

<u>White</u>: J W Flournoy and Lucile C McAfee.

<u>Colored</u>: Sam Ford and Sallie May; Sam B Hayes and Corine Bradford; Louis Ely and Lottie Carpenter; Lewis Starks and Hattie Johnson; Clab Coats and Addie Jones.

DEATHS

<u>White</u>: Z T Dwyer, 7 months; A L Curry, 4; Adalade Yesbeck, 5 months; J S Moore (no age shown); Oscar Forsman, 44; Jim Cates, 42.

<u>Colored</u>: Stephen Marks, 66; Carrie Harris, 39; Albert Fredrick, 3 months; Hattie Gibson, 37; John Macen, 45; James Pickett, 33; Frank Williams, 55; Samuel Jones, 63; Nathanel Rogers, 32; Lewis Walker, 47; Joe Amos, 17.

<u>Issue of June 25, 1905</u>:

Board of Health Statistics ending June 24, 1905

MARRIAGES

<u>White</u>: C V Allman and Leona Perrin; E M Adger and Elizabeth Hayden.

<u>Colored</u>: Will Walker and Mary Crowder; Will Bartlett and Penny Chambers; Robert Goch and M D Mock; H S Steins and Mary Graham.

DEATHS

<u>White</u>: August Zorn, 56; Miss Severne Wadley, 16; Tom Herold, 15; J A Dunn, 79; Julia West, 6.

<u>Colored</u>: Edna May Howard, 1 months; George Nickerson, 77; J W Butler, 20; Brinnie Loyd, 28; S J Sims, 42; Rebecca Birge, 29; Nellie Williams, 18; Matthew Chapman, 24; Isaac Thompson, 47; Archie Calloway, 28.

<u>Issue of June 27, 1905</u>:

The Caucasian received by mail today the following: Mrs. Kate Schaeffer announces the marriage of her daughter, Loire Dorine, to Dr. John Head Gayle, on June 15, 1905, at Chattanooga, Tenn. Born in Shreveport, the bride is the daughter of Charles Schaeffer. The groom is the son of John L. Gayle.

Issues of June 28, 1905-
Jan. 2, 1907

All issues are missing.

Issues of Jan. 6, 1907-
Dec. 29, 1907

Issue of Jan. 6, 1907:

Board of Health Statistics ending Jan. 12, 1907

MARRIAGES

White: Andrew Hendrickson and Lilla Riley; M C Trichel and Lillian Hall; W L Shyrock and Annie L Simpson; Ed Blount and Mamie Harris; Floyd Hankins and Dalzell Kennedy.

Colored: Will Lewis and Lula Wilson; Robert Neally and Christiana Rabb; Allen Jackson and Mary Taylor; William Hamilton and Tillie Raunche; Wesley Hearn and Mary Turner; John Hanks and Louise Rose; Joe Morris and Ella Todd; Joe Wagner and Mary Lott; A White and Hattie Marshall; John Marshall and Lucy Walls; E Courets and Pearl Thomas; H Hayes and Lula Wesley; J Cook and Lula Robinson; A Hilliards and Laura Collins; George Washington and Mary Oden; J Warring and Margret Thomas.

Issue of Jan. 13, 1907:

Board of Health Statistics ending Jan. 12, 1907

MARRIAGES

White: C L Avery and Myrtle Brodie; Charles N Neson and Minnie Batchellor; H H Fisher and Flossie Preslar.
Colored: James Willis and Carnelia Robinson; Preston Washington and Leona Garrett; Sam Seacer and Belle Kye; George Olda and Australia Andrews; M I Stewart and Main E Flapion; Tobe Gwin and Cora Washington.

DEATHS

White: Elias Lake, 44; Virginia Barron, 69; Susan Evans, 76; Clarrence Auld, 50; M A Belcher, 67; George Simon, 55.
Colored: Francis Young, 46; Easter Palmer, 55; Robert Hutchinson, 24; George Taylor, 80.

Issue of Jan. 20, 1907

Board of Health Statistics ending Jan. 19, 1907

MARRIAGES

White: J C Buckells and _____ Wagner; Arthur Kennedy and _____ Underwood; Jim Hayes and Susie Anderson.
Colored: Willie Howard and Emma Thomas; Horace Williams and M Haines; M Tyler and F Fields; Z Henderson and Effie Lee; S Walls and Rose Williams; Calvin Smith and E Beard; Fred Wright and Pearl Comeau; John Washington and Mallie Brown; Walter Snell and L Smith; H Williams and Mary Green.

DEATHS

White: Blanche W Hunter, 32; W S Currey, 48; J P Hamel, 16 months; Samuel Fazio Jr, 3 months; Kathleen E Jones, 15 months; Sarah Semans, 66; J M Cook, 20.
Colored: Dave Reace, 44; Ruline Jones, 39; Henry Jones, 20; Alma Eistner, 34; Davey Addington, 24; Della Gills, 16; Hilliard Eskridge, 38; H Castor, 30.

Issue of Jan. 27, 1907

Board of Health Statistics ending Jan. 26, 1907

MARRIAGES

White: W H Harris and Pearl Leseur; R S Tatum and Emma Stewart.
Colored: Joe Ellis and Mattie Gaines; Ed Walker and Lou

Turner; Walter Carter and Carmelia Worley; Albert Forker and Nellie Frazier; Jeff Young and Jessie Lee Sanders; George Triplet and Virginia Collins; William Taylor and Ella Miles.

DEATHS

<u>White</u>: Mrs. Mattie Jones, 29; Pauline Perry, 1.
<u>Colored</u>: Henry Howard, 53; F T Parkham, 26; Josephine Matrany, 37; Allen Brown, 40; Willie Henderson, 42; Susan Hammer, 37.

Died at her home yesterday morning, Mrs. Matthew Van Lear, a resident of Shreveport since 1887. She was the widow of Rev. John Van Lear, First Presbyterian Church. Mrs. Van Lear is survived by eight children: Rev. John Van Lear, Tuscaloosa, Ala.; Mrs. W H Morton, Spartanburg, S.C.; Mrs. Edward McAfee, McAfee, Ky.; and Will G Van Lear, Minden; Mrs. A M Leary, Bille Van Lear, Thomas and Matthew Van Lear, of this city.

Issue of Feb. 3, 1907:

Board of Health Statistics ending Feb. 2, 1907

MARRIAGES

<u>White</u>: P S Young and Ella Basset.
<u>Colored</u>: Nelson Hymes and Ella H Thurman; Willie George and May E Hall; Ed Sullivan and Minnie Brown; M Jones and Elnora Johnson.

DEATHS

<u>White</u>: Mildred McCracken, 7 months; Mrs. Carrie M Lehman, 59; Mrs. M Van Lear, 79.
<u>Colored</u>: Taylor Segue, 59; Melissa Brown, 30; Walter Taylor, 9; Alex Norman, 56; Willie Jones, 20; Henry Dean,

75; John Loney, 26.

Issue of Feb. 7, 1907:

Married yesterday at St. Mark's Episcopal Church, Lamar Campbell of New Orleans and Cora Hart of this city, by Rev. J H Spearing.

Married yesterday at the bride's home, Dr. S Y Alexander and Florence Jacobs. She is the daughter of the late Walter B Jacobs, the groom the son of S A Alexander of Greenwood. The ceremony took place at Holy Trinity Church, Father Bertels officiating.

Issue of Feb. 10, 1907:

Died in this city February 5, Mrs. D E Nicholson. She was Nannie Kervin of Kingston. Burial was in Evergreen Cemetery, Frierson. Survivors include her husband, sons Edward and Anthony Kervin, sisters, Mrs. Agnes Kervin, Mrs. Barton Nelson and Mrs. L A Scott, all of Frierson.

Issue of Feb. 12, 1907:

Married at St. Mark's Episcopal Church yesterday, Hamilton E Sharpe and Mary Hearn by Rev. J H Spearing. She is the daughter of H B Hearn.

Issue of Feb. 17, 1907:

Board of Health Statistics ending Feb. 16, 1907

MARRIAGES

White: Dr. S Y Alexander and Annie F Jacobs; L L Campbell and Cora J Hart.
Colored: H M Abbott and Mabie Mathews; Sam Jones and

Martha Kemp; C D Hoover and Lillie Matson; Henry Miller and Susie Howard; Henry Jones and Mary Gordon.

DEATHS
White: Dr. H Barncastle, 41; Mrs. Mary Carroll, 34; Mrs. T J Jordan, 67; A J VanDusen, 50; Mrs. Mamie Nicholson, 52.
Colored: Ida Bias, 18; Charles Johnson, 29; Charley Ashley, 35; Eliza Mason, 48; Frank Jones, 22; More Squire, 33; Jim Ford, 29; Malliso Brown, 30; Will Colbert (no age shown).

Issue of Feb. 24, 1907:

Board of Health Statistics ending Feb. 23, 1907

MARRIAGES
White: Charles Bass and Virginia Maxwell; Frank Derban and Iona Herson; Io Mozique and Pearl Fisher; Henry Stephens and Emma Nelson.
Colored: Andrew Jackson and Verna Williams.

DEATHS
White: Crystal Price, 5 months; Illmond Ice, 2; J S Macklin, 57; Sam Miller, 29; S A Anderson, 60; C M Felton, 22; Effie Hall, 7.
Colored: Henry Mitchell, 27; Exzena Boisseau, 21; A J Williams, 80; Julius Jones, 1; Aline Gipson, 70; Exzena Wilson, 2; S F Vicus, 56; H Grant, 65.

Issue of Mar. 3, 1907:

Died March 2, at the home of his brother, Walter J Crowder. Born in Oglethorpe, Ga., in 1834, he moved to Caddo Parish with his mother, brother and sisters in 1854. He is survived by a sister, Mrs. W H Wise of this city, brothers, Walter, of this city, and A B Crowder of Houson, Tex. On

April 18, 1861, he volunteered in the Shreveport Grays as a second Corporal and saw service in the Virginia Peninsula. In 1862, he transferred to Vicksburg, Miss., where he surrendered with General John C Pemberton's army.

Burial was in Oakland Cemetery beside his brother, Ben Crowder.

Issue of Mar. 2, 1907:

Board of Health Statistics ending Mar. 1, 1907

MARRIAGES

White: E H Loper and Effie Baird.
Colored: H Scott and Julia Bunkin; L Smith and Bertha Moore; J Gibson and Annie Hinkle; A Williams and May Thompson; F Mack and Julia Tyler; L H Thomas and Florence Dickson.

DEATHS

White: Mrs. Katherine Lichia, 73; El Roquemore, 59; Frances X Austen, 31; Mrs. _____ Odum, 45; D R Hoke, 25; Ben Crowder, 70; Pennie Colquitt, 11; F J Humphy, 56.
Colored: Stella Jackson, 29; Henry Watkins, 65; Mattie Carter, 53; Ann Robinson, 55; Emma J Williams, 11 months; Lucy Goss, 29; Fidelia Booker, 30; Henry Barnes, 80.

Issue of Mar. 10, 1907:

Board of Health Statistics ending Mar. 9, 1907

MARRIAGES

White: J W Brown and Manda Koa; T B Venson and Miss Melvin Sims; J E Raminge and Minnie L High.
Colored: Thomas Page and Georgia Toney; Eddie Brown and Jimmie Snowder; B Johnson and S Allen; Isiah Frenchies and

Matilda Washington; Alfred Curry and Belle Johnson; Allen Pennywell and Flora Williams; James Banks and Mary Quarles.

DEATHS

White: Prudie Coker, 1; Emma Kerry, 1; Shalboy John, 60; C E Simpson, 68; W J Crowder, 72; J F Foran, 44; John Lemon, 40; Joe Whittaker, 60.
Colored: Emma Cottonreader, 32; Wesley Ford, 40; Prudie Rochelle, 77; A P Gipson, 7 days; Albert Glen, 25; M Boone, 24; Carrie Williams, 48; Fannie McDonald, 33; Melvin Floyd, 1; Albert Walsey, 60; Elijah Williams, 27; Charles Burns, 65; Alexander Brown, 24.

Issue of Mar. 14, 1907:

Died today, John Patzman, 64, born in Germany. In 1842 he arrived in the United States. He settled in Shreveport in 1872. He is survived by his son, John H Patzman and daughter, Mrs. M H Dowling, of Chicago, Ill.

Issue of Mar. 17, 1907:

Board of Health Statistics ending Mar. 16, 1907

MARRIAGES

White: C C Cain and Sallie Sims; D E Peebles and Evelyn L Anderson.
Colored: R Lowe and Frances Primer; S Palmer and Stella Wilson; Dan McBride and K Henderson; P White and Mollie Bies; Walter Hill and Tina Crotchett; L Neucent and Mattie Simmons.

DEATHS

White: J R Watts, 5; John Patzman, 64; Rosa Costansa, 1

month; Henry Peters, 50; J R Jones, 41.

Colored: Adam Oliver, 55; Willie Wesley, 28; Cain Turner, 67; Percilla Martin, 76; Pearl Harris, 20; Thomas Thompson, 1; Robert Wilson, 27; Lizzie Standeird, 48; Stephen Morgan, 60; Peter Rollins, 23.

Issue of Mar. 31, 1907:

Board of Health Statistics ending Mar. 30, 1907

MARRIAGES

White: J A Alch and Yetta Benson; Otis Dickson and Florence Waldrup; K T Crews and Media C Spilker; C C Hardman and Mrs. L A Houston; F Hearn and May Brown.

DEATHS

White: Henry Jacobs, 54; Harry Ravinia, 5; Pauline Blattman, 20; Mike Maloney 44; Joe Merrell, 26; Leonard Hughes, 22; J Craig Hopkins, 26; Omey Barber, 17.
Colored: Susan Patton, 63; Margret Page, 39; Sam Shandle, 73; Wyley Hicks, 34; Mattie Newton, 1; Loveley Johnson, 16; Belle Roberson, 22; M M Richard, 26; Walter Piliot, 49.

Issue of Apr. 7, 1907:

Board of Health Statistics ending Apr. 6, 1907

MARRIAGES

White: J J Dillman and Effie May Bryan; A M Calkins and Donnie Bickham; H A Poleman and Maude Blackmer; J N Gates and Artella Washington; Domica Fazio and Entonia Feducia.
Colored: Albert Johnson and Roberta Anderson; William Slack and Ida Henry.

DEATHS

White: C C Wagner, 47; Mrs. Amelia New, 78; Frank Sofia, 66; Frank Bourdette, 38; C H Garner, 52; Emas Liginis, 16.
Colored: Lettie Brown, 49; Eliza Pryor, 20; H W Washington, 28; August Fontenette, 30.

Issue of Apr. 14, 1907:

Board of Health Statistics ending Apr. 13, 1907

MARRIAGES

White: W M Shepshire and Florence Parsons; L Porter and Dolly Jones.
Colored: Henry Smith and Litta Brimmer; E S Bush and Inez Stokes; Y Anlin and A A Glappion; Joseph Jacobs and R Gilford; B Prirna and C M Gyspi.

DEATHS

White: Hessie Maxey, 21; Mrs. L Sims, 80; E J Guetter, 47; Louis Tekulski, 67; R F Burnside, 43; J Hannan, 47.
Colored: E S Kirvin, 6; Mack Johnson, 28; Joe Harris, 21; Maggie Hayes, 42; Annie Hill, 2; John Stewart, 28; Victor Tabor, 1 month.

Issue of Apr. 21, 1907:

Board of Health Statistics ending Apr. 20, 1907

MARRIAGES

Colored: Ace White and Mary J Brown; Isaiah Jones and Alice Lockhart; D M Redwine and Grace Craig.

DEATHS

White: C W Hutchens, 50; Margia F Raviana, 2.
Colored: Racel Roberson, 50; Gus Gibson, 24; Frank Smith,

1; Ima Lee, 12; Adline Lewis, 59; Mary Anderson, 40; Tom Atkins, 19; Robert Jones, 37; Robert Atkins, 19; Robert Jackson, 21.

Issue of Apr. 28, 1907:

Board of Health Statistics ending Apr. 27, 1907

MARRIAGES

White: D A Breard and Annie L Ridley.
Colored: Allen Marks and Lena Jackson.

DEATHS

White: Walter Norsworthy, 6 months; Allen Culpepper, 1; Louis Gahagan, 12.
Colored: John Brock, 49; Willie Murphy, 19; Nora Walker, 42; John Fench, 50; John Bingston, 15; Pink Quinn, 44.

Issue of May 5, 1907:

Board of Health Statistics ending May 4, 1907

MARRIAGES

White: M M Jacobson and E Blum; A L Grenieux and F L Gunthier; Dr. H L Prikle and Mrs. E A Greening.
Colored: Ed Green and Alice Sims; B Hale and Nanie Bailey; Dave Armstead and Polly Young; Jones Commelias and Della Clark.

DEATHS

White: A W O Hicks, 90; Ellen Ward, 76; J P Brady, 64; T E Bannon, 64.
Colored: Robert Johnson, 60; R E Carter, 33; H A Tony, 74; Rena Johnson, 24; Henry Green, 20; Peggy Hopkins, 61.

Issue of May 12, 1907:

Board of Health Statistics ending May 11, 1907

MARRIAGES

White: L E Hinds and Mattie B Boynton; J F Cox and Hellen L Sumrell; J E Tucker and Nina Culpepper.
Colored: Will Murdock and May Bell Johnson; John McKinney and Ola Adams; M Graham and Ella McGee.

DEATHS

White: Allie Mai Wilkinson, 11; Willie Forshee, 1; J H Gilliland, 61; L H Howard, 26.
Colored: Ida B Ealy, 26; Mattie Huffine, 56; Pheba Smith, 17; George Davis, 43; Wash Johnson, 49; Lewis Carey, 21; Lizzie Jiles, 32.

Issue of May 19, 1907:

Board of Health Statistics ending May 18, 1907

MARRIAGES

White: Walter Gillian and Marietta Bell; A C Scriber and Margaret Potenza; Milton Breman and _____ Boylston.
Colored: John Crocknell and May L Powell; Charlie Smith and Lillian P Lewis.

DEATHS

White: M Stoner, 25; H C Gordon, 40.
Colored: Will Robertson, 45; Octavia Russ, 67; John Kelly, 21; Rachel Embers, 23; M Johnson, 58; Fisher Johnson, 16.

Issue of May 26, 1907:

Board of Health Statistics ending May 25, 1907

MARRIAGES
Colored: J Leggin and Jennie Crowder.

DEATHS
White: Julia A Hughes, 71; Clopha St. Germain, 70; C Greelie, 64.
Colored: Estella Dalia, 22; Mary Martin, 22; Parthenia Jones, 45; Melvin Cole, 10; Tom Powell, 53.

Issue of June 2, 1907:

Board of Health Statistics ending June 1, 1907

MARRIAGES
Colored: Thomas Witherspoon and Lizzie Brown; Elonzo Johnson and L C Colquitt; James Miles and May Shan.

DEATHS
White: C Griggs, 47; Mrs. E Knoble, 28; Willie Wells, 31; Mrs. J M Bagley (no age shown); T L Stevens, 65; R J Phillips, 51; G L Adams, 36.
Colored: Harriett Coleman, 66; Ella Holman, 32; Logan Curry, 72; M Johnson, 23; Charity Richardson, 45; John Harris, 57.

Issue of June 9, 1907:

Board of Health Statistics ending June 8, 1907

MARRIAGES
White: C M Miller and Minnie J Ridley; Cal D Hicks and Annie Sibley.
Colored: R E Robertson and Nellie Tanner; J Vanzant and Mary Mann; Willie Hill and Ada Boone; Mathews Johnson and Roberta Rose; Henry M McNeil and Carrie Bell; Jim

Saction and Pearl Robertson.

DEATHS
White: Mrs. W K Sutherlin, 34; Sallie Nelson, 49; Bennie Johnson, 28; G W Graham, 22; Ernest Schuler, 63.
Colored: A Dandolds, 63; William Lumas, 40; S Jordan, 40.

Issue of June 16, 1907:

Board of Health Statistics ending June 15, 1907

MARRIAGES
White: J Hewitt and Minnie Williams; E Levy and Bertha Donner; Julian E Whiteworth and Bertha W Harp.
Colored: A Smith and Edna Willis; Joe McKinney and Lou Ellen Bulleson; Jerry Thompson and Emma Edward; J C Daniels and Julia Carter; Frank Ragsdate and Dora Williams.

DEATHS
Colored: Ella Huey, 14; Julius Prince, 40; Perry Ivory, 25; Annie Freeman, 24; George Phillips, 23; Eddie Lee Porter, 22.

Issue of June 30, 1907:

Board of Health Statistics ending June 29, 1907

MARRIAGES
White: C W Rose and Lucile Mashaw; G W Waisman and Addie Wolfrk; T G Winn and A K Kruhen; F P McCord and Pearl Gillepsi.
Colored: E J Nelson and R Johnson; F Hodge and A Andrews; C D Hopkins and Rose Smith; Gus Slater and May Lewis.

DEATHS

White: Marie Curtis, 21; Sidney T Jones, 8; Goldie Phillips, 20; W J Head, 50; Hartley Headwick, 12.
Colored: Dollie Warters, 68; Maggie Neal, 30; Della Miles, 51; J M Powell, 10; Albert Booker, 28; Polly Perry, 21; Rose Washington, 20.

Issue of July 7, 1907:

Board of Health Statistics ending July 6, 1907

MARRIAGES

White: George N McPhee and Nettie E Finnegan; Charles Venson and Cassie McPherson.

DEATHS

White: J P Cunningham, 4; W S Penick, 71; Albert Jones, 60; C E Thompson, 59.
Colored: Oscar Ford, 22; Monroe Graham, 45; Ruth Thomas, 17; Robert Ford, 33; K Jones, 34.

Issue of July 14, 1907:

Board of Health Statistics ending July 13, 1907

MARRIAGES

White: H C Kree and Esah Allen White.
Colored: George Hall and Clara Crowder; Frank Wallace and May Byas.

DEATHS

White: F W Bell, 40; M Kelly, 28; A Lewis, 27; Ola Wafer, 20.
Colored: Laurence Smith, 30; Florence Jackson, 45.

Issue of July 21, 1907:

Board of Health Statistics ending July 20, 1907

MARRIAGES
White: Sam Heffte and Nellie P McCartney; E E Hettler and May McCabe.
Colored: Fred Mim and Will Ann Parder; John Minden and Minnie Hale; J L Shelton and Rebecca Watts.

DEATHS
White: Joe Abrantes, 49.
Colored: Margaret Prior, 45; Rosa McConnell, 21; Richardson Blankenship, 78.

Issue of July 28, 1907:

Board of Health Statistics ending July 27, 1907

MARRIAGES
Colored: John Freeman and Palsey Oden; Noble Green and Daisy Duke.

DEATHS
White: Claudia Harvey (no age shown); James M Griffin, 12; Mrs. W S Lynch, 60; Clyde Cartwright (no age shown); Mat Auhelze, 48; Dr. _____ Graham (no age shown); W F Bell, 40.
Colored: C A Wilson, 37; Brown Dickson, 29; C E Ketter, 1; Hattie Humphrey, 63; James Prymans, 1; Rose Gilmore, 25; Violet White, 11; Alex Williams, 27; Isam Varner (no age shown).

Issue of Aug. 4, 1907:

Board of Health Statistics ending Aug. 3, 1907

MARRIAGES
White: F J Price and Katie Mullins.
Colored: J R King and Susie Hines; Charles Oats and Julia Garrett.

DEATHS
White: H Hebert, 1; Ethel Havell, 5.
Colored: Prudence Armstead, 5; Mose Cook, 62; G W Washington, 45; P E Ketter, 3; Robert Thompson, 36; Russell Scott, 6; Caroline Robinson, 83; Sarah Pierson, 35; Ella Hyams, 22; Sallie Bingham, 18; A R Bozie, 3; Elsie Patterson, 28; L Lee, 30; Tom Johnson, 60.

Issue of Aug. 11, 1907:

Board of Health Statistics ending Aug. 10, 1907

MARRIAGES
White: A B West and Lena Wellman; T M Brown and Ellen Hill; W L Dickson and Bertha Harman; J Valentine and Nora Thomas; D F Dickleberry and Sadie Mozely; Frank Oglivie and Abie Douglas; J F Shahan and Minnie Lou Crisp; E C Roach and Hellen Nixson.

DEATHS
White: J W Parker, 1; Miss Sallis Champion, 40; Emma Mercer, 29; Mrs. Jennie Hargis, 38; Joe Sartino, 69; W J Townsend, 52; Myrline Watts, 4.
Colored: Louis Jackson, 35; George Williams, 26; Eliza Strong, 80; Ed Thomas, 30.

Married on Wednesday evening at the home of the bride's parents, Mr. and Mrs. L N Crisp, J F Shahan and

Minnie Lou Crisp, Rev. R G Kendrick Officiating.
Married Tuesday at the residence of Dr. W H Morgan, Scott Fowler and Gussie Fauntleroy, only daughter of Rev. T A Fauntleroy, recently deceased.

Issue of Aug. 13, 1907:

Died at his home yesterday, Abe Kirsch. He was born in Alsace, France, in 1854. He is survived by his wife and several children. Interment will be tomorrow at Jewish Cemetery, Rabbi Moses P Jacobs officiating.

Issue of Aug. 18, 1907:

Board of Health Statistics ending Aug. 17, 1907

DEATHS
White: L P Perry, 76; Mary L Prudhomme, 1; Abe Kirsch, 43; J F Boykin, 51; Annie Turner, 30; Artie Welldon, 27; J W Duggars, 32; W M Fowler, 26; R L Thompson, 36.
Colored: Helen Shivers, 16; Clarence Ealy, 1; Primous Gideon, 1; Joe Dickson, 83; Allison Porter, 49; Sarah Blue, 75; Elsey Patterson, 60.

Issue of Aug. 25, 1907:

Board of Health Statistics ending Aug. 24, 1907

MARRIAGES
White: H V Smith and Mary Leta Hicks; T W Farmer and Alice Hargis; S A Parker and C Whitlatch; J D Milheam and Fannie Welborn.

DEATHS
White: Mrs. Amanda Patterson, 76; R F Lawson, 51; W S

DeWitt, 33.
Colored: Nancy McClue, 85; Cora Williams, 19; Sallie Murry, 65; Henrietta Lee, 53; Katie Maiden, 35; Harrison Mathews, 25; Dave Woodward, 23; George Robinson, 52; Minnie Waldon, 27.

Issue of Sept. 1, 1907:

Board of Health Statistics ending Aug. 31, 1907

MARRIAGES
White: B A Russell and Jessie McGellery; W A Hunhanallen and A M Jones; D V Frazier and Maggie Wain; J M Sojoumen and Josephine Smith.

DEATHS
White: T P Pennywell, 51; Mamie I Culverson, 55; Irvin Glass, 60.
Colored: Charity Oliver, 58; Hobson Harrison, 56; Mary Dansby, 3; Murphy Gibson, 5; J F Newman, 32; Lavelle Beach, 4; Armstead Nettles, 20; Augusten Tyler, 1; L B Dupree, 35; Peter Williams, 60; Louis James, 25; Ranse Terrell, 48.

Issue of Sept. 8, 1907:

Board of Health Statistics ending Sept. 7, 1907

MARRIAGES
White: J P Elliott and Mary L Thornton.
Colored: George Mixon and Bulah Atkinson; A J Parham and Mabel Marsden.

DEATHS
White: Ben F Guilliland, 60; G Stewart, 27; L L McKee, 63.

Colored: Green Hanley (no age shown); Janie Reed, 2; Nathaniel Shivers, 1.

Issue of Sept. 14, 1907:

Board of Health Statistics ending Sept. 13, 1907

MARRIAGES
Colored: J W Watson and Mary Green.

DEATHS
White: William Adams, 22; Emma Smith, 40; Levi Freedman, 54; Ben Hodges, 49; Mrs. J D Collins, 37.
Colored: Alfred Wyatt, 22; Virginia Jackson, 34; Charles Johnson, 84; George Marion, 18; Polly Davenport, 107; Charley Carter, 17; George Long, 70.

Issue of Sept. 22, 1907:

Board of Health Statistics ending Sept. 21, 1907

MARRIAGES
White: Charles H Adams and Eliza Ruff; Rube Whittington and Leslie Key; B G James and Carrie Williams; J C Vowell and R E English.
Colored: Joe Rafe and Inez Boon; G Norman and Emily Preso.

DEATHS
White: Willie C George, 2; Sue M Pennington, 75; C S Ramange, 34; George W Latham, 53; F Johnson, 24.
Colored: Henry McDuffie, 66; Alma Green, 2; Felicia Lewis, 105; Rebecca Williams, 5; Minnie Pugh, 35; S Huki, 35.

Issue of Sept. 29, 1907:

Board of Health Statistics ending Sept. 28, 1907

MARRIAGES
Colored: William Coyten and Rosa Sims.

DEATHS
White: Martin Guysler (no age shown); W C James, 38.
Colored: Little Smith, 50; Julia Duboles, 48; John Simmons, 53; John Ford, 43; John Smith, 19; Tony Coel, 18; Annie Thomas, 20.

Issue of Oct. 6, 1907:

Board of Health Statistics ending Oct. 5, 1907

MARRIAGES
White: J G Morten and Cora E Tripp.
Colored: Monroe Kelly and Lula Wesley; R D Richardson and Bartee Green.

DEATHS
White: Nathan Myer, 60; George Hanson, 24; Willie May Dowden, 1; Nat Nunery, 70; James E Hennerty, 52.
Colored: Sarah Nelson, 40; Eleese Murray, 3; Lizzie Edwards, 33; Celest Richardson, 70; D M Brelford, 45; Gus Smith, 24.

Issue of Oct. 13, 1907:

Died at her home October 9, Mrs. Mary Frances Sample, wife of O H Sample. Born in Mansfield, she was Miss Fannie Guy. Survivors include besides her husband two sons, Guy and Arthur Sample, sisters, Mrs. J D Pickens, Mrs. Lily Guy, Mrs. Charles Elam, Mrs. R M Bryan, and a brother, J E Guy.

Issue of Oct. 13, 1907:

Board of Health Statistics ending Oct. 12, 1907

MARRIAGES

White: F T Henson and Ethel Watson.
Colored: George Nelson and Julia Daniels; Henry Brooks and Hattie Johnikin; Mack McCain and Hattie Reece.

DEATHS

White: Mrs. _____ McGill, 60; Fannie Guy Sample, 54; J Furk, 44.
Colored: Cue Washington, 28; Julius Besset, 36; Dave Williams, 22; Snyder Heard, 2.

Issue of Oct. 20, 1907:

Board of Health Statistics ending Oct. 19, 1907

MARRIAGES

Colored: Rufus Atkins and Mary Lee Words.

DEATHS

White: James George, 18; S Gosher, 33; James A Norman, 50; Mary C Ansley, 56; Sarah Teague, 50; Tony Bynake, 30.
Colored: Rose Calmez, 3; Joe Smith, 26; A J Beaty, 43; Maggie Battle, 19; Comick Will, 7.

Issue of Oct. 17, 1907:

Board of Health Statistics ending Oct. 16, 1907

MARRIAGES

White: Robert F Floyd and Lizzie C Rines; C M Watson and Minnie V Chandler.
Colored: A P Thompson and Martha Mankham; B Bryant and Lillie Letson; Jake Nichols and Flora Ware; Warren Calhoun and Roberta Harvey; F G Freeman and Josephine Jones.

DEATHS
White: Margaret F Harrison, 33; Manny Carnes, 35; Genevieve R Collins, 18; Alice Atkins, 5; Annie M Nuett, 37; M L Rawls, 32; R McCauley, 15; Harry Oneal, 34; Arthur Daggs, 15; Ed Desimer, 31; Carrie Caffray, 18.
Colored: S B Smith, 2; Grandison King, 50; John Dozier, 32; Harriett Thomas, 70.

Issue of Oct. 31, 1907:

Died October 28, Captain William Kinney. He was born in Dublin, Ireland, August 17, 1836. He moved to Shreveport in 1856. On May 17, 1861, he volunteered in Louisiana Rangers, later Company F of Louisiana Third Regiment. He was promoted from sergeant to captain in May 1862. He was in battles at Elkhorn and Oak Hills, Ark. Being paroled at the surrender of Vicksburg, Miss., he returned to Shreveport. In 1870 he married Clara Geise, who, with five children, Annie, Bressau, Leonard, Paul and Francis, survive him. Burial was in Catholic Cemetery, following funeral at Holy Trinity Church.

Issue of Nov. 3, 1907:

Board of Health Statistics ending Nov. 2, 1907

MARRIAGES
White: J H Webb and Blanche Tiffin; C L Amiss and Cora M

Hanley.

Colored: L Heiter and Fannie Hicks; H J Thomas and Virginia McPherson; James Jacobs and Callie Smith.

DEATHS

White: Mrs. Leslie Tignor, 30; Mrs. Linda Parker, 21; William Kinney, 71; Mary House, 29.

Colored: Alice Easley, 30; Mattie Jackson, 2; John Nelson, 60.

Issue of Nov. 10, 1907:

Board of Health Statistics ending Nov. 9, 1907

MARRIAGES

White: John J Kraldich and Antonia Sterle; J W Norton and Jessie Kirk; Emile Jacquet and Maude E Brassill.

DEATHS

White: Juliett R Norton, 77; H P Thomas, 56; Emma Roberson, 61; R N Sibley, 40; I N Hitchcox, 40.

Colored: George Gilbert, 23; Nanie Gay, 28; Margaret Bloom, 65; Virginia Thomas, 15; Benton Clark, 40.

Died November 12 at the residence of his daughter, Mrs. Nathan T Penick, Major A F Stephenson. In 1861 he volunteered at Fort Smith, Ark., in Company B, First Arkansas Mounted Riflemen, was elected to captain in 1862 and promoted to major in 1863. In 1864 he was wounded at Pleasant Hill. He is suvived by three sons, D F, A F and George Stephenson, two sisters, Mrs. M T Crawford of Union Springs, Ala., and Mrs. V A Hamil of Talledaga, Ala. He was aged 62 years.

Died yesterday, age 62, M B Parker. Born in Alabama he volunteered and was in Confederate campaigns in

Tennessee and Georgia. In 1872 he married Mary Lou Ardis, daughter of Colonel C H Ardis. He had no children.

Issue of Nov. 17, 1907:

Board of Health Statistics ending Nov. 16, 1907

MARRIAGES
White: R D Webb and Neomie Skannal; George B Garrett and Edith M Bainer; R A Clanton and J L DeSoto.
Colored: John Polly and Arnett Rabon; L Freeman and Lillie Wilson; Frank White and Ruby Haughton.

DEATHS
White: M B Parker, 64; Trebie Hartman, 1; Major A F Stephenson, 74; D E Moss, 40; Fred Cobel, 30; L J Fixary, 32; James McVee, 61; Anna H Kelly, 61; Carl Kraft, 40; Will Cameron, 29.
Colored: John Barber, 46; Jacob Pinkney, 46; Mariah Abbott, 26; Mary J Bell, 60; Sam Handy, 27; John Green, 65; Charles Rijoe, 27; Henry Miller, 55; Ansie Jewitt, 94.

Issue of November 24, 1907:

Board of Health Statistics ending November 23, 1907

MARRIAGES
White: Perry Parish and Frances O'Dwyer; A H Sightler and Rosie Brante.
Colored: Will Young and Ollie Thomas; Napoleon Webb and Lina Peterson.

DEATHS
White: Charles Wagner, 40; Temmie Miller, 6; I I Helpman, 62; Raymond Daniels 2; A Moline, 27; E W Patton, 28;

James Shepherd, 50; Joe Stank, 36; J P Jones, 50; J R Robinson, 60.
Colored: Jim Boone, 75; Henry Cooper, 44; Alice Green, 26; Lum Coffer, 45; Mose Johnson, 23; Ralph Howard, 37; Frank Josiah, 48; E Cook, 57.

Issue of December 1, 1907:

Board of Health Statistics ending November 30, 1907

MARRIAGES

White: C C Cooper and Willie L Walton; W S Orr and Annie M Williams.
Colored: Tom Brown and Belle Campbell; Robert Brown and Annie Armstrong; James Davenport and Hattie Mims.

DEATHS

White: Robert Rigdon, 38; Rosa Blumberg, 32; E T Ousley, 27; Susie B Barber, 46; R F Wilson, 28; Jessie Gray, 31.
Colored: P H Coty, 2; Lucinda Napoleon, 52; Jim Figgins, 28; Willie Bell, 19; Jesse Edwards, 18; L Haynes, 21; Ed Little, 24.

Issue of Dec. 3, 1907:

Died last night, Dr. John J. Scott. He was born in Edgefield S.C. in 1837. At the war's start he volunteered in Company B Bossier (Louisiana) Cavalry and also served in the Sixteenth Texas Infantry. Survivors include his wife, and daughters, Mrs. Pollie Abel of Hope, Ark., Mrs. Letta Little, Augusta, Ga., Mrs. Leola Palmer, of this city, Mrs. Eugenia Wolz, Marshall, Tex., and Mrs. Birdie Blackman, Ruston.

Issue of Dec. 8, 1907:

Board of Health Statistics ending Dec. 7, 1907

MARRIAGES
White: W M Pate and Mattie Grosjean; T L Kimbrough and Ann Garity; Jim Omlas and Angiline Iosas.
Colored: S C Smith and Allice Williams.

DEATHS
White: Dr. J J Scott, 70; August Wagner, 59; B W Williams, 59; Elbert Weaver, 13; Barbara Wingate, 4.
Colored: Henry Snow, 3; Dora Orr, 30; Bill Lewis, 50; Monroe Dark, 16; Jackson McFarland, 66; Nettie Burrs, 30; Ben Robinson, 20; A Williams, 22.

Issue of Dec. 15, 1907:

Board of Health Statistics ending Dec. 14, 1907

MARRIAGES
White: T M Barnwell and Mary Morgan; J H Johnson and E A Lymer.
Colored: J G Cannon and Elvira Washington; J W Johnse and Cora Johnson.

DEATHS
White: Harry Zimmerman, 15; L J McCool, 42; F H Branin, 20; J T Johnson, 28; D W Quarrier, 61.
Colored: Joanna Cook, 11; Annie Miles, 1; Ed Sullivan, 29; Lucy Crow, 10.

Issue of Dec. 22, 1907:

Board of Health Statistics ending Dec. 21, 1907

MARRIAGES

White: E A Mogan and Hilda LeVasser.
Colored: H A Rohman and Ella J Levy; John Parsons and Julia Williams; Julius Oden and Arbella White.

Issue of Dec. 29, 1907:

Board of Health Statistics ending Dec. 28, 1907

MARRIAGES

White: W M Reland and Cora C Frames; F N Louis and Florence Moss; V A Roans and Maud Miller; John Melzer and Marie Page; D H Cathey and Alice Tucker; Sam Hughs and Pearl Jones; L C Blanchard and Maggie P Holbert; J W Rushing and Maud Caldwell.
Colored: Charles Bennett and Jessie Jones; Clifton Williams and Selma Pellars; Silas Conado and Fannie Turner.

DEATHS

White: Annie M McMahon, 33; Sallie Chester, 54; W M Roache, 49; Ed Warren, 27.
Colored: Northe Nelson, 27; Bessie Drain, 25; Jesse McCoy, 27; H Collins, 30.

Issues of Jan. 1, 1908-
Dec. 31, 1908

All issues are missing.

Issues of Jan. 3, 1909-
Dec. 28, 1909

Issue of Jan. 3, 1909:

Board of Health Statistics ending Jan. 2, 1909

MARRIAGES

White: Albin Thompkins and Vera L Taylor; W H Platt and Isabelle Wayman; J H Shepherd and Philena Fairth.
Colored: Andrew Wiggins and Mamie Trudean; Homer Whittaker and Carrie Johnson; Will Johnson and Pearl Edwards; W C Roberson and Ada Hamilton; Pleas Sessions and Julia Crawford; Mellow Bradford and Hattie B Johnson; Hy Brown and Ella Marshall.

DEATHS

White: Ula Thompson 25; John Marshall, 23; Antone Kramer, 35; W K Nash, 68; J J Blanton, 42; Dr. S H Hicks, 44; Randolph Nevell, 8; W E Earp, 27; James Parnell, 34; Mrs. Ida Florsheim, 62; Dr. F W Dortch, 38.
Colored: J Miles, 86; Frank Royston, 51; George Wilson 1; Hattie Sims, 22.

Issue of Jan. 10, 1909:

Board of Health Statistics ending Jan. 9, 1909

MARRIAGES

White: Roy McPherson and Ethel Pretz; Joseph Kosakofsky and Sadie Grays; Charles Turner and Rosa Adams; Allen Samuels Jr and Mary Ann Mosique; Willie Clemer and Leonia Wiggins.

DEATHS

White: Ella Houston, 10; Helen Blackwood, 30; Ida Bain, 34; George W Sproul, 48; Caroline Lemle, 46; Mrs. Dorlean Kennedy, 23; William North, 16; Abe Moseley, 49; Mary Gibbs, 40.
Colored: Sam Johnson, 31; Mariah Rose, 54; Charlotte Staton, 48; Julius Miller, 24; Willie Simons, 22, Charity Armstrong, 39.

Issue of Jan. 14, 1909:

Died January 12, Simon Herold. He was born in Ellerstadt, Rhenish Bavaria, February 16, 1835. In 1853 he settled in Vicksburg, Miss., and moved to Shreveport in 1866. He married Sophie Kaufman in 1869. Surviving is a daughter, Mrs. Nettie Herold Hoffheimer, Richmond, Va., and a son, Joseph K Herold, St. Louis, Mo. In 1879 Mr. Herold married Rosa Simmons. They had the following children: Sidney H, Dr. Arthur, Lech, Flora, Henrietta, and Sallie Herold, all of Shreveport. Rabbi M P Jacobson officated at burial in Jewish Cemetery.

Issue of Jan. 17, 1909:

Board of Health Statistics ending Jan. 16, 1909

MARRIAGES
White: Joe Fretta and Ida Fulco; Alfred E Filhiol and Ida Clawson.

DEATHS
White: Maude Mongogna, 30; Simon Herold, 73.
Colored: Carrie Brown, 22; Annie Jetta Pierce, 22; Helen Simon, 4; Peggy Dondy, 80; J R. Houston, 38; Henry Percell, 30; Hy Fisher, 38; George Haurn, 38; Will Aiken, 25; Sherman Wright, 21; Sibella Wellborn, 26; Rosetta

Flanager, 21.

Issue of Jan. 24, 1909:

Board of Health Statistics ending Jan. 23, 1909

MARRIAGES
<u>White</u>: W J Roland and Loula Boyd Martin; W H Marshall and Susie Sullivan; J C Morris and Angeline Armstrong; Leonard Avery and Mira Dowden.

DEATHS
<u>White</u>: C E Havell, 38; Mira Smith, 12; H B Robertson, 42; Robert Elliott, 29; Lillian Upchaw, 13; T J Moore, 50; Cornelius Pillows, 11; S Walker, 53; Ella Sheldon, 21.
<u>Colored</u>: Geneva Scott, 38; Sara Wouds, 45; Henry Clark, 22; Rila Flimmins, 75.

Issue of Jan. 28, 1909:

After an illness of three weeks, James A Burnside died at his home in this city early today. He was born here July 1, 1860. He is survived by his wife and two sons, James W and Poland Belmont.

Issue of Jan. 31, 1909:

Board of Health Statistics ending Jan. 30, 1909

MARRIAGES
<u>White</u>: J B Christopher and Viola Croch.

DEATHS
<u>White</u>: T M Hunt, 71; J R Burnside, 48.
<u>Colored</u>: Katie Green, 44; Julia Anderson, 46; Laura

Johnson, 20; H Boyles, 24; Henry Flint, 54; Ernest Kelly, 12; Fritz Walker, 56; Henry Shre, 26; Henry Gooche, 19.

Issue of Feb. 7, 1909:

Board of Health Statistics ending Feb. 6, 1909

MARRIAGES
White: Sam Cannon and Mary Tucker
Colored: Roy Frost and Mary Franklin; Frank Coleman and Carrie Power.

DEATHS
White: M R Wait, 40; Howard Wells, 25.
Colored: Lizzie Chips, 19; Alice Butler, 25; Charles Sanders, 57; Ben Henderson, 55; Leo Kelly, 40.

Issue of Feb. 14, 1909:

Board of Health Statistics Ending Feb. 13, 1909

MARRIAGES
White: Thomas W Ford Jr and Mabel M Currie; H D Poole and Rila Ponder; S J Flores and Fannie Parnell.
Colored: Joe Mat and Sophina Smith; William Robertson and Dora Lamplain.

DEATHS
White: Harriett R Irven, 8; J A Griffin, 50.
Colored: Louis Jackson, 68; Evans Holmes, 30; Penny Theo, 25; A Jackson, 44; Annie Outerside, 18; S R Porter, 39; John Smith, 40; Sarah Waites, 30; Fred Jones, 38; John Lewis, 7; Rachel Williams, 24.

Issue of Feb. 16, 1909:

Died in Nashville, Tennessee Feb. 15, Alice G Dale, eldest daughter of Mr. and Mrs. V. Grosjean. Funeral service will be tomorrow at St. Mark's Episcopal Church, with burial in Greenwood Cemetery.

Issue of Feb. 21, 1909:

Board of Health Statistics ending Feb. 20, 1909

MARRIAGES
White: Charles E Alley and Maude Crew; D Attaway and Bessie Fisher.
Colored: William Burrell and Susie Porter; Ed Brown and Lula Knox.

DEATHS
White: Alice G Dale, 34; Palmyre Fraenkel, 42; J E Everhard, 65; Shaag Finestein, 26; R D Meade, 44; Harry Johnson, 44; Belle Thomas, 56; Wes Hagan, 28; Henry Wright, 28; Jackson Neal, 23; Will Jackson, 25; Lea Bradley, 17.
Colored: A White, 81; Mollie Allen, 60.

Buried yesterday in Greenwood Cemetery, Mrs. C M Christian, who died February 20 in this city. She is survived by her husband and four daughters: Mrs. J P Hammell and Mrs. Charles Hammell, of Texas; and Grace and Bertha Christian, and one son, Charles, all of Shreveport.

Issue of Mar. 7, 1909:

Board of Health Statistics ending Mar. 6, 1909

MARRIAGES

White: Jessie Johnson and Ethel Oden; W W Shirrelle and Julia Todd; Howard Bremen and Roberta Frie.

DEATHS
White: Mrs. B C Crandall, 25; Luther Sims, 28; Mallie Green, 34; Elsie Bonney, 30; Riley Gordon, 28; Henry Miller, 30.
Colored: Mandy Anderson, 50; Rapp Flynn, 28; Ruby Washington, 1; Cornelius Sanders, 37; Edithe Norman, 5; Ira Cooper, 26.

Issue of Mar. 14, 1909:

Board of Health Statistics ending Mar. 13, 1909

MARRIAGES
White: George Lambert and Phebe Doris.

DEATHS
White: F J Wandell, 52; Mrs. M Weinstock, 74; T E Flournoy, 70.
Colored: J B Penn, 29; Emeline Kelly, 65; Wash Parker, 38; Lucindy Boswell, 45; A J Johnson, 36; Oliver C Massey, 2; J C Orr, 39.

Issue of Mar. 21, 1909:

Board of Health Statistics ending Mar. 20, 1909

MARRIAGES
White: Andrew Melady and Mrs. M A Bonnegent; John Notini and Maria Proveza.
Colored: Lee Mohooffey and Mary Turner; Charles Williams and Ella Parker; Gilbert Washington and Nancy Davis.

DEATHS

<u>White</u>: Earl Fouts, 29.

<u>Colored</u>: George Haynes Jr, 21; Andrew Johnson, 65; John Spears, 57; J A Ragan, 7; Bessie Constantia, 26; Mattie Hinckley (no age shown); Henry Washington, 22; Millie Peace, 24; Mandy Moore, 45; Archie Solomon, 22; Horace Parker, 45.

Issue of Mar. 21, 1909:

Died in this city Mar. 19, Mrs. Isabelle Williamson Hodge, wife of Arthur G Hodge. She was a daughter of Colonel George Williamson and Mrs. Isabelle Butler Williamson. Funeral service at St. Mark's Episcopal Church. Other survivors include, sisters, Mrs. Caro B Frierson and Mrs. Edgar Sutherlin, this city; brothers, Prof. George Williamson, Natchitoches, Roland Williamson, this city, and George Freeman, Monroe.

Issue of Mar. 28, 1909:

Board of Health Statistics ending Mar. 27, 1909

MARRIAGES

<u>White</u>: George Morrison and Goodin Black; Andrew Reed and Lena Simmons.

DEATHS

<u>White</u>: Mrs. Arthur Hodge, 53; August Mayer, 49; Patrick McGrory, 69; Mrs. Leha Peddy, 26.

<u>Colored</u>: Lavina Dockwell, 57; Richard Smith, 23; Aaron Brown, 24; Ben H Wilson, 49; James Williams, 19; Theodore Hanchey, 21.

Issue of Apr. 4, 1909:

Board of Health Statistics ending Apr. 3, 1909

MARRIAGES
White: L Lieto and Elizabeth A Brantes; Thomas H Wooldridge and Virginia Wilson; V I Miller and Annie Smith.

DEATHS
White: Howard Rigdon, 37.
Colored: Angeline Johnson, 7; Jeff Davis, 28; Henry Carter, 22; Olie Idon, 25; Cora Phillips, 28.

Issue of May 9, 1909:

Board of Health Statistics ending May 8, 1909

MARRIAGES
White: Strother Mitchell and Florence Tadd; George White and Lydia Leddenham.
Colored: John Hall and Susie W Redden.

DEATHS
White: F L Marionneaux, 50; Christopher De Graffenreid, 36.
Colored: Julia M Henderson, 4; Emery Green, 64; Pearl Carl, 30; Lucindy Cotton, 50; Ophelia Redwine, 1; Elizabeth Stewart, 70; V N Page, 58; Rosemary Harding (no age shown); Laura Johnson (no age shown); Lizzie Williams, 28; Mary Williams, 24; E B Alexander, 34; Sarah Tidwell, 27; Henry Baker, 29; Mary Bell, 29; Kattie Moore, 25.

Issue of May 16, 1909:

Board of Health Statistics ending May 15, 1909

MARRIAGES
White: M T Bellah and Nellie Barie; J T Raburn and Josie M Willis; L Boykin and May Geagler; R E Midgett and Bertie Holland; W M White and Margaret Wingate.
Colored: Horace Hardy and Ella Gustus; Richard Hall and Bertha Chestnut.

DEATHS
White: Charles Morizat, 1; K T Stevens, 2; John Fuchs, 19.
Colored: Lena Edwards, 50; Eliza Norrington, 74; Anna Boon, 3; Henry Taylor, 65; May Lichner, 24; Amos Burr, 69; Arthur Jackson, 35; Dock Pierce, 29; Mary Simmons, 75.

Issue of May 23, 1909:

Board of Health Statistics ending May 22, 1909

MARRIAGES
White: G H McAdams and Mannie Waldron; Leman Lee and Ethel Christian.

DEATHS
White: Hiram J Allen, 78.
Colored: Mandy Campbell, 56; Lurline Witt, 29; Julia Beach, 58; Jim Terry, 31; Edgar Wall, 55; Mirah Brown, 60; Dinah Rettig, 95; Albemonia McRay, 23; Zell Scott, 46; Riley Taylor, 18; Alice Johnson, 30.

Issue of June 6, 1909:

Board of Health Statistics ending June 5, 1909

MARRIAGES

White: Fabio Martinez and Jesua Palacio; John T Gamlin and Rebecca Cox; W C Ford and Carrie Russell; Leo B Shouds and Maude Spearman; John L Gibson and Pauline Legg; B B Watson and Bessie Sibley; E W Ebert and Pearl B McCloud; Joe W Walker and Ida Kroll; F J Latter and N Yarbrough; L M Mulford and May Sullivan.

Colored: L B Hatcher and Mary Gates; Leonard Johnson and Sallie Battle; Ned Simmons and Estella Chase.

DEATHS

White: Ellie Self, 53.

Colored: Margaret Green, 43; Ben Hearn, 100; T M Lee, 21; W H Brown, 70; George Reed, 48.

Issue of June 13, 1909:

Board of Health Statistics ending June 12, 1909

MARRIAGES

White: J A Cook and Evie Farmer; Theodore Hutchinson and Callie Johnson; Nelson Hynes and Carrie Jefferson.

DEATHS

White: J J Wilcox, 67; Jackson Calloway, 9; H Douglas, 85; Jessie Washam, 39; Anna May White, 1; Emanuel Johnson, 36; R H Hall, 32; Annie Jonas, 28.

Colored: Lelia M Patton, 21; Crawford Holland, 20; Ernest Gardner, 23.

Married June 12, Simon Patrick Fox and Susie Elizabeth Hunsicker, the daughter of Henry Hunsicker.

Issue of June 20, 1909:

Board of Health Statistics ending June 19, 1909

MARRIAGES
White: W A Stanton and H Weber; E Avis and R Robertson; S C Fox and Susie Hunsicker; J L Tarpley and _____ Coffind; George Johnson and Ida Stephens.

DEATHS
White: Joe S Bond, 47; Herbert Frankel, 19; Harry Bluestein, 26.
Colored: Matilda Kimble, 48; Oscar Robertson, 15; Eva R Pierce, 5; Bubble Ragles, 8; J B Browning, 55; Eddye Hilburn, 21; T J Wells, 68; Sallie Lawrence, 26; Lizzie Ranger, 27; Albert Phillips, 31; Anderson Henry, 39; Charley Johnson, 58.

Issue of June 27, 1909:

Board of Health Statistics ending June 26, 1909

MARRIAGES
White: J F Tanant and Lizzie Dillinger; J D Youngblood and Georgia Stringfellow; E R Flood and Frances O Allen; W M Watson and Pearl Jernigan; West Bailey and Susie Gray; J I Jackson and Ada Merritt.

DEATHS
Colored: Henry Smith, 39; Tom Gillan, 35; Fannie Gay, 38; Mamie McGloken, 15; Julia Thurston, 19; Alice Thomas, 53; Martha Scott, 21; Anna Miller, 54; Hazel M Hunter, 15; James Irwin, 21; Wash Neal, 60; Robert Gilmore, 60; Ed Vaughn, 19; Jane Parks, 45; Fannie Richards, 22.

Issue of July 4, 1909:

Board of Health Statistics ending July 3, 1909

MARRIAGES
<u>White</u>: W T Borkland and A Goldenburg; D Fazio and M Fiducio; R L Smith and E Alexander; Dan Denman and Julia Bell; Ed Hunter and Emma Walker.

DEATHS
<u>White</u>: M E Gutler, 65; Henry Karam, 16.
<u>Colored</u>: Mattie Burns, 42; Nancy Napolian, 52; E M Adams, 24; E Smith, 51; Wilson Davidson, 8; L S Stewart, 40; Walter Ford, 21; A O ONeal, 25; Ernest Preston, 6; Henry Harvey, 26; Ned Cherry, 69; Fisher Thompson, 20; Mattie Goin, 33.

Married recently at the home of bride's sister, Mrs. Howell Robinson, Esther Alexander and Robin L Smith, by Rev. Charles J Jones, at Christian Church. The groom is the son of Mrs. Margaret Smith.

Issue of July 11, 1909:

Board of Health Statistics ending July 10, 1909

MARRIAGES
<u>White</u>: Jake G Levy and Lee Harris; O A Lundsford and Ora Lee Cooper; Henry Clifton and Mary Davis.

DEATHS
<u>White</u>: W J Simon, 55; J M Richardson, 71.
<u>Colored</u>: Rebecca Collins, 43; Lucille Bryant, 22; C E Ogilvie, 12; Edna Graves, 7; Eva Cooper, 23.
<u>No Race Shown</u>: James Kennedy, 34; G H Bond, 31; Jerry Wilson, 38; J H Neal, 57; Howard Williams, 27; Gabe Jackson, 41.

Issue of July 18, 1909:

Board of Health Statistics ending July 17, 1909

MARRIAGES

White: J B Smith and Mina Grayson; Tony Zefato and Mary Rappolo; Charles Curruth and Bernice Carley; J D Price and Zola Dixon; T R Mulligan and Lillian Havrell; Mose Morris and Alberta Jacobs; Mayfield Williams and Viola Ross.

DEATHS

White: Bonnie B Welch, 1; H Henderson, 90; Mrs. H B Strosnide, 21; Nettie B Effinger, 25; F L Drake, 45; Thornton Perkins, 23; Alf Banks, 51; Sy Jenkins, 62.
Colored: James Wright, 26; Odessa High, 6; Katie Green, 36.

Issue of July 25, 1909:

Board of Health Statistics ending July 24, 1909

MARRIAGES

White: A N Craddock and Mary L Pentecost; Henry Weir and Florence Goldman; I S Kaufman and Stella Winter; Mack Hubbard and Julia Douglass; Thomas Woods and Beatrice McLean.

DEATHS

White: Floyd Prestridge, 4; Lem Hall, 25; Marthy Fleming, 35; Oliver Bonner, 24.
Colored: James Williams, 19.

Issue of Aug. 1, 1909:

Board of Health Statistics ending July 31, 1909

MARRIAGES
<u>White</u>: Sam Emery and Hattie Robinson.

DEATHS
<u>White</u>: Jim Scrogins, 60; Emma Compton, 32; J R McClain, 54; Daniel Young, 55; Mary Robertson 20; Arthur Bell, 42; Charles St. Clair, 76; Melissa Timmons, 38.
<u>Colored</u>: Jessie Taylor, 10; Jessie Harris, 1; Emanuel Whitted, 34; John Clark, 16; Maggie Jones, 20.

<u>Issue of Aug. 8, 1909</u>:

Board of Health Statistics ending Aug. 7, 1909

MARRIAGES
<u>White</u>: R M Hill and Charity Dunlap.
<u>Black</u>: Ike Jones and Mira Brown; Sam Johnson and Gertrude Miner.

DEATHS
<u>White</u>: Harriett Ruth Ann Waring, 57; Nathan Johnson, 20.
<u>Black</u>: Dick Cimer, 42; Mary Lee Jones, 24; Nellie Beasley, 75; Effie Edwards, 26; Sibel Smith, 14; N Martin, 31.

Died August 6, 1909, Harriett Ruth Ann Waring, wife of W W Waring. She was before marriage Harriett Ruth A. Tanner. Funeral services at First Baptist Church, burial in Greenwood Cemetery, Rev. H A Sumrell officiating.

<u>Issue of Aug. 15, 1909</u>:

Board of Health Statistics ending Aug. 14, 1909

MARRIAGES
White: Charles Jones and Mandy Breemin.

DEATHS
White: Grafton Dixon, 21; Ella G Bagley, 31; Arthur S Toombs, 64; R E Austin, 34; Lucy Carter, 25; John Coy, 70; West Steward, 35.
Black: William H Thompson, 10; James Wilkerson, 65; Alva Janerson, 2; Will Hamilton, 28.

Issue of Aug. 22, 1909:

Board of Health Statistics ending Aug. 21, 1909

MARRIAGES
White: Arthur White and Sue Heitzman; J R Burkett and Josie Adams; Charles E West and Mary Backard.
Black: A Cutliff and Ophelia Avery.

DEATHS
White: Amelia Ford McCutchen, 64; Mattie Robertson, 36; Will Davis, 37; Arthur Blake, 17.
Colored: Jimmie Chambers, 30; H Burough 21; Rosanna Bell, 28; Mason Brown, 69; Booker T Anderson, 1; Dan Walker, 21; Emma Carter, 38.

Died August 19, at her home, Amelia Ford McCutchen, wife of Captain S B McCutchen. She was a daughter of Judge Thomas Ford of Caddo Parish. Besides her husband, other survivors include daughters, Bessie McCutchen and Mrs. J C Foster, sons, A M, Sam B McCutchen and a brother, Dr. T G Ford. Burial was in Greenwood Cemetery, Rev. Felix Hill, officiating.

Issue of Aug. 29, 1909:

Board of Health Statistics ending Aug. 28, 1909

MARRIAGES

White: Sam J Meyers and Flora Strauss; James Tanner and Adeline Moseley; Robert Stewart and Lela Boney; Henry Brown and Hattie Robinson.

DEATHS

White: Mrs. Minnie Snyder, 56.
Black: W M Armstrong, 36; Lillian Marshall, 39; Ella Cheatham, 18; Henry Green, 105; Earl Waling, 22; Mat Caperton, 85; Mary J Colome, 34; Holcombe Perry, 35; Lewis Pickett, 35.

Issue of Sept. 5, 1909:

Board of Health Statistics ending Sept. 4, 1909

MARRIAGES

White: George H Frenche and Addie Shahan; Charles A Barnes and Amanda Rumkin; James A Bailey and Annie Peffer.

DEATHS

White: Thomas J Kelly, 12; Florence May Moorehead, 10; Alice Holsinger, 32; Sumie Clark, 29; Carrie Crittenden, 60; Charlie R Cookson, 26; Lennie Ford, 19; Della Jackson, 45.
Black: Mathew Ray, 28; Mollie Henderson, 50; Isy Brown, 25; John Gant, 50; Annie Mayer, 52.

Issue of Sept. 6, 1909:

Died in this city September 7, Ameline Joseph, 25, wife of Miller Joseph. Funeral services at Holy Trinity

Catholic Church with burial in Catholic Cemetery.

Issue of Sept. 11, 1909:

Board of Health Statistics ending Sept. 10, 1909

DEATHS
White: Eli H Signor, 67; Dr. M M White, 31; J W Overture, 28; W C Kelly, 50; Emiline Joseph, 25; Louise Van Hoose, 1; Harvey Wilson, 44; John Custer, 47; Ollie Harrie, 31; Rachel Shelton, 21; Will Smith, 25.
Colored: Walker Hardy, 23; Alice Smith, 38; Nannie Oats, 40; Leola Bass, 19.

Issue of Sept. 19, 1909:

Board of Health Statistics ending Sept. 18, 1909

MARRIAGES
White: B F Snider and Hattie Rascoe; W B Whitmeyer and Essie Ford.
Colored: Tom Solome and Molly Knox.

DEATHS
White: John Budrow, 33; J W Rainey, 78; L B Custer, 35; John Driscoll, 58; J C Craft, 40; John Martele, 22; Eva Brown, 28; Augustus Love, 70; Oscar Jenkins, 21.
Colored: Lizzie Hauton, 32; John Barnes, 39; Zoe Hill, 1; Kissie Washington, 60; Lizzie Dawson, 70.

Issue of Oct. 3, 1909:

Board of Health Statistics ending October 3, 1909

MARRIAGES

White: Isaac Wilson and Maude McClaney.

DEATHS
White: Mary W Keith, 43; Joe Hebler, 32; Clarnes Thomas, 27.
Colored: Adell Parham, 23; Elgin Stoaks, 1; Quilla Hardy, 17; Matt Hall, 70; Lucindy Stackhouse 67.

Issue of Oct. 10, 1909:

Board of Health Statistics ending Oct. 9, 1909

MARRIAGES
White: C E Maltby and Marion A Miller; C P Handy and Ella Oglesby; J C Harkrider and Lillian S Walford; E R Dorian and Maude M Allen; Carl McCoy and Mabel G Steers.
Black: Arthur Brown and Lena Collins; C Bryam and Laura Williams; Minor Holliday and Idona Jackson.

DEATHS
White: John Lucas, 18; B Fahan, 42; Rena Pillips, 34; Mrs. Irene Findley, 39; Cladys Burrio, 4; Francis Praytor, 32; Julia Delkee, 18.
Black: Ella Jackson, 28; Charles Thomas, 25; Jarrett Dawson, 71.

Issue of Oct. 17, 1909:

Board of Health Statistics ending Oct. 16, 1909

MARRIAGES
White: Wesley Wheles and Bettie M Johnson.
Black: J B Green and Sifana Turner; Luke B Brown and Lizzie Marshall.

DEATHS
White: John Blattman, 67; D W Johnson, 49.
Black: Clara Patterson, 27; Jerry Johnson, 59; Lucy Young, 54; Lizzie Lambert, 40; Effie Cox, 27.

Issue of Oct. 24, 1909:

Board of Health Statistics ending Oct. 23, 1909

MARRIAGES
White: W B Miller and Annie Tipps; Charles B Turner and Vera M Holsted; Elias A Connell and Rose L Roberts; W M Sebastion and Susie M Keith; Henry Prudhomme and Dora McCabe; J A Pinchera and Mabel MacIntosh; Lee Nolan and Jennie Ashland.
Black: D Gaulder and Lula Burk; Peter Green and Esther Chandler; Charles Harris and Charlotte Fields; Harry Furgerson and Gussie Wiggins; C Horace and Mollie Thomas.

DEATHS
White: Mrs. Mary V Hunt, 71; Thomas Lynn, 57; Walter Williams, 30; Charles Vann, 31; John Sloane, 20.
Black: James Boyd, 27; Willie Levistone, 16; Frank McCoy, 90.

  Died October 12, E W Jackson, husband of Rebecca Jackson. Besides his wife other survivors include daughters, Misses Sallie Belle and Vera Jackson, sons, Howard of Oklahoma City, Okla., Eugene of Bunkie, and Hugh and Charlie of Shreveport. Burial was in Greenwood Cemetery.

Issue of Nov. 7, 1909:

Board of Health Statistics ending Nov. 6, 1909

MARRIAGES
<u>White</u>: R D Wells and Maude Williams; Alfred Haynes and Edyth Allman; R T Huson and Celeste Young.
<u>Black</u>: Prymus Hall and Cora V Parry; Moses Spears and Minnie Taylor.

DEATHS
<u>White</u>: William J Dyer, 7; Rose Williams, 38.
<u>Black</u>: Henrietta Houston, 35; Henry Cason, 90.

Issue of Nov. 14, 1909:

Board of Health Statistics ending Nov. 13, 1909

MARRIAGES
<u>White</u>: C Edwin Clancy and Mrs. D A Clancy.
<u>Black</u>: Silas Hatton and Eliza Smith; W A Williams and May P Gilbert; Lee Johnson and Carrie King.

DEATHS
<u>White</u>: Jannie K Coggin, 50; Peter J Trezevant, 65; William Porter, 7; Clara Cooper, 39; Pearl Borling, 19.
<u>Black</u>: Harriett Richards, 32; Dolph Underwood, 70; Judge Batom, 20; Fannie Jackson, 30.

Issue of Nov. 21, 1909:

Board of Health Statistics ending Nov. 20, 1909

MARRIAGES
<u>White</u>: Clyde A Collins and Grace E Steere.
<u>Black</u>: Joe Martin and Florie Bacon; John Scott and Mollie Jemee; Gus Logan and Mary Williams.

DEATHS

White: Dock Reed, 70; Howard Bunston, 7; Carl Balding, 22; James R Wright, 1; L L Harvey, 38; Charles D Harris, 37; Edward Lomnepie, 69.
Black: Helen Wilson, 2; Effie Winn, 34; Ruth Armstrong, 2; Betty Scott, 58.

Issue of Dec. 5, 1909:

Board of Health Statistics ending Dec. 4, 1909

MARRIAGES
White: F C OLeary and Isabella Curtis; J M Adams and Ella Burns.
Black: Will Langster and Laura Hall.

DEATHS
White: Eliza Daniels, 22; James Yerser, 56; Jules Dreyfuss, 53; Mrs. Ada Ford, 25; Pat Duffy, 40; W G Hall, 48; William Woodward, 35; Elizabeth Chapman, 38; Fannie Woodard, 35.
Black: Estella McCoy, 28; Simmie Rochelle, 25; Ben Ware, 38.

Issue of Dec. 12, 1909:

Board of Health Statistics ending Dec. 11, 1909

MARRIAGES
White: Floyd Kendrick and Sallie Woodworth; George H Ray and Nellie Jones; Oscar T Galloway and L E Garrett; C B Hebert and M Williams.
Black: Gus Thomas and Adeline Washington; Burt Henton and Annie Robinson.

DEATHS

White: S Hynes, 77; Mrs. I McDonald, 54; E D Tucker, 38; Mary Davanie, 54.
Black: Josephine Barrett, 55; Dan Carthan, 45; Dixie Jones, 50; J W Abbott, 71.

<u>Issue of Dec. 28, 1909</u>:

Died December 26, Mrs. Caroline Bernstein, wife of Jacob Bernstein. Born in Reidtselz, Alsace, she came to the United States 78 years ago, and resided in Shreveport for the past 34 years.

Issues of Jan. 9, 1910-
Oct. 22, 1910

Board of Health Statistics ending Jan. 8, 1910

MARRIAGES

White: V H Hughens and L Morrison; Walter Cooper and May McCabe; L Lemle and Rosa B Lemle; Harry Balcom and Isa Bollinger; August Shultz and May Flint; Frank Vaccaro and S Leggio.
Black: Charles Clay and Lizzie Watts.

DEATHS

White: Rube Richards, 21; Rhoda Edwards, 93; E Adams, 24; Ethel Kennedy, 26; Mary Pemerton, 60; Mrs. James O Spence, 59; Sarah Dreyer, 49; Silas Jenkins, 60; Elsie Jacobs Lloyd, 28; Frank Warder, 43; Mrs. Susan Scanlon, 51; Julie W Bogel, 72; T J Stoner, 59; Jim Robinson, 45; John Williams, 60; Salina Riley, 36.
Black: Tosy Cains, 48.

Issue of Jan. 16, 1910:

Board of Health Statistics ending Jan. 15, 1910

MARRIAGES

White: Waddy Joseph and Jennie Stamm; W C Price and Sadie Metcalf; Pink Williams and Zola Nelson.

DEATHS

White: Sara Rogers, 25; W Rogers, 19; Richard M Coty, 45; Percy Parish, 25; Cora Dunn, 24; M Andrew, 30; James Coulson, 19; J H Cornwall, 49; H Laysome, 72; George Thomas, 28; A S Salmonson, 56; Allen Fauss, 49.
Black: Amanda Calhoun, 49; Joe Byrd, 30; Virginia

Johnson, 45; Randall Reed, 49; J Abraham, 40; Effie Jones, 27.

Issue of Jan. 18, 1910:

Died January 18, James J Jeffries. A Texan by birth, he volunteered for service in the Confederacy in a command of the Army of Tennessee. He moved from Alexandria to Shreveport ten years ago. He is survived by a niece, Mrs. Field Scott, Calvert, Tex., and a son-in-law, E H Randolph. Burial was in Greenwood Cemetery.

Issue of Jan 23, 1910:

Board of Health Statistics ending Jan. 22, 1910

MARRIAGES
White: T J Matthews and C Holden; J T Whitten and Lena Lunsford.
Black: Cole Young and Lena Robinson.

DEATHS
White: J W Ridder (no age shown); Ardis Mills, 20; Mrs. Ann Johnson, 82; J A Deveness, 55; Mrs. Maltilda Wehkie, 70; Viola Robertson, 30.
Black: Mary Jones, 67; Julia Conway, 17; Georgie Williams, 27; Lawrence Lafall, 15; Chief Bondey, 109; John Williams, 30; Thomas Warren, 90; W H Smith, 52; L Smith, 11; Jimmie Reed, 50; Peter Parker, 120.

Issue of Jan. 30, 1910:

Board of Health Statistics ending Jan. 29, 1910

MARRIAGES

White: Harry Roux and A Mustachia; Thomas F Hodges and Alma Moybrem; Joe Moranto and May Provenza; Edgar Peppler and C Welsh.
Black: Willie Crenshaw and C Minden; Sam Emery and Sue Freneber; Charles Wells and Ethel Christian; P Payne and Ictavia Edwards; Will Prunty and Annie Hord; C Howard and Annie Stone.

DEATHS
White: Joe Goff, 23; Joseph Pedro, 55; Mrs. John Cashore, 44; Howard Edwards, 32; Mrs. Helen Fish, 58; Oma Jacobs, 17; Caroline Scott, 17; John Moore, 35; Jack Perry, 38; George Beardon, 21.
Black: Lettie Christian, 8; L Rowder, 42; Sam Anderson, 46.

Issue of Feb. 5, 1910:

Board of Health Statistics ending Feb. 4, 1910

MARRIAGES
White: Robert McAnn and Ida Brown; C P Keese and Sarah Williams; C E Palmer and E Moines; C B Williams and Cecile Flower; Clarence W King and Julia W Alcocke.
Black: Olivar Williams and Frances Taylor; Hilliard Taylor and Mattie P Walker; Willie Grant and Gertrude Johnson.

DEATHS
White: R E Flores, 54; Mrs. Mary E Hearne, 71; Calcida Acencia, 56.
Black: Bertha McPherson, 3; Rebecca Beaver, 52; Mack Davis, 28; Simon Harris, 55; Alberteen Fields, 1.

Issue of Feb. 13, 1910:

Board of Health Statistics ending Feb. 12, 1910

MARRIAGES
White: J R Thweatt and E Brewer; Phillips Norvinsky and P Hawley; L Watson and Rainie Law.
Black: Thomas Reed and Louisa Roberson; Will Jones and Willie Reed; Bennie Hicks and Martha Washington; Sam Johnson and Louisa Caffa.

DEATHS
White: William McAdams, 70; Albert H Jones, 63; M V Johnson, 63; M Kline, 38; Willie Miles, 28; William Marks, 22; Hilton Emley, 43; Emma Jackson, 27, King McClain, 26; Robert Horn, 23; Wayne Attaway, 1.
Black: Aleck Bass, 43; Dora Roberson, 22; Eliza Simms, 26; Albert Harris, 22; Cora Lee Prichard, 30.

Issue of Feb. 20, 1910:

Board of Health Statistics ending Feb. 19, 1910

MARRIAGES
White: Walter White and Corine Ross; R C McCoy and May Black.

DEATHS
White: 0 W Mullins, 75; W P Cole, 57; Catherine Mueller, 31; S L Coleman, 65.
Black: Harry Edwards, 16; Bella Gins, 60; Victoria Jones, 40; L Z Booher, 65; Julia Depree, 30; Jennie Anderson, 27; Bill Linson, 78; Charles Johnson, 14; Luella Williams, 17; Lavinia Washington, 80.

Issue of Mar. 13, 1910:

Board of Health Statistics ending Mar. 12, 1910

MARRIAGES
White: F G Jones and Effie Bishop; Ben Bonner and Esther Schwartzberg.
Black: George Hazel and Maggie McCoy; John Jones and Jane Davis.

DEATHS
White: S H Crunk, 52; Anthony F Hayes, 4; Mollie Hunt, 55; A B Blocker Jr, 32; John Kelly, 60; Mrs. A E Hobby, 36; John Nelson, 22; R H Wade, 43.
Black: Rube Thomas, 54; Cora Prude, 18; William Jackson, 92; Prince Albert, 70; Ernest Lewis, 17.

Issue of Mar. 20, 1910:

Board of Health Statistics ending Mar. 19, 1910

MARRIAGES
Black: George Woods and Mattie Woods.

DEATHS
White: T C Jordan, 41; Nancy Landrum, 24; John Culliney (no age shown); C B Wheeler, 67; W H Lawley, 57; J M McDermott, 30; Willie Coleman, 50; W M Hutchinson, 18; Maria Beans, 50; George Jones, 65; Albert Thomas, 68; John Kelly, 23; Evyline Hawkins, 26.
Black: Peter Fergerson, 52; Camille Johnson, 28; Bertha Ford, 60; Clara Johnson, 61; Melvini Vensin, 14.

Issue of Mar. 26, 1910:

MARRIAGES
White: E Boatcap and Dona Harris; William R Fogle Jr and Lillian Gillen; Emile Jacquet and Julia B Hood; Hugh W McGill and Annie Hester; R Viola and Ida Feducia.

Black: Ed Foster and Minnie Daniels.

DEATHS
White: W E Maples, 60; John N Hicks, 64; Marie Hall, 19; Binum Dansby, 50; F Conada, 23; Ennis Banks, 19.
Black: Annie Shivers, 14; Sofa Chatain, 76; Anna Soliter, 1; Rosetta Nobles, 61; Jeff Hampton, 24.

Issue of Apr. 3, 1910:

Board of Health Statistics ending Apr. 2, 1910

MARRIAGES
White: B K Jarrett and E Sandell; William Samuels and Florence Western; A E Parham and Annie Cris.
Black: John Robinson and Fannie Herrett.

DEATHS
White: Lizzie Tarrant, 34; W H Lawley, 57; R C Carroll, 32.
Black: Caroline Arkansas, 20; John Whaley, 75; Dan Johnson, 26; Jester Anderson, 6; Annie Brown, 25; Will Murry, 29.

Issue of Apr. 10, 1910:

Board of Health Statistics ending Apr. 9, 1910

MARRIAGES
White: T Burroughs and Girtie Zimmerman; B W Jones and Mary E Hughes; George W Church and Sallie Ivy.
Black: Robert Miller and Laura Booms.

DEATHS
White: Albert Barnett, 30; Mrs. J F Shafner, 30.
Black: Andrew Douglass, 49; Sam Hardia, 42; Julia

Wilfong, 30; Handy Green, 22; Willie White, 2.

Issue of Apr. 17, 1910:

Board of Health Statistics ending Apr. 16, 1910

MARRIAGES
White: J M Colter and Arnie L Pennywell.

DEATHS
White: Ruby McDonald, 9.
Black: Ada Reed, 32; Charles Thomas, 44; William Williams, 4; Andrew Jackson, 65; Alexander Fields, 8; Odell Collins, 24.

Issue of Apr. 18, 1910:

Died yesterday, Mrs. Lena Benjamin, 68, at home of her daughter, Mrs. M Blustein. She was a resident of Shreveport for 35 years. Other survivors include a daughter, Mrs. Sara Marks, Selma, Ala., and two sons, Louis and Joe Benjamin, of this city, grandchildren, Isadore Bluestein, Pine Bluff, Ark., Mrs. H L Heilperin and Mrs. A M Kaufman, Beaumont, Texas. Burial was in Hebrew Rest, Rabbi Moses Jacobson officiating.

Issue of Apr. 23, 1910:

Board of Health Statistics ending Apr. 22, 1910

MARRIAGES
White: Oswell Simmons and Marian Giesen; J E Jackson and Beni Bryan; A S Reeves and Mrs. Hettie Murphy.

DEATHS

White: Mrs. Lena Benjamin, 71; Mrs. Louisie Kerley, 83; John Curn, 60; Grover Hill, 20; Albert Winfred, 35; Aron Jackson, 60; Wilten Parker, 32; Caroline McShow, 65; Willie Lee, 23.
Black: Newton Williams, 13; Viola Cole, 43; Adline McDonald, 64; William Morin, 28; Hallie Friend, 28; John L Howell, 27; Mary Carter, 17; George Rolleigh, 38.

Issue of May 3, 1910:

Board of Health Statistics ending Apr. 30, 1910

MARRIAGES
White: Charley Criss and Willie A Biril; Joe Blackshear and Rebecca Reed; Sam Ward and Martha Robinson.

DEATHS
White: John Hobson, 45; John Frater, 78; Gregory Cruse, 18; Henry J Walls, 41; John Wright, 50; W T Poole, 50; Mary Sanders, 35; William Luck, 68.
Black: Rosa Johnson, 40; Martha A Allen, 39; Eliza Mathews, 16; William A Davis, 1; Victoria Beard, 29; Keno Long, 76; H Frank, 27; Lizzie Wiggins, 17; Eleanor Cade, 23; John Harrell, 40.

Issue of May 17, 1910:

Board of Health Statistics ending May 16, 1910

MARRIAGES
White: W G Moffin and Lula Milton; Richard Nelson and Agnus Noble.

DEATHS
White: Henry Youree, 52; Juna Adair, 1; Justice Baird, 5;

Walter L Cheesman, 13; J C Gibbs, 58; Eugene Bell, 19; Robert L Hampton, 36; James D McDade, 7.
Black: Harriet McLemo, 45; Frank Brooks, 16; Lula Nelson, 60; Thomas Jones, 50; Joe Simmons, 30; Annie Simpson, 70; Jessie Norman, 30.

Issue of May 22, 1910:

Board of Health Statistics ending May 21, 1910

MARRIAGES
White: Ernest Wiseman and Broadie McDade.
Black: Ras Mosley and Lelia Woods; Sandy Holmes and Dora Marshall; Winfred Johnson and Jennie Norris.

DEATHS
White: Nancy Jones, 64; Grace Beaird, 1; Hortense Marionneaux, 28; Leon Lee, 20.
Black: Caroline Washington, 49; Ernest Drew, 10.

Issue of May 29, 1910:

Board of Health Statistics ending May 28, 1910

MARRIAGES
White: W H Lindsay and M E Kenyon; L M Rudy and Lillie W Harrison.
Black: W J Walker and Ella Jordan.

DEATHS
White: Llewellyn L Tomkies, 54; F Barnett, 83; John Anderson, 59; Joe Vance, 31.
Black: Bethusel Jones, 29; Sam Washington, 29; Mack Boons, 26; Jim Hall, 28.

Issue of June 5, 1910:

Board of Health Statistics ending June 4, 1910

MARRIAGES
White: J H Oneal and Annie C Kinney; John M Knighton and M E Smith; J B Williams and B Shepard; Marian Young and E Baisch; R G Collins and Margret Jefferson; L R George and Georgie Walker

DEATHS
White: Ruth Adams, 22.
Black: Glen Miles, 25; Constant McCoy, 24; Z Richmond, 12; Robert Randolph, 2; Laura A Marville, 54; Joe McKinney, 50; Mary Moore, 36; Bettie Jackson, 43; Patsy Bryant, 15; Leana Oliver, 24.

Issue of June 12, 1910:

Board of Health Statistics ending June 11, 1910

MARRIAGES
White: W S Dunkin and Veva Henderson; Dolph G Frantz and Elda V Weaver; S S Watts and B Robinson.
Black: Blake Parker and Caroline Collins.

DEATHS
White: C B Johnson, 52; A G Hodge, 59; Mrs. Barbette Weil, 77; Della Boyett, 53; Owen Hill, 55; Singleton Jones, 20; Jane Gestine, 60; John Morris, 50; Steve Ellis, 60.
Black: John Hooker, 30; Henry Jackson, 24.

Died June 5, Babette Weil, a native of Strasburg, Alsace-Lorraine, 77. A native of Shreveport for 51 years, she was the mother of Mrs. Henry Bodenheimer, Mrs. M

Strauss, Charles and H M Weil. Burial was in Hebrew Rest.
Died June 5, Arthur G Hodge, 59, eldest son of Hon. B L Hodge and Mrs. Carrie Dudley Hodge of this city. He married Isabel Butler Williamson, daughter of Col. George Williamson. Burial was in Oakland Cemetery, Rev. D V Philson of Episcopal Church officiating.

Issue of June 18, 1910:

Board of Health Statistics ending June 17, 1910

MARRIAGES

White: Grover Hall and Ruby L Neal; J F Schilling and M. Findly.
Black: James Pipkins and E McPherson; Richard Ford and Martha Washington; J B Anderson and Hattie Turner; Fletcher Ward and Carrie Turner; Willie Carter and Emma Smith; James Carter and Ruth Christian.

DEATHS

White: F A Sellers, 50; Mrs. Josephine Henry, 59; Mrs. E E Loe, 47; Lou Page, 38.
Black: Emile Smith, 27; Charles Burnham, 72; Alfred Bull, 46; Alice Hatler, 30; Ella Rose, 22; Noah Green, 47.

Issue of June 26, 1910:

Board of Health Statistics ending June 25, 1910

MARRIAGES

White: E R Bauer and Hester Jeffries; M G Aldrich and Ola Cook; William North and Annie Ringgold.
Black: Sam Williams and Adeline Williams; Joseph Mason and Lula Johnson; Richard Grant and Beatrice Walker.

DEATHS
<u>White</u>: Mary Wortman, 77; H C Stokes, 55; Harold Grant, 2; Mrs. E C Coburn, 44; John Donohue, 41.
<u>Black</u>: Dave Green, 70; Clint Campbell, 55; Gracy Smith, 34; Georgie Scott, 28; Sallie Ward, 85; Annie Miles, 25; Alex Johnson, 51; Joseph Brooke, 13; Frank Bradford, 30; Perry Wilson, 90; George Poleman, 50; Evangeline Burrow, 30; Lucy Low, 28.

Issue of July 3, 1910:

Board of Health Statistics ending July 2, 1910

MARRIAGES
<u>White</u>: H Sartini and P Notini; S J Braunig and Rosa Miller; C L Hut and N Stanford; E H Small and Mai Jones.
<u>Black</u>: Willie Bryant and Leola Dundo.

DEATHS
<u>White</u>: Rosa Jones, 16; Francis Williams, 65; Charles Reagan, 53; W H Hyde, 4.
<u>Black</u>: Lizzie Smith, 24; Henrietta Johnson, 21; John Hines, 31; Lavinia Washington, 50; Julia Ganvial, 35; Daniel Dickson, 32; H Valerin, 51; Sella Patterson, 23; Dallas Johnstone, 17; Wilson Anderson, 60.

Issue of July 10, 1910:

Board of Health Statistics ending July 9, 1910

MARRIAGES
<u>White</u>: J S Baifield and Lillian Jones; M A Haydon and Emma H Quinn; J M Monroe and Willie Beazeale; Isa Froner and Jennie Recher.
<u>Black</u>: Mose Chelson and Beatrice McKiney.

DEATHS

<u>White</u>: J C Beasley, 60; Mrs. Kate Dalton, 61; Lizzie Dewitt, 40; Andrew Collins, 35; C Garcia, 23; Jim Gray, 78; I Sims, 86; Ike Davis, 28.

<u>Black</u>: Francis Rollin, 50; M Goder, 49; W H Lee, 4; Ethel Zeigler, 23; Ellen White, 23; Gertrude Jamison, 11; Carrie Davis, 28; Octavia Reede, 26.

Issue of July 17, 1910:

Died July 13, Mrs. N M Furman, mother of Dr. Frank Furman, Mrs. Paul Means and Mary Furman, of this city. She was the daughter of the Hon. Henry M Marshall of DeSoto Parish, widow of the late Dr. F S Furman. Services were at St. Marks's Episcopal Church with burial in the family burying ground near Gloster, Rev. Dr. Thorp officiating.

Issue of July 17, 1910:

Board of Health Statistics ending July 16, 1910

MARRIAGES

<u>White</u>: W H Stockwell and Hilda Rosenberg; J D Williams and Mary L Rolston.
<u>Black</u>: Zach Washington and Dora Garrett.

DEATHS

<u>White</u>: Coltis Davis, 25; Mrs. H Dreyfuss, 52; Mrs. Mattie Furman, 70; Ed Lynch, 35; Sam Ellins, 25.
<u>Black</u>: Mattie Ricks, 24; Elen Johnson, 65; Bob Mitchell, 45; Sarah Jones, 60; Mandy Williams, 21; Pickins Patterson, 30; Eta Oneal, 25; Aaron Vansen, 18; Charlie Mitchell, 40; Francis Packleck, 40; Julia Sims, 36; Arthur Jones, 36.

Issue of July 24, 1910:

Board of Health Statistics ending July 23, 1910

DEATHS
White: Sara Aseunes, 60; Lena Ann Robinson, 74.
Black: Maggie Washington, 31; Reace Lee Brown, 22; George Howard, 29; John Dunaway, 20.

Issue of Aug. 7, 1910:

Board of Health Statistics ending Aug. 6, 1910

MARRIAGES
White: John J Kline and Julia Mayer.
Black: Carlia Earls and Roberta Clayton.

DEATHS
White: Al Johnson, 42; Arnold Martin, 14; Stef Kytrnike, 45; Clara Rouget, 18.
Black: Jim Banks, 71; Nathan Walker, 74; Prince Love, 29; Edmonia Allen, 54; Dessie Beasley, 23; Andrew Thomas, 59.

Issue of Aug. 14, 1910:

Board of Health Statistics ending Aug. 13, 1910

MARRIAGES
White: George Beck and Belle McDonald; W H Mayo Jr and U B Jordan; J Davis and Mattie Coleman; Will Taylor and Rosa Clark; Robert Freeman and Alice Johnson; Kirby S Jones and Ernestine White.

DEATHS

White: Sallie M Allison, 30; John Breffieh, 1; Euna Cargile, 28; Lizzie Ruiter, 22; R L Gilbert, 31; Isaiah Grantham, 29; P Moody, 38.
Black: Fannie L Sims, 42; John Crimmeal, 25; Louis Rix, 28; Earl S Dorch, 6; Sarah White, 14; Cy Williams, 24; Ben Goodrich, 66.

Issue of Aug. 20, 1910:

Board of Health Statistics ending Aug. 19, 1910

MARRIAGES
White: D E Shaw and Girlsie Vise.

DEATHS
White: J E Powell, 22; H M Rutherford, 67; John T Enright, 63; J W McClelland, 45; Mrs. Mollie Fisher, 38; M L Maybright, 27; C G Rife, 63; Joe Simmons, 39.
Black: Zannie Taylor, 15; Polly Taylor, 68; Jenny Minor, 45; Nathaniel Byas, 3; Jeff Shaw, 67.

Issue of Aug. 28, 1910:

Board of Health Statistics ending Aug. 27, 1910

MARRIAGES
White: W E Condon and Martha Hauser.
Black: C Anderson and Ella Stewart; James Lewis and Alice Samuels; D Gibson and Carrie Robinson; W Robinson and Josephine Robinson.

DEATHS
White: George Sutherland, 45; J C Backus, 44; Elva Killinger, 34; R O Walters 30; T C Grey, 70; John Beefe, 60; B F Berry, 35; Addie Dillard, 36; A Farly, 20; Hat Higgins,

41; Angie Johnson, 28.
Black: Bettie Pettic, 53; W R McDonald, 41; Roda Johnson, 80; Mose McCray, 96.

Issue of Sept. 4, 1910:

Board of Health Statistics ending Sept. 3, 1910

DEATHS

White: W P Philibert, 57; Willie Harper, 39; D J Crowley, 38; William B Cox, 38.
Black: Fanny Lawson, 22; S B Jones, 48; Susan Wilson, 59; Emanuel Bennings, 29; Annie Fisher, 49; Ann Mclean, 66; Matt Scott, 74; Jim Smith, 26; Sam Williams, 33; Charles Johnson, 1; Erwin Charles, 85; Della Mitchell, 40.

Issue of Sept. 13, 1910:

Board of Health Statistics ending Sept. 12, 1910

MARRIAGES

White: George C Rimes and Lucile Voisin.
Black: Willie Blackshire and Elmora Brown.

DEATHS

White: Pauline McBrady, 28; Willis Alston, 86; Robert McDonald, 5; Marian Rockmore, 56; Rose Lavell, 73; Jacob Brack, 40; Annie McLemore, 1; Willie Watson, 4; Wesley Fuller, 18; Mariah Daniels, 70; Marion Maltby, 20; Wallace Breckenridge, 29; Lee Massey, 22; F Ruby, 24; Ben Farley, 25; Viola Parks, 26; Florence Ginabirth, 24.

Issue of Sept. 15, 1910:

Board of Health Statistics ending Sept. 14, 1910

MARRIAGES
White: Henry McCain and Adelia Thomas.

DEATHS
White: Ben Landman, 67; J T Ponder, 53; Dora Johnson, 31.
Black: Hortense Rowling, 25; Fred D Collins, 13.

Issue of Sept. 18, 1910:

Board of Health Statistics ending Sept. 17, 1910

MARRIAGES
White: John Sandora and Vincenzo Rizzo; G W Adams and Nora Maroney.
Black: George Jackson and Lilie P Smith; George Cobb and Corine Williams; Alex Ross and Josephine Jackson.

DEATHS
White: Blanchard Spurline, 22; Charles Hamilton, 46; N B Franklin, 60; Robert Bray, 18; Mrs. M Dubois, 31; Joe L Walker, 24.
Black: Ivie Pugh, 13; Mary Jelks, 21; F S LeGardy, 66; Mazie Hicks, 40; Everlina Sims, 23; Eddie Lee Smith, 8; Annie Dupree, 19; Isaac Wade, 68; Will Drake, 25.

Issue of Oct. 16, 1910:

Board of Health Statistics ending Oct. 15, 1910

MARRIAGES
White: Henry McCain and Adelia Thomas.

DEATHS
White: Ben Landman, 67; T S Ponder, 53; Dora Johnson, 31.
Black: Hortense Rowling, 25; Fred D Collins, 13.

Married September 27, Emerson Bentley and Sue Eleanor Watson at home of bride's aunt, Mrs. Mattie H Williams, by Dr. Jasper K Smith, First Presbyterian Church. She is the only daughter of Mrs. H D Watson and the late Harry Douglas Watson, and grandchild of Colonel Matthew Watson.

<u>Issue of Oct. 22, 1910</u>:

Board of Health Statistics ending Oct. 21, 1910

MARRIAGES

<u>White</u>: Oscar Schliepak and Mainie O Specht; Albert M Bourquin and Carrie L Booth; Bert F Carter and B F Dorian; Joe Clociso and Annie Fulco.
<u>Black</u>: John Hickman and C Jones; John Sims and Estella Bridger; George Mathews and B White; H Gardener and Hattie Wilson.

DEATHS

<u>White</u>: Mrs. A F Roscoe, 58; Clarke Wabers, 4; Frank Harris, 34; J M Williams, 65; J M Pugh, 70; F Hanson, 43; George M Garmony, 19; Pennie Glasper, 20.
<u>Black</u>: Mattie B Miles, 1; Isom Hill, 84; Margaret Hamilton, 52; Julia Carter, 37; China Green, 75

(The Board of Health did not publish any statistics from November 12, 1910 to February 18, 1911)

Issues of Nov. 14, 1910-
Dec. 25, 1910

Issues from Nov. 14, 1910, to Dec. 25, 1910:

Nov. 14, 1910: Died November 13, 1910, Estelle Logan Dalzell, widow of Dr. W T D Dalzell, rector of St. Mark's Episcopal Church for 30 years. She is survived by daughters, Mrs. A J Ingersoll and Mrs. William Boyd, Coushatta, and a son, Dr. W G Dalzell. Funeral services at St. Mark's, conducted by Dr. White, burial in Greenwood Cemetery.

Nov. 29, 1910: Died November 23, Nellie Long Foster, at her home in "Curraghmuir". She was the widow of James Martin Foster. Two sons, W L and Jim Foster, and two daughters, Mrs. Benton McMillan and Mrs. Felix Williams, survive. Burial was in Oakland Cemetery.

Dec. 6, 1910: Married December 2, M S Slagle and Susie Dunsmire.

Dec. 6, 1910: Married December 5 at St. Mark's Episcopal Church, by Rev. Luke White, James McCann and Chloe Ridenboch. She is a daughter of Mrs. Ida Collier. The groom is a son of Professor T E McCann, leader of the Majestic Theater orchestra.

Dec. 11, 1910: Died December 6, Annie Burt Land. A daughter of Dr. William Miles Burt of Edgefield, S. C., she first married Captain Pierce Butler in June 1875. After years of widowhood, she married Thomas L Land, son of Judge T T Land. Survivors include brothers, Jim and Ed Burt, and a daughter, Pawnee Butler, Benton.

Dec. 8, 1910: Married December 7, by Rev. C L Jones,

Pressley W Smith and Gertrude Sightler.

Dec. 25, 1910: Died December 23, Mrs. Jennie R Elstner. She is survived by daughters, Mrs. Daisy Wimbish, Mrs. Lloyd Bowers, Nacogdoches, Tex., sons, Hayden Elstner, Texarkana, Ark., and Lee, Monroe and Richard Elstner. Burial was in Oakland Cemetery.

Issues of Jan. 8, 1911-
Dec. 31, 1911

Jan. 8, 1911: Married January 5, William Peyton and Bessie Scott by Rev. Luke White at St. Mark's Episcopal Church.

Jan. 8, 1911: Married January 4, Carl Skoog and Carrie Hunsicker, daughter of Henry Hunsicker. The bride's attendant was her sister, Mrs. Simon Fox. The best man was the groom's brother, Grover Skoog.

Jan. 15, 1911: Died January 9, Wilbur F Buckelew, husband of Nettie Wood Buckelew, who died several years ago. Surviving is a daughter, Mrs. Minnie Melton, Longview, sons, Newton, Will, Fred and Andrew Buckelew, and a sister, Mrs. T F Bell. Burial was in Greenwood Cemetery.

Jan. 22, 1911: Died January 19, Mrs. Marie Benus Lawrason, widow of Dr. G B Lawrason. Survivors include two daughters, Belle and Zelia Lawrason.

Feb. 8, 1911: Married February 8, Clarence Reid and Elizabeth Edmonds at First Presbyterian Church.

Issue of February 19, 1911:

Board of Health Statistics ending Feb. 18, 1911

MARRIAGES
White: Gus Young and Carrie Brown; Horace Carter and Zenabia Williams; Henry Kendall and Anna Kendall; Louis Williams and Bulah Miles.

DEATHS
White: Jim Williams, 82; Rosa Sloan, 45; John Rogers, 10;

Ben Rhines, 24; Fred Feutiess, 3; Lillie Cameron, 73.
Black: Charles Flowers, 3; Hulda Underwood, 61; Robert Perry, 23.

Issue of Feb. 26, 1911:

Board of Health Statistics ending Feb. 25, 1911

MARRIAGES
White: F L Thomas and E M Fellows; Victor H Wenk and Ida Porath; S C McConnell and Rosalie Clanton; Eugene E Senord and Mary Harkey; T L McClean and Sarah Stinson; George Freeman and Sarah Sebastian.
Black: Jim Baily and Pearl Hewitt; E O Hucher and Hary Hewitt; George McCally and Ella Silman; Mance Williams and Tevey Tanner; Add Hall and Bessie Mayo.

DEATHS
White: Dr. W L Egan, 53; Mrs. Elizabeth Fisher, 67; J W Gaudin, 64; M Spelman, 74; Mary Willis, 28; S Thomas, 6; Mary Z Pegues, 24; E P Sexton, 22; F Winstead, 18.
Black: Carrie Green, 46; Julia McKenney, 3; Elvira Taylor, 60; James Doughtery, 33; Mattie Sims, 3; V E White, 14; H Moser, 35; Aron Jones, 60; Bruner Lambert, 39; Will Morris, 28.

Died February 24, Mrs. Elizabeth Fisher, widow of Dr. L H Fisher. Survivors include daughters, Mrs. Susie Kline, Mrs. Douglas Attaway and Delinda Fisher, sisters, Mrs. Mattie Sewall, Mrs. Maggie Bourquin and Mrs. Annie Carlton. Burial was in Oakland Cemetery.

Issue of Mar. 5, 1911:

Board of Health Statistics ending Mar. 4, 1911

MARRIAGES
White: Duncan L Campbell and E L Umberhagen.
Black: Morgan Washington and Annette Peterson.

DEATHS
White: Robert K Williams, 22; Julian Morizot, 61; Sarah Moore, 56; Jefferson Lewis, 8; J L Waldrop, 34; Burt Murray, 69; Effie Boone, 30; Jim Skinner, 69.
Black: George Roberson, 40; Clifford Thomas, 19; Susie Russell, 59; Emerline Reed, 3; Maggie Banks, 53; L Pipkin, 2; Edgar Connor, 10; Virginia Wells, 37; Charley Wiggins, 40; William Sims, 43; John Richardson, 29; Leila Garborough, 20; Will Johnson, 23; Anna B Laftin, 20; Mabel L Lewis, 5.

Issue of Mar. 12, 1911:

Board of Health Statistics ending Mar. 11, 1911

MARRIAGES
White: J A Bell and Mollie Gooley; Walter F Kennedy and Barina Dragon; D C Peniff and Zella Childers.
Black: Ananias Brown and Tyra Taylor; Will Beasley and Estelle Rupell; A Williams and Julia Harrison.

DEATHS
White: Birdie Jester, 20; Herman Linman, 82; Mrs. Emma Lawrence, 49; G B Peck, 70; Allana Cooke, 4; C A Alston, 65; W R Furlow, 38; John B Margrove, 45; George Smith, 68.
Black: Mary Legardy, 40; Sam Adams, 23; Ida Stephens, 28; Georgie Woodard, 22; Addie Mitchell, 20; Fanny Tally, 24; Emma Lewis, 27; Jim Hollis, 18; A Wiley, 51.

Issue of Mar. 17, 1911:

Board of Health Statistics ending Mar. 16, 1911

MARRIAGES
White: F Selger and Mary V Stevenson; W C Morris and Clio Nicholson; Clarence E Trichel and Codilia Roberts.

DEATHS
White: P A Maxwell, 29; George Turk, 53; Peter Raccich, 11; Martin L McDonald, 46; Sam Huffman, 3; A Williams, 30.
Black: Randell Pemberton, 58; Mable Cloud, 1; Lizzie Garden, 28; Sallie Dean, 103; Carl McKinney, 17; Charles Brown, 48; Tomey Cole, 45; Joseph Mutchinson, 22; James Daniels, 60; Jennie Morley, 50; Mandy Brown, 30.

Issue of Mar. 26, 1911:

Board of Health Statistics ending Mar. 25, 1911

MARRIAGES
White: C C Phillips and Myra Bickham; J O Summerhill and Elsie Foster.
Black: Sims Rayford and Maude Eleson; Sam Ogilvie and Lula Steers.

DEATHS
White: C G Kornegay, 30; P Horregue, 62; A R Davis, 51.
Black: Lula A Hooker, 1; Dell Baily, 45; Mathew Ankron, 20; Eliza Thompson, 24; Leo Beaty, 16; Phil Smith, 75; C Young, 28; Alen Curry, 25; Rufus Rice, 39; Tom Ross, 26; James Williams, 35.

Issue of Apr. 2, 1911:

Board of Health Statistics ending Apr. 1, 1911

MARRIAGES
<u>White</u>: Tug Boyd and Virginia Lucas; Charles Lewis and Orilla Banks; T J Edwards and Leala Collins; Joseph Allen and Lulia Watts; J Rafe and Frances Holliner; E D Williams and Virginia Tyler.

DEATHS
<u>White</u>: Myra Whitman, 1; Vera May Shirley, 21; Mrs. Emma Moore, 58; D J Showers, 52; Irene J Heartman, 22.
<u>Black</u>: Lela Jenkins, 40; Katie Mose, 40; Jeannett Wright, 20; Will Washington, 45; Charlie Harris, 35; Robert Walker, 26; Allen McCall, 70; Sarah Bird, 32; Charles Jackson, 30; Anderson Author, 20; Mannie Russell, 40; H Collins, 30; George Flemming, 36.

Issue of Apr. 9, 1911:

Board of Health Statistics ending Apr. 8, 1911

MARRIAGES
<u>White</u>: S A Johnson and Inez Morgan; Jeff Rigsby and Rufle Williams; W E Wallace and Mrs. J M Brewster; G D Seay and Mrs. Leah Prudhomme Jackson.
<u>Black</u>: Phil Gales and Lula Johnson; Fran Braden and Sybe Johnson; Willie Oneal and Florintine Frazier; Nathan Chew and Josephine Williams; T H Davis and Ella Taylor.

DEATHS
<u>White</u>: Mrs. Ernestine Jacobson, 47; Carry M Matovich, 44; Johnnie Moore Barnes, 14; R J McLemore, 55; Nan Crews, 3.
<u>Black</u>: Mary Henderson, 8; Willie Hill, 29; Anna Lewis, 19; Clara Wilson, 67; Thelma Gaulden, 4; Dallas Cassier, 18;

Henrietta Harris, 14; Cary Wood, 63; Pessiro Berry, 1; Willie Brown, 17; Harriett Goodrich, 80; Tom Davis, 50; Burt Smith, 2; Walter Jones, 12.

Issue of Apr. 16, 1911:

Board of Health Statistics ending Apr. 15, 1911

MARRIAGES

White: J R Crownrich and Mary Finday; P B Meyer and Matilda Loeb; W Smith and May Holmes.
Black: Charles Harrell and Sallie Lewis; J W LeJoy and Willie F Blue; W Beazley and Essee Harris; T Johnson and Mary Coleman.

DEATHS

White: Carrie Lee James, 29; Annie May Kendrick, 1; Thomas Halstead, 31; Frank C Wells, 57; Sarah Woods Pearce, 23; Charles Purnell, 53.
Black: Effie Williams, 44; Moses Shackleford, 57; Ella Gilbert, 30; Archie Richardson, 26; Nina Robinson, 30; Mattie Marshall, 30; Mary Henderson, 31; Nina Montgomery, 25; Pinky Sullivan, 22; George Wiley, 66.

Married April 11, Percy Meyer and Tillie Loeb, daughter of Mr. and Mrs. Herman Loeb. Attending were bride's sisters, Mrs. Leon Loeab, Eda Loeb, the groom's parents, Mr. and Mrs. Gabe Meyer, the bride's brothers Herbert Loeb and Sol Loeb.

Issue of Apr. 23, 1911:

Board of Health Statistics ending Apr. 22, 1911

MARRIAGES

White: B C Crandall and Alvina Rottsebal; James C Hall and Annie Woods; Richard Gustine and Elizabeth Deas; Robert Elmore and Zeta M Mobley.
Black: Clark William and Florence Sims; Louis Hall and Flora Williams; D Fulcher and Georgiana Callay; L McDaniel and Amanda Polly.

DEATHS
White: Henry Schwartzberg, 13; P Toney, 46; William Sprouse, 55.
Black: Major Moseley, 2; Lewis Green, 80; Alice Cook, 46; Abner Battle, 31; Lucidy Wilson, 19; Thomas Forsythe, 44; Green Rider, 58; E Baker, 3.

Issue of Apr. 30, 1911:

Board of Health Statistics ending Apr. 29, 1911

MARRIAGES
White: J M Holden and Maggie Ramsey; A C Bains and Lizzie Robertson; W C Morgan and Myrtle Bridges; W E Pecor and Lina Crowder.
Black: Dennis Patterson and Mira Hickson; Tom Smith and Lucy Frierson; Elijah Carter and Maddie McCain; Andrew Banks and Mary Dixon; Bert Brown and Matie Adams; Joseph Dillingham and Julia Clark; Charles Boardman and Ruby M Franklin; Leonard Franklin and Annie Cary.

DEATHS
White: Thomas G Roberts Jr, 3; Dennis J McMahan, 76; Mrs. Virginia Pugh, 82; Mrs. Annie Smith, 45.
Black: Elvira Wilson, 15 months; Bettie Pringle, 38; Eliza Porter, 67; Ann Jackson, 80; Preston Tyler, 4; George Oars, 80; Littie Smith, 45; Nicie Prescott, 2; P Williams, 29; Richard Jackson, 45; Henry Thomas, 19.

Issue of May 6, 1911:

Board of Health Statistics ending May 5, 1911

MARRIAGES

White: J A Burris and Maude Williams; D F Harding and Eveline Ashly.

Black: E D Wilson and Susie Bauman; Fred McElveen and Edna Hartsfield; Isiah Maiden and Rebecca Player; Floyd McMillan and Jennie Alexander.

DEATHS

White: Obedia B Ferrel, 9; Martha E Allen, 69; Bow Stephenson, 17; Joe Wilmore, 22; Miriam Hudson, 16 months; E C Morrie, 20; Annie Craft, 11; Ruth Pruitt, 32.
Black: Willie Pore, 1; Dan Blunsen, 58; Fanny Burns, 20; Gertrude Taylor, 14; Maggie Chotlin, 23; Lee Emmett, 24; Lige Fuller, 41; Tom Wart, 22.

Issue of May 14, 1911:

Board of Health Statistics ending May 13, 1911

MARRIAGES

White: Pete Froib and Sallie Schutz; H C Shuchley and Frankie Jones; Toney Parlavecio and Ida Fulco.

DEATHS

White: William Singleton, 52; S F M Barnard, 67; John G Noles, 32; Charles Spurling, 70; Charles Laenger, 14; Ida Lee Chapman, 10; June Jacobs, 101; Nona McDade, 43; M Hanley, 31; George Reynolds, 45; Ruth R Vincent, 30; Aaron Perkins, 51.
Black: Ambers Howard, 24; Maple Gardner, 17 months; Willie May Lewis, 25; Ralph Peterson, 2; Nathan Dunmire,

24; W Sushner, 25.

Issue of May 21, 1911:

Board of Health Statistics ending May 20, 1911

MARRIAGES
White: W D Judkins and Lucy Flanagan; William Morent and Julia Strong.
Black: John Watson and Mary Byrd.

DEATHS
White: William Chase Jr, 27; Ruby Wells, 27; Herman Poleman, 49; Mary Cohn, 69; J F Bates, 50; Josephine Maas, 55; Frank Truss, 24; Florence Bertrand, 7; Ruth Butler, 10.
Black: Willie Biles, 20; Mollie Field, 53; Frank Watson, 63; Ella Nettles, 17; Robert Collins, 19; Sopha Blachins, 44.

Issue of May 28, 1911:

Board of Health Statistics ending May 27, 1911

MARRIAGES
White: Thomas R Bounds and Jennie Prudhomme; Thomas Grimes and Lelia Bell; E S Dorser and Rosa Odem; William Andreola and Caroline Bowers.
Black: Elias Banks and Elizabeth King; Hy Young and Lavinia James.

DEATHS
White: David Weiller, 50; William J William Jr, 16 months; G N Bates, 54.
Black: Ed Rowdy, 53; Noma Glassco, 48; George B Crisp, 26; Luke Loyd, 65; Willie Stephens, 26.

Issue of June 4, 1911:

Board of Health Statistics ending June 3, 1911

MARRIAGES

White: F Bailey and S Johnson; Ernest Smith and Sarah Wiley; Oscar Richardson and Hattie Perrin; B S Taylor and Susie Edmonds; Will E Boyd and Annie Lanier; J B Haris and P Schwartzburg.

DEATHS

White: Corsoro Gonzalez, 47; Frank Blocker, 25; Jesse W Braswell, 38; Will Thomas, 25; A Creton, 25; Clarede Wells, 36; A Hill, 22.
Black: Abe Wells Jr, 9; Lillie S Brown, 27; Francis Dupree, 37; Sydney Wyatt, 37; Major Simon, 78; G F Bell Jr, 28; Jackson Moran, 51.

Issue of June 11, 1911:

Board of Health Statistics ending June 10, 1911

MARRIAGES

White: W C Hatie and E Bonnette; J D S Brown and Alma Zimmerman; Charles Rogers and Nina Gillen; L Mayor and H Dreyfuss; Carey Ratcliff and D Fisher; W H Swearinger and B Hudson.
Black: Paul Williams and Clara Gates; William Johnson and Stella White.

DEATHS

White: Emma S Frick, 31; Fred Davidson, 41; Antionette Voisin, 47; Eunice F Kirby, 23; J H Gilliland, 67; Mrs. K Moncrief, 28; Lewis Tipa, 64; E Miller, 24; Etta Jones, 21.
Black: Ernest Hover, 6; Rachel Scott, 28; Savannah Thomas,

41; Mary J Harris, 1; R N Williams, 1; Harris Anderson, 19; Ebenezer Morris, 35; Mattie Griffin, 37; Henry Love, 28; Joe Lewis, 20; Albert Falkner, 33; Dink Roberts, 45; Anderson Cato, 45; Oscar Williams, 28.

Issue of June 18, 1911:

Board of Health Statistics ending June 17, 1911

MARRIAGES

<u>White</u>: F E Peatross and Neva Kerley; E D Miller and Grace Hinsey; M Weisman and Bertha Goldstein; H Heelmers and Marie Ertz; Thomas P Manuel and E Hughens.
<u>Black</u>: Robert Hoyer and Clara Banks; Louis Braden and Pearl Gatlin; H Andrews and Lavinia Thomas.

DEATHS

<u>White</u>: Charles A Roger, 25; Ruby F Wells, 27; Jerrimia Sanford, 70; Bunkly Coston, 18; W P Grayson, 36; Mary Sloane, 43.
<u>Black</u>: Clay Stewart, 66; Lula Edwards, 20; Florence Williams, 76; Caterine Harper, 20; Nicholas Williams, 12; Rock A Mitchell, 54; Rochelle Bird, 41; Susanna Love, 35; H L Lewis, 60; Sam Monis, 18; Richard Allen, 54; V Tolliver, 40.

Issue of June 25, 1911:

Board of Health Statistics ending June 24, 1911

MARRIAGES

<u>White</u>: E S Cayce and E T Moore; J A McDonald and Emma W Collins; M G Stewart and Frances Lacy; E S Tiffen and Shurley J Parish.
<u>Black</u>: Robert Christman and Alice Jackson; E Buttler and

Alice Thomas; H Woods and Frances Jones; Tyler Watts and Virginia Blackman; I Wilson and Susie E Moore.

DEATHS

<u>White</u>: C W Keiser, 53; Mary C Wiley, 68; Judith E Dunlap, 85; Joe Travis, 45; E Luke, 28.
<u>Black</u>: Harriett Boone, 52; Casey Nickerson, 87; Lucindy Champion, 32; Matildy Frinchell, 22; Gus Edwards, 49; Francis Jackson, 64; Charles Chandler, 75; Sallie L Howell, 3; Nina White, 28; Olive Coleman, 21.

Issue of July 2, 1911:

Board of Health Statistics ending July 1, 1911

MARRIAGES

<u>White</u>: J Williams and Mary D Hunt; S Gray and Jennie Henderson; Clifford Garrett and Evie Pickett; George S Dickson and Martha Holmes; B Switzer and Dixie Talley; Moss McCalish and B Holloway.

DEATHS

<u>White</u>: Catherine Whitmeyer, 59; Mary Saritina, 45; Charles Halen, 62.
<u>Black</u>: Pearl Timbler, 17; Mary Henderson, 38; Eddie Greer, 45; West Bailey, 58; Jessie Hersey, 22; C Scott, 65; David Stephens, 42; Nancy Franklin, 70; Dora Fagans, 48; Levi Lewis, 20.

Issue of July 9, 1911:

Board of Health Statistics ending July 8, 1911

MARRIAGES

<u>White</u>: James W Sanders and Mary Jones; R C Alexander

and Mattie Bowers; Yancy Collins and Pearl Richardson; W D Whilby and Carrie Johnson; Dr. S A Dickson and B Dillingham.
Black: William H Smith and Necie Oliver.

DEATHS

White: Florence N Fullilove, 26; Rafin Degan, 18; Noma Dickerson, 20; John Johnson, 17.
Black: Almer Brown, 8 months; Louise Ford, 23; Mary Simpson, 50; Mattie Walker, 30; Memphis Rosell, 20; Irene Beldon, 35; Joe Woods, 40; Oliver Wright, 31; Kittie Cross, 65; Richard White, 27; Foster Blackman, 34.

Issue of July 23, 1911:

Board of Health Statistics ending July 22, 1911

MARRIAGES

White: J J Jones and C Rudy; W J Krameroski and N Clanegan.
Black: Eastman Cage and Ione Hodge; H Poston and Clara Boyd.

DEATHS

White: John W Westenbroke, 15 months; Zack Howell, 77; Mary T Little, 36; Mrs. Dan Smith, 39; Laura Randall, 16; Liza Jones, 35; Jim Williams, 67; Charlie Neighbors, 38.
Black: Albert Hanaday, 60; Adkins Dennis, 18; Willie Davis, 10 months; L L Scott, 29.

Died July 19, Zack Howell, 77, a soldier of the Confederacy. Survivors include daughters, Amanda Howell, Mrs. Levert Stringfellow, Mrs. J S Harman, Mrs. S C Fullilove, and Mrs. J D Youngblood. Funeral services at Methodist Church, burial at Forest Park.

Issue of July 30, 1911:

Board of Health Statistics ending July 29, 1911

MARRIAGES
White: R A Tierney and Ellen A Slattery.
Black: Sidney Carr and Minnie Allen; Henry Thomas and Maimie Prescott; Willie Williams and Maggie Smith; Willie Mims and Edith Taliaferro; Bert Brooks and Nettie Fincher.

DEATHS
White: Mrs. Philip Dillingberger, 84; Binnie E Moore, 4; John Johnson, 51; Eli White, 42.
Black: Foster Marshall, 41; Laura Harris, 22; Fannie Johnson, 51; Lettie Ford, 35; Levi Dupre, 2 months.

Issue of Aug. 13, 1911:

Board of Health Statistics ending Aug. 12, 1911

MARRIAGES
Black: Richard Gains and Victoria Coron; D M Young and Eliza Donahue; Vic Poindexter and Linda Davis; A Calhoun and Annie Walker; John Ward and Hattie Turner.

DEATHS
White: Mary Johnson, 27; Arthur Kahn, 50; Della Williams, 25; John Watts, 35; W H Burnham, 32; W H Harbeson, 55; John Adlin Byrd, 31; George Russell Jr, 29; Mrs. L Brownlee, 55; Bert Talton, 26; M Hall, 61; W A VanHoose, 1.
Black: Manury Jones, 1; Paula Jones, 72; Charles Tucker, 50; Leon Roberson, 1.

Issue of Aug. 20, 1911:

Board of Health Statistics ending Aug. 19, 1911

MARRIAGES
<u>White</u>: Jim Harmon and Lucy Barton; Dick Shepherd and Daisy D Watts; Robert Fulton and Mrs. C Clark

DEATHS
<u>White</u>: S N Wooten, 61; J M Sutlington, 60; Caroline G Daniels, 58; Emma Mountford, 80; Fannie E Bennett, 32; William Watson, 64; Bertie Grayham, 17; J R Evans, 57; Ben Hall, 26; Cally Williams, 21; Will Calloway, 18; Jim Crisp, 56.
<u>Black</u>: Corry Smith, 33; Lucindy Berry, 50; Mother Eve, 100; Sam Davenport, 38.

Issue of Sept. 10, 1911:

Board of Health Statistics ending Sept. 9, 1911

MARRIAGES
<u>White</u>: E P Haynes and Josephine Frazier; J H Brauer and Alphar Yeiser; Madison Rube and Lillie Galloway; Antonio Cardaro and Etta Robinson; A Hargson and Adrian Fields.
<u>Black</u>: V A Henderson and Claudia Reeves; Richard Smith and Ella Robson.

DEATHS
<u>White</u>: Mrs. Julia F Bickham, 46; John Lawrence, 46; Amandy Skidmore, 2 months; Barbara Monsour, 84; Jesse Debo, 37; F M Icher, 38.
<u>Black</u>: Mary Moore, 42; Jerry Williams, 75; Lucy Reeves, 54; Thomas Youngblood, 29; Emmett Page, 19; John Stuart, 30; Charlie Mack, 26; Pouncey Cash, 20; Gilbert Wiler, 78.

Issue of Sept. 17, 1911:

Died Sept. 14, George Russell, 62, a native of North Carolina and for many years a resident of Shreveport. He is survived by his wife, daughters, Mrs. Clark Ford, Mrs. Walter Prescott, Mrs. Jack Shelan, all of Dallas, Tex., and sons, Don and Leon Russell of Shreveport.

Issue of Sept. 17, 1911:

Board of Health Statistics ending Sept. 16, 1911

MARRIAGES
White: E C Osborne and Mrs. L P Blunt; A Evans and Julia Sheppard; F E Montgomery and Callie E Roberts; F W Temple and Fannie Willey.

DEATHS
White: George H Russell, 62; Mollie Kosakofsky, 47; Bessie Robertson, 2; Henry Westfall, 61; Eva Hall, 31; Mrs. Ada Smith, 51; Mary Ann Print, 74.
Black: Vallie Battle, 32; Mose Stokes, 35; Bab Washington, 11 months; C Tillman, 23; W George, 23.

Issue of Sept. 30, 1911:

Board of Health Statistics ending Sept. 29, 1911

MARRIAGES
White: E C Bryant and Ruby Galloway; Marvin Shoul and Cevil Rolston; Floyd Southern and Cora Greenwood; Charles Wilson and Esther Martin; Jimmie Blackburn and Rebecca Wesley; Tom Hampton and Lucy Carter; Sims Small and Hannah Jackson.

DEATHS
White: Millie Stevens, 37; L Williams, 58; Ophelia Sargent, 4.
Black: Martha A Jenkins, 27; Stephen Wilson, 38; Ida Thomas, 23; Will Atkins, 23; Will Ranson, 23; John P Robinson, 3 months.

Issue of Oct. 8, 1911:

Board of Health Statistics ending Oct. 7, 1911

MARRIAGES (No race shown)
Andrew Bower Jr and Tomye Day; Robert McDonald and M Coleman; V C Graves and Anna McKittrel; Roy E Bonner and A Jolly; F M Marsden and Charlotte Files; Will Rose and Jane Jones; William Greenhill and Hannah Kism; N Lawson and Georgia Stephens; John Whitlatch and Rosa Blacker.

DEATHS (No ages shown)
White: Harry Bailey; E O Budderbrock; Martile Ray; Roy Dickson; S H Shreadgill; Dena Howell; J C Farley; John W Caldwell.
Black: Donnie Z Lewis; Millie Wilson; Sarah Smith; Ann Monroe; Sam Thomas; Sally Edwards; Melvin Orange.

Issue of Oct. 15, 1911:

Board of Health Statistics ending Oct. 14, 1911

MARRIAGES (No race shown)
John E Prudhomme and Willie Gray Pegues; Joe Fate and Myra Dorden; Jack McGruene and N Lucas; Bob White and Nancy Stroud; G T Crow and L Kbourz.

DEATHS

White: Mrs. L T Ford, 62; Thomas E McCann, 46; Dr. Edgar Moore, 25; N J Belton, 67.

Black: Esther Johnson, 65; Gus Simpson, 45; Cora Clairborne, 34; Francis Huntly, 65; Bettie Davis, 37; Martha Jackson, 50; Minnie Mason, 1; J L House, 51; Henry Booker, 28; Harry Robinson, 26; Ollie Scott, 23.

Died October 14, Mrs. Zachary Ford, born in Mobile, Ala., in 1848. Survived by husband, Zachary Taylor Ford, daughters, Mrs. Anna Bell Brannon, Mrs. Kate Lowry, Allie Gae Ford, and sons, Herbert G, Archie M, William D, Lucius L and Zack A Ford.

Issue of Nov. 25, 1911:

Board of Health Statistics ending Nov. 24, 1911

MARRIAGES

White: J F Russell and Alice M Jolly; James S Cole and Ada P Ford; B F Kelly and Una Bounds; T W Burson and Lizzie Wood; Dave E R Peniff and Ora Chumley.

Black: Charles Holman and Florence Hulden; U B Hagen and Eliza Moss; Will Clark and Alice Baker, Marshall Stevens and Annie Winn; J Evans and Verna Williams; Phil Brown and Georgie Johnson; Johnie Lyons and Eddie Love; Eugene Reves and Kate Renchil; Burrus Johnson and Sarah Smith; H Carpenter and Mary Wiggins; Eugene Asken and Bertha Butler; Mitchell Mason and Laura Hasket.

DEATHS

White: Emilie DeGraffenreid, 3; Annie Leigh Hicks, 1; Earl Wright, 23; J M Jones, 61; Will T Williams, 67.

Black: Bettie Davis, 74; Mary Tillman, 53; L C Harris, 43.

Issue of Dec. 3, 1911:

Board of Health Statistics ending Dec. 2, 1911

MARRIAGES

<u>White</u>: D Larant and F E Smyrmoudis; G G Eilbott and Hattie Goetschel; B F Ford and Elizabeth Stephens; A M Fraley and Maggie Frasure; R J Wilcox and Annie E Hughes; E A Chapman and Inez M Potter; John Harris and Nellie Handy; E Bullock and Willie M Melton.

<u>Black</u>: Will Walker and Lula Kennedy; W B Hagen and Eliza Moss; Willie Clark and Alice Baker.

DEATHS

<u>White</u>: Frank Carpenter, 4; T E Bird, 64; J R Prince, 36; Salina Thompson, 29; John Sims, 46; S J Hicks, 60; M Morris, 70; Estelle L Kennedy, 26; M D Thorp, 47; Walter Bryant, 34; Martha Pace, 84; Marie Brandenburg, 43; Alex Hicks, 20.

<u>Black</u>: Willie Mathews, 30; Francis Chambers, 58; Jerry Lewis, 41; Effie Johnson, 23; W F Allen, 2; Mary Adkins, 110; Minnie Woodward, 65; Manerva Coleman, 51.

Issue of Dec. 10, 1911:

Board of Health Statistics ending Dec. 9, 1911

MARRIAGES (No race shown)

Madison J Dennis and Edith Glemmons; Ira W Stance and Maria Corcett; Eugene Conway and Louisa Brown; Richard Brown and Esther Taylor.

DEATHS

<u>White</u>: Francis Otelia Jacobs, 21; Eldridge H Hamans, 1; A L Mayhem, 35; Ben Henshow, 70; J T Millif, 48; Tom

Roswell, 23.

Black: Bessie Bravelle, 70; Perlina Dickson, 14; Ord Roach, 28; Beatrice Minor, 15; Sam Oliver Jr, 60; Lizzie Williams, 36.

Issue of Dec. 17, 1911 :

Board of Health Statistics ending Dec. 16, 1911

MARRIAGES

White: J E Wooten and Nellie M Campbell; Joe Johnson and Lillie Porter; Buford R Hayden and Marie T Leck; A Mandel Jr and Edith Moore.
Black: Charles Parker and Daisy Stratton; Hamilton Lowe and Lizzie Adams; L Merldon and Trelie Hart; E P Blair and Sallie Andrews; Anderson Boeton and Susan Brice; James Williams and Cloteal Grimstead.

DEATHS

White: W R Bridges, 60; W M Rabb Jr, 25; Ora Anderson, 33.
Black: Calvin Bryant, 30; Walter Howard, 1; Watson Ruby, 4; Luelia Roberson, 23.

Died December 15, Dr. J C Egan. Survived by daughters, Mrs. A L Gilbert, Mrs. C H Irion, Lavina H Egan, a nephew, Bryan Ardis and a niece, Mrs. Pennie Ardis Mills.

Issue of Dec. 24, 1911:

Board of Health Statistics ending Dec. 23, 1911

MARRIAGES

White: C C German and Lily McCoy; W A Bryson and Kattie L Bagley; F L Parsons and Emma L Ingram.

Black: Rafe Davis and Gussie Thomas; John W Stephens and Mattie Edwards; Will Renon and Victoria Williams; Fred Lewis and Ophelia Jones; E Garner and P Swift; Rufus Hill and Lena Trosper; Henry Manuel and Edith Johnson.

DEATHS

White: Henry Astor Sumrell, 51; Evelyn Goetschel, 19 months; James Ray, 57; Charles Smith, 52; C F Decker, 16.
Black: Rosa Marshall, 21; Alex Maxie, 66; Louisa Kitchens, 61; Lucil Thomas, 17; Julia Bryant, 70; Willie Edison, 26; Dave Mathews, 36.

Issue of Dec. 31, 1911:

Board of Health Statistics ending Dec. 30, 1911

MARRIAGES

White: J Ben Wise and M E Wortman; W P Duncan and Maggie Conell; E A Conway Jr and Mary A Glassell; Rev. O M Posey and Mrs. L E Deck; Q A Hargis and Maud Dean.
Black: Ed Hunter and Hattie Kendall; David Babers and Lillie Williams; Arthur Randolph and Mattie Davis; Jim Lockets and Mattie Crenshaw; James Williams and Willie Hackback; Augustus Cutliff and Estelle L Hampson; G Douglas and Hiser Scott; Wiley Wright and Nannie Edwards.

DEATHS

White: J D Clements, 29; Mrs. Ella Tompkins, 76; C Methwin, 49; Theo LaConn, 21; Tom Johnson, 42; Leon Johns, 6 months; Margret Moro, 60; Paul Reese, 36.
Black: Grant Berry, 44; Hamp Kuckler, 17; Willie Freeman, 28; Clara Wilson, 60; Rosie Peterson, 26; John Hulond, 61; L B Corners, 40; Sango Connel, 30; Robert Thomson, 27.

Issues of Jan. 12, 1912-
July 21, 1912

Issue of Jan. 12, 1912:

Board of Health Statistics ending Jan. 11, 1912

MARRIAGES

White: W L Ogle and Mary Dennis; Sidney Smith and Marguerite Martin; George T Martin and Mrs. Addie C Maples; T Russell and Leala Putteyman; A N Newman and Mrs. Ella Erickson; Joseph B Oneal and J Perritt.

Black: James J Williams and Julia Dickinson; L Mason and Irma Banks; A Chambers and Susie Sell; Gus Sims and Maggie Conway.

DEATHS

White: Emma C Dickinson, 75; George W Crooks, 65; G M Johnson, 39; Claude Bennice, 29; J C Cuff, 53; H M Purser (no age shown).

Black: M V Albert, 40; Julia Baker, 40; Sadie Nash, 26; Georgie Murry, 35; Mary Smith, 55; Sarah Green, 66; Vink Huler, 22; Annie Hall, 32; Henry Green, 43; Charlie Cook, 40.

Married January 1, Sidney Smith and Marguerite Martin at Parkview Baptist Church, Rev. A D Kendrick officiating. She is the daughter of Mrs. Alice Guenemer Martin and the late James L. Martin. The groom is the son of Mrs. Mary F Smith and the late Joseph Smith.

Issue of Jan. 14, 1912:

Board of Health Statistics ending Jan. 13, 1912

MARRIAGES

White: L C Thebold and Dena Nelson; F Seiberthale and N Landrum; H P Powell and Marie Brice; H A Morris and L Dingle; J J VanCleve and Zetta Alch; V Cascio and Marie Vaccaro; A C Daly and M C Smith; A C Jordan and E R Devit.

Black: Alfred Bakefield and Eliza Gaskin; James Arthur and Lucy Presley; Dan Mozuque and Mary Williams.

DEATHS

White: Foster Carter, 58; Maggie B Dance, 16; Ben J Rudder, 67; W S Lewis, 48; Della Randolph, 32; Sallie Day, 39; Charley Jackson, 32; Viola Meyers, 28; Johnie Love, 4; Freddie Hamilton, 35; Rosa Clark, 25; Will Fait, 41.

Black: Nancy Eldors, 79; Charles Ellis, 25; Wash Allen, 60.

Died January 8, John J Marshall, a soldier of the Confederacy, son of John James Marshall Sr. Survived by nieces, Mary and Fanny Marshall, nephews, W C Marshall and Roland Williams, all of Shreveport.

Issue of Jan. 21, 1912:

Board of Health Statistics ending Jan. 20, 1912

MARRIAGES

White: J A Causley and Mrs. C D Harris; John J Felschker and Marian Levy; R W Blake and Margaret Brown; Joseph Carrigan and Nettie Lewis; O W Stanley and Dora Denler.

Black: Will Zeigler and Lenora McLaughlin; Frank Sanders and Annie Adams; Henry P Lucien and Leadie Keer.

DEATHS

White: Mrs. E J Cain, 68; Ruth Leayer, 2; Rev.V Journet, 83; Charles Heineman, 53; A T Peterson, 45; J M Henshaw, 41.

Black: Topsy Anderson, 21 days; Clint Howard, 32; Ellen Thornton, 72; Annie Rice, 80; James Williams, 41; Abram Maiden, 20; Benny Revlin, 20; Channy Stewart, 65; Robert Leslie, 38; Frank B Bennett, 36.

Issue of Jan. 28, 1912:

Board of Health Statistics ending Jan. 27, 1912

MARRIAGES

White: F N Harris and Caro Lee; A A Herold and Eda Loeb; C H Lucas and Maude D Guse.
Black: Henry Jones and Helen Clark; Orange Gilliam and Dennie L Puch; C Whilton and Mabel Maloy; Ben Boxley and Mollie Washington; F A Brown and Martha Johnson; John McLemon and Corine Williams.

DEATHS (No ages shown)

White: W B Porter; James R Giles; George Hall; W T Bradford; Harris Wallace; Estelle Ellison.
Black: Darkes Walker; George Handy; Parthinia Wilson; Emiline Matthews; John Thomas; Julie Nickolas.

Issue of Feb. 4, 1912:

Board of Health Statistics ending Feb. 3, 1912

MARRIAGES

White: Lloyd Ellis and Mrs. Estelle Lewis; R A Durio and Sallie Parnell; A D Rushdon and Ruth Craighead; Albert Harper and Cora Allen.

DEATHS (No ages shown)

White: Mrs. S E Morton; Mertil E Houston; William B Durkee; Annie Smith.

Black: Abbie C Hughes; Ellen Brown; James Taylor; C R Mims; Reed Young; James Henson; Laura Love; Thomas Hayes; Jesse Harris.

Issue of Feb. 13, 1912:

Board of Health Statistics ending Feb, 12, 1912

MARRIAGES

White: C M Messenger and M Baker; H S Hodges and Mrs. Hallie Gills; Marshall Courtney and Lucy Pritchard; L H Walker and Mrs. Fannie Walker.
Black: John Thomas and Bessie Brown; Ben F Thompson and Gazelle Robertson; George Brown and Paralee Dumont.

DEATHS (No ages shown)

White: R Wylie; E Colbert Moss; Edgar Elhihes; N B Williams; Leon Legrone.
Black: Duglass Coleman; Emile Harris; Hosey Hardy; Bernard Brazelle; Cleveland Hynes; Emma Wilson; Josephine Oliver; Mary Whipps; Dela Black; Rosa Jackson; Elizater Jackson; George Phillips; Joe Martin; Virgie Burke.

Issue of Feb. 8, 1912:

Board of Health Statistics ending Feb. 7, 1912

MARRIAGES

White: J Imbrogulio and S Raffolo; W H Robinson and Mary B Flournoy; William C Best and Ruby E Leaton; Murray G Quigler and Rosalee Miller.
Black: F Dearborn and Mable Bennett; F Thompson and Ada Johnson.

DEATHS (No ages shown)

White: Anton Grundgonk; Marian D Wylie; Sister Loretta; Edwin S Preston; Annie L Miller; Mrs. E J Alexander; Bird M Wells; Rev. George Jackson Manuel; John McFarland.
Black: Simon White; Andrew Jackson; Ella Adams; Minnie Adams; Louis Jackson; Henrietta Smith; Marrietta Jones; Archie Woodson; Jim Biggers; Largo Smith; Wiley Harden; Vinie Johnson; B Fearal; Victor Carpenter; Eva Hawkins; Charlotte Mays; Clober Johnson; H Butler; Jerry Martin.

Issue of Feb. 24, 1912:

Board of Health Statistics ending Feb. 23, 1912

MARRIAGES

White: D C Richardson Jr and Lena Christian; William Vickers and Bertha Hanna; James J McDermott and Alice McCabe; Jake Rosen and Beckie Lafin.
Black: William Roach and Lizzie Williams; F Newman and Minnie Thomas; Leonard Randolph and Lizzie Brazier; William Brady and Nora Armstrong.

DEATHS (No ages shown)

White: Nora Horn; Addie T. Morgan; W U Carlton; G W Ward; J Y Sanders; Cyrus V Cegar.
Black: Rachel Churchill; George Richards; Henry Williams; Theodore Lashwish; Anthony Dougless; Viney McDuffy; Joseph Simon; Leroy Lockett; Mary Isaacs; Jonnie Johnson; Rachel Ingram; Emily Lewis; George Cullins; Lizzie Robinson; Virgie Williams; Francis Robinson; Sallie Whittaker; Mary Webb; Thomas J McIntyre; Arthur L Allen.

Issue of Mar. 3, 1912:

Board of Health Statistics ending Mar. 2, 1912

MARRIAGES

White: Thomas M Gross and Sadie Brown; E D Bird and Elean Dyar; H V Hardwick and Marie Moore; Oscar M McDuff and Mary A Robinson.
Black: E P Marinz Jr and Cora Washington.

DEATHS (No ages shown)

White: Mrs. Dollie Amond; Emma M Miller; Maggie Miller; R M Montgomery; Ben Lacash; J N Strickland; Mrs. J Sibley; Mrs. Alice Thomas.
Black: Mandy Williams; Millrage Smith; Andrew J Evans Jr; Adeline Mason; Sarah Johnson; Ollie Hardy; Jessie M Butler; Winston Edwards; Angeline Sinclair; Amanda Henderson; Felix Soliter Jr; Silas Harnbill; Ellen Wells; Wesley Goodwin; Miles Lewis; Cacey Edwards.

Married March 1, Alfred C Glassell and Fannie Elvie Lane at First Presbyterian Church by Rev. H M Mclain. Bride is daughter of Mr. and Mrs. Charles Lane and grand daughter of Mr. and Mrs. J S Noel. The groom is the son of Mr. and Mrs. John Glassell, Belcher.

Issue of Mar. 17, 1912:

Board of Health Statistics ending Mar. 16, 1912

MARRIAGES

White: T Beeson and Clara N Cargill.
Black: Barney Isaacs and Mary Clayton; Ivey Bird and Edith Bind.

DEATHS (No ages shown)

White: Frank Bicknell; Floyd Alexander; Mrs. Annie McGrath; John Herbert.
Black: Jesse Davis; Derry Hunter; Amile Chester; Clarence

Haynes; Edward Joseph; Robert Dorsey; Elizabeth Gray; Edward Hunter; Mittie Johnson; Robert Dickson; Maggie Patterson.

Issue of Mar. 24, 1912:

Board of Health Statistics ending Mar. 23, 1912

MARRIAGES

<u>White</u>: Hugh Collins and Myrtle Williams; Henry L Jones and Charlotte Jamions; Durand F Milton and Fannie Carns.

DEATHS (No ages shown)

<u>White</u>: W J Curtis; Rev. W M Alford; John H Patzman; Sam L Jones.
<u>Black</u>: Will Jones; Willie M Ridley; Herbert Sharpe; George Coleman; Adam Johnson; Bob Graham; Polly Washington; Seany Anderson; Fannie Bell; Amanda Hamilton; Fannie Searis; Eliza Slater; Adam Mays.

Died March 21, William Curtis, age 21. Survivors include his father, J J Curtis, brothers, Aubrey and Louis Curtis, sisters, Mrs. J J Nalin, Mrs. Frank O'Leary, Erath and May Curtis. Burial was in Greenwood Cemetary following service by Father Wilkinson.

Issue of Mar. 31, 1912:

Board of Health Statistics ending Mar. 30, 1912

<u>White</u>: Louis P Lemoine and Irene L Lemoine.
<u>Black</u>: Frank Johnson and Stella McIntyre; William Jones and B Oliver.

DEATHS (No ages shown)

White: Lizzie Barron; Eugene L Studebaker; Julian Elliott; George D Ramsay; Mary E Sebastian; J B Bradley; A Carr; Joe A Stephens.
Black: Jenette Ogden; Bill Williams; D C Brown; Dinah Henderson; Albert Benjamin; Leah Hewey; Martha Dagl; Claude Williams; Ida Ferguson; Wallie Law; Florence Willis; Dinkey Davis; Sallie Mallard; Ed Geer; Lizt Heron; Jim Spivey; Peter Jones; Thomas Jones; Albert Johnson.

Issue of Apr. 7, 1912:

Board of Health Statistics ending Apr. 6, 1912

White: James M Hudgins and M Mereer; John Stewart and Fanny Winston; Will Lewis and Beatrice Farnier; Christopher Burdock and Frances Miller; Robert Morgan and Beatrice Wilson.

DEATHS (no race shown)
Edward E Matthews, 6; Jonie Burch, 7 months; Alex Jamerson, 21; Susie A Howard, 68; Albert Woods, 28; Leo Edwards, 16; Lula A Lewis, 40; Patsy Willis, 63; Mack Farnell, 81; Alex Johnson, 30; Cleo Harris, 2; Lindsy McCoy, 23; Lillie Murray, 34; Curtis Franklin, 46; Dennis Wiggins, 54; Fanny Evans, 38.

Issue of Apr. 14, 1912:

Board of Health Statistics ending Apr. 13, 1912

MARRIAGES
White: L E Parker and N M Guice; Louis A Morizot and A Rotsenberger.
Black: John Caley and Maggie Jacobs; John Brown and Mary Dees; Willie Lees and Mattie Harris; Dallas Jay and

Emma McAdams; H Wassinger and C Abby; Will Thompson and Lula Timmons; Oscar Moore and Mary Harts; Jim Forest and Georgie Harris; Eddie Johnson and Lizzie Shelton.

DEATHS
<u>White</u>: W J Platt, 62; John Bonner, 52; F W Neill, 37; J H Watson, 57; J B Williams, 76; George McCain, 87; Mary Williams, 39.
<u>Black</u>: Prince Albert, 65; Carrie Thomas, 33; John Sorrel, 20; Cleo T Green, 9; John Shelton, 25; Nellie Orr, 27; Emma Hubert, 15; Tom Miles, 28; Jim Lake, 35; Silvia Smith, 50; Harrison Stokes, 22.

Issue of Apr. 20, 1912:

Board of Health Statistics ending Apr. 19, 1912

MARRIAGES
<u>White</u>: Horace C Vaughn and Josephine Keith-Carlson.
<u>Black</u>: Sam Jackson and Sarah Jamison; Albert West and Louisa Shannon; Robert Carter and Roberta Haymes.

DEATHS
<u>White</u>: Mary A Yeiser, 55; C L Vaughn, 40; Mary J Coty, 74; Mrs. Susie Alford, 76; Charles Caplis, 16; Rex Brite, 24; Mildred Brady, 20.
<u>Black</u>: Julius Johnson, 30; Temple Holly, 14; Leonard Harris, 2; F S McKeel, 70; Delia Gray, 36; Mollie Johnson, 63; Abe Marcus, 18; Oscar Seales, 12; Edith Dennis, 35; Roberta Roberson, 2; Adline Norman, 60.

Issue of May 12, 1912:

Board of Health Statistics ending May 11, 1912

MARRIAGES

White: Arthur Freeman and Sarah Brown; Roy Pruitt and Mollie Manon.

DEATHS

White: E D Nelson, 29; Dr. John I Schumept, 79.
Black: Alice H Johnson, 40; Alfred Davis, 63; Robert Gardner, 1; Lloyd Hankins, 25; Yale Brown, 3; Lula Williams, 65; Virginia King, 21.

Issue of June 9, 1912:

Died June 1, Mrs. E L Kirk. Surviving are daughters, Mrs. E K Johnson, Mrs. J W Norton, Mrs Van Simon Allman, Mrs. Percy Webb, Mrs. F O Hudson, and son N I Kirk.

Issue of June 16, 1912:

Married June 15, R A Bryson and Gussie Attaway at Methodist Church by Rev. G E Cannon. Attending were the groom's mother, Mrs. S Bryson, his sisters, Martha and Agnes Bryson, Mrs. John Wynn and Mrs. Margaret Flournoy.

Issue of June 20, 1912:

Married June 19, at home of bride's parents, L C Butler and Mary Lou Doll, daughter of Mr. and Mrs. H F Doll. The groom is a U. S. Assistant District Attorney.

Issue of June 25, 1912

Married June 24, Lally C Clauson and Allene Matthews at St. John's Church by Father Wilkinson.

Issue of July 2, 1912:

Died July 1, Frank Surrett, a Confederate veteran of service in units in South Carolina. Burial was in Confederate Bivouac, Greenwood Cemetery.

Issue of July 21, 1912:

Died July 14, Wimberk Boney. He is survived by his wife, and children, Gaston and Jack Boney, Mrs. Kate Landrum, and Gertrude Boney, and a brother, Dick Boney.

Married July 17, George Hardwick Mills and Caro Prudhomme at Baptist Parsonage by Rev. Doad. She is the daughter of Mr. and Mrs. A J Prudhomme. The groom is a son of Mrs. Pennie Ardis Mills and nephew of Bryan Ardis.

Issues of Sept. 1, 1912-
Nov. 28, 1912

All issues are missing.

Issues of Dec. 1, 1912-
Dec. 29, 1912

Issue of Dec. 1, 1912:

Board of Health Statistics ending Nov. 30, 1912

MARRIAGES (No race shown)
Lucius Gant and Hattie Stoney; J B Green and Nita Whited; George Thomas Rose and Leta Banks; Millard Joseph and Lydia Brosington; Charles Swann and Caroline Smith; C W Kirkpatrick and Georgie Washington; John A Williams and Mary Helen Hubbard; Ed Washington and Emma Williams; Lewis Grant and Mandy Henderson.

DEATHS
White: Dudley B Anderson, 31; H Davidson, 58; Chester L Fletcher, 23; William F Porath, 78; Joseph F Barlow, 23; Jessie H Fisher, 30; Edua L Stephens, 9 months; Mrs. S M Roahity, 54.
Black: James Wolf, 55; Banister Johnson, 44; Hardy Smith, 80; Will Taylor, 35; Marcello Dorsey, 31; Jane Stanley, 59; Savanah Harber, 53; Rocksie Hicks, 40; Jane Flanagan, 40; Sallie Young 47.

Issue of Dec 8, 1912:

Board of Health Statistics ending Dec. 7, 1912

MARRIAGES (No race shown)
Cleveland H Brooks and Eloise H Chew; Robert B Moss and Leola C Hughes; John Jackson and Rebecca Jones; Henry C Burks and Mrs. Elener E Burks.

DEATHS

White: John C Allen, 72; Jim Swift, 30; Pat Callahan, 52; William H Eddins, 56; Samuel H Heine, 54; C B Parker, 28; Elizabeth Jack, 10.
Black: Jim Heard, 35; Clint Hollis, 16; Tommie York, 21; Calvin Scott, 62; James L George, 2 months; Alberta Henderson, 23; James Taylor, 24; Susan Gilmer, 54; Mary Boykin, 27; Winnie Hicks, 41; Rebecca Mackroy, 23; Mary Ann Jackson, 47; P Harris, 25; Hattie Gideon, 56.

Issue of Dec. 24, 1912:

Board of Health Statistics ending Dec. 23, 1912

MARRIAGES

White: Mack Boring and Annie Lockett; Alonza Patterson and Marke Parker; Chatham McKie and Grace McKie; Emmett Grace and Lummi Boyd; Roy Bringer and Mary Hendrick; John Edwards and Birtie Chandler; Richard Ethridge and Lula Rambris; Owen Larnum and Ethel Cripper; Arthur Andrews and Jennie Reneau; Edgar Mariselli and Florence Nelson; Frederick Ratzburg and Adelina Robinson; John Westmoreland and Mary Palmer; William Owens and Blanche Hays; Robert LaJames and Eva Cook; Frank Wynn and Minnie Williams.

DEATHS

White: Prof. Daniel Donovan, 84; G F Weatherly, 38; A Katz, 78; Ed Murphy, 55; Samuel Beckwith, 78; George F Clanton, 53; Isah Jerome Rudy, 63; C C Barfield, 63; Albert C Westcott, 50; Mrs. P A Bedard (no age shown).
Black: Ben Edwards, 33; J Schills, 28; Vink Jones, 55; Will Newton, 28; Filmore White, 18; C Johnson, 78; Gib Kendall, 22; Mary Washington, 17; Emma Donehue, 21; Mary Divens, 43; Rebecca Williams, 28.

Issue of Dec. 29, 1912:

Board of Health Statistics ending Dec. 28, 1912

MARRIAGES (No race shown)
W A Owens and Blanche M Hayes; Luther Waites and Josephine Edwards; Isaac Webb and Eva Williams; Joe Ellis and Louisa Patterson; J A McNeil and Margaret Evans; John S Henderson and Lizzie B Grover; Frank Ellmore and Parthena Brooks; Nathaniel Farmer and Mary Shelby; Fred E Beatty and Alma Berry; Henry Stringer and Ada Hawkins; John Fuller and Hazel Dell Hagen; Henry Johnson and Rosalie Miller; Jeff Allen and Precious Sonden; Claude R Kenyon and Margaret D Robie; Wilson McClemore and Rosa Chapman.

DEATHS (No age or race shown)
A C Montgomery; J H Hudnall; C H Andrews; W J Franks; Wilber I Oliver; Ralph Watson; Charley Bell; Dave Watson; Julius Jordan; Henry Marina; Newton F Berret; Henry West; Ezra Turner; Jim Davis; Robert Calhoun; William Trappier; Bob Gibson; O C Smith; Nancy Roberson; David Hanks; Mamie Bell Hatcher; Betsy Galoway; Jane Hicks; Della Owens.

Issues of Jan. 4, 1913-
Dec. 31, 1913

Issue of Jan. 4, 1913:

Board of Health Statistics ending Jan. 3, 1913

MARRIAGES (No race shown)
Columbus Brown and Frances York; H C Runnels and Mrs. Katie Mullen; Harry J Sheaman and Clara Florsheim; Newt Edwards and Sadie Mays; Mack Richardson and Susie Thompson.

DEATHS
White: Jim Calley, 50; J Murray Wilkinson, 25; Emilie Wortman, 52; Tony Kezerle, 54; Maybelle Windham, 31; Mrs. Angline High, 74; Mrs. Julia Saxton Parker, 62.
Black: Luther Shiven, 6; Mark Hanna, 50; Hayellen Woodlard, 11; Jobe R Lottimore, 70; Asief Wilson (no age shown); George Walker, 60; George Thomas, 15; Jerry Bryant, 54; J T Johnson, 40; Paul Gentry, 36; Maggie Camp, 34; Hanna Taylor, 33; Mandy Chatman, 44; Rozello Washington, 19.

Issue of Jan. 12, 1913:

Board of Health Statistics ending Jan. 11, 1913

MARRIAGES (No race shown)
Richard L Reed and Mathilde Smith; I Politski and C Allen; Alfred Davis and Katie Bell Thomas; Anderson Williams and Adeline Scott; Welborn N Clark and Susie Murray.

DEATHS
White: Jack Powell, 3; P A Robertson, 22; Mrs. T B Warren,

46; G Roberson, 37; C D Roberts, 30; Thomas H Kelly, 30; J Cillulon, 50; Kate Henderson, 38; Mrs. T L Voigt, 50; Catherine Dudley, 74.

Black: Dock Jackson, 31; Lee Haven, 33; D C Pander, 24; H Smith, 40; Sam Stewart, 30; Nathan Rutledge, 50; Daniel Wells, 35; Leon Roberson, 7 months; Willie Cooper, 11; Mazie Bryant, 6; Nettie Venell, 41; Patsy Smith, 52; Sarah Turner, 72; Mary Golsten, 48; Rosa Brown, 70; Elizabeth Anderson, 65; Cozie Green, 31.

Died January 1, Thomas H Kelley, 30, son of the late Thomas Kelly. He was unmarried and lived with sisters, Annie and Nelly Kelly. His brothers are Hank, Paul, Joe, and Will Kelly.

Issue of Jan. 19, 1913:

Board of Health Statistics ending Jan. 18, 1913

MARRIAGES (No race shown)

Oliver A Stiles and Martha Barnett; Willie Moss and Clara Woodson; Oscar Moore and Pollie Armstrong; W J Hurst and Mrs. Alice Y Renefrae.

DEATHS

White: Edward Aaron, 50; G W Hutchins, 78; Henry Sartin, 29; C D Feeney, 28.

Black: Richard Dudley, 29; Alex Barett, 22; Albert Hasson, 23; George Stephens, 64; Eliza Henderson, 17; A Lewis, 48; Minnie Walker, 15; Martha Armstrong, 48; Henrietta Lindley, 22; Comfort Wimberly, 72.

Died January 18, Mrs. Ida B Bounds, 53, wife of F B Bounds. Survivors include four daughters, Mrs. B F Holly, Mrs L B Hamilton, and Alva and Budie Bounds, all of this city. Burial was in Greenwood Cemetery.

Issue of Jan. 26, 1913:

Board of Health Statistics ending Jan. 25, 1913

DEATHS

White: Sam Debargo, 60; N Zeigler, 48; Floyd Blanchard, 9; Bob Brumfield, 35; Ruben L Phelps, 72; Annie E Ferguson, 60; Sarah J Odell, 77; Ida B Bounds, 53.

Black: Arthur Williams, 23; Robert Blarkman, 65; George Hill, 15; Andrew Thomas, 30; Will Smith, 25; Julius Williams, 75; Anny Perry, 30; Kathleen Alexander, 3; Bertha Boyston, 24; Susie Johnson, 32; Jenie Andrews, 27; Fanny Dunn, 29; Will Beasley, 26.

Issue of Feb. 2, 1913:

Board of Health Statistics ending Feb. 1, 1913

MARRIAGES (No race shown)

Isadore Block and Florey Josey; J B Cook and Ollie Reed; Ellis Roynor and Lena Gold; Volney McDaniel and Ida Gleberman; I B Rogers and Rosa Lee Clyde; C Brady and Marcella E Brady; L S Winham and Lola Shaw; Van Glover and Hannah Stuart; Lewellin Freeman and Josephine Thomas; Collie L Gardner and Pearly Bates; W C Huston and Eula Thompson; Johnnie Hart and Josephine Blane; J Paul Turner and Effie L Wilson; Albert Lowe and Emma Lucas; Joseph Wilson and Nancy Darrow; Donovan N Larkin and Edna Ward; Watson Heaves and Fanny Wash.

DEATHS

White: Claude Jones, 42; Charlie George, 5; Mrs. Willie Moore, 23; J B Schwartzberg, 53; Zeb Springer, 21; Mrs. J

W Courtney, 36.
Black: John Dorsey, 21; Charles Jackson, 19; Frank Harris, 23; John Page, 50; Bessie Lopez, 19; East Tyler, 56; Malinda Tigner, 15; Mattie Jackson, 36.

Died February 1, John C Vance, 70. Born in Cross Hill, S.C., August 4, 1843, he enlisted in service of the Confederacy in 1863. He was in various battles, such as Manassas, Gettysburg and Sharpsburg. In 1872 he married Helen Pratt, who died May 10, 1885. Survivors include daughters, Mrs. W G Dalzell, Mrs. Allen Rendall, of Shreveport, Mrs. Leon Huckins, Oklahoma City, Okla., Mrs. J A Bailey, Clinton, S.C., Mrs. Etienne Bourgeois, Jackson, Miss., a son, Horwood K Vance, and a sister, Mrs. W C Vance.

Issue of Feb. 9, 1913:

Board of Health of Statistics ending February 8, 1913

MARRIAGES (No race shown)
Henry Allen and Rosa White; Chester Powell and Ada Green; R L Prudhomme and Roberta V Aubrey; Albert W Peterman and Rosa Lee Reggio; Joseph W Marioneoux and Carrie B O'Neil; John P Chandler and Nellie E Veal; Thomas Mullins and Mattie Lee Williams; Charles D Stone and Lois Turney; D L Cornelius and Anna Crossman; S M Stouts and Clara Garrett; Preston Washington and Myrtle Gloster.

DEATHS
White: J D Norman, 42; C R Tuttle, 37; John C Vance, 70; J E Breda, 71; O E Kresse, 38; W C Evans, 21.
Black: J C Ratcliff, 23; John Draughn, 25; Don Harris, 23; Coleman Watson, 50; Martha Smith, 70; Dora Ford, 48.

Issue of Feb. 16, 1913:

Board of Health Statistics ending Feb. 15, 1913

MARRIAGES (No race shown)
T H Hill and Ardath Easley; Joe H Schendle and Pauline Braunig; R L Anderson and Willie Henderson; Albert Bates and Ada Richardson; L C Capers and Rosa Gamble; William Johnson and Mrs. Agnes Griffiths; John Neal and Fannie Pearson.

DEATHS
White: Andrew J Ingersoll, 6; George Filmore, 52; E M Vallett, 55; George I Goodenow, age unknown; Joe Fulso, 5; E F Nelson, 43; F Cholker, 23; E Z Gaskins, 71; Caroline Le Pard, 34; Mary Monsour, 52.
Black: Wes Barnes, 35; Tom Rives, 56; Hasker Bird, 30; Adam Lee, 65; Henry Collins, 39; Charley Weeks, 44; J Taylor, 55; Charles Johnson, 57; Willie Floyd, 22; Andrew Thomas, 30; W D Gooden, 10; Jim Lewis, 30; Nettie Balark, 60; Lissie Grant, 35.

Issue of Feb. 23, 1913:

Board of Health Statistics ending Feb. 22, 1913

MARRIAGES (No race shown)
Will Anderson and Ella Hamilton; Frank R Butler and Eliza Thomas; Frank Conway and Mrs. Lester Schultz.

DEATHS
White: Mike McMahon, 48; Harry Skideit, 28; H N Tanner, 48; John Booth, 70; W F McAdams, 64; Mrs. M C Jordan, 76; Mrs. Ora McDangeal, 30; Bessie Jones, 33; Mrs. C F Ray, 24; Alie Clos, 1.

Black: Kid Frazier, 65; Willie Melton, 3; Tom Joiner, 24; William Sims, 45; Cli Gidion, 45.

Issue of Mar. 3, 1913:

Board of Health Statistics ending Mar. 2, 1913

MARRIAGES (No race shown)
Bill Watkins and Susie Turner; W A Troegel and Eva C Bates; Luke Parnell and Mary White; C W Glasspool and Ora Irene Murray; Gus Jackson and Athlene Lewis; Alfred Edgar and Johnnie C Maxing.

DEATHS
White: B P Talley, 36; Roy Butler, 3; Edwin Hawkins, 44; Henry Lorenz, 25; Henry Canglialosi, 21 months.
Black: Paul Jackson, 19; Will Rogers, 23; Walter Ullums, 31; Eugene Campbell, 2; John Randall, 21; Pink Haris, 37; Gus Goodwin, 62; Dan Pettiway, 40; Halie Ross, 50;

Hattie M Howard, 20; Evy Marshall, 29; Corrie Sawyer, 24; Alvie Moore, 28.

Issue of Mar. 9, 1913:

Board of Health Statistics ending Mar. 8, 1913

MARRIAGES (No race shown)
Robert A Hill and Genevieve Stephenson; Bill Bailey and Crese Milton; W E Hulman and Lillie Flores; Willie Johnson and Mary Harvey.

DEATHS
White: W E Seay, 51; B G Kirn, 53; W O Tatune, 49; Mrs. B T Crews, 67; Mrs. Mary Kelley, 71; Mrs. Amelia O'Brien,

46; Mollie Webb, 32; Mrs. N P Vlahoyames, 43; Mrs. J C Klethey, 34; Mrs. W A Keith, 28.
Black: Harrison Buse, 20; Henry Jackson, 22; Columbus Owen, 20; John Balden, 95; Andrew Jones, 39; John Adkins, 30; W Hendricks, 21; Lawrence King, 50; Lee McDonald, 41; W Whitaker, 58; M White, 43; Mary Gallagher, 18; Nancy Logan, 79; Corrie Scott, 16.

Issue of Mar. 23, 1913:

Board of Health Statistics ending Mar. 22, 1913

MARRIAGES (No race shown)
Howard Thomas and Willie Fields; J B Mosely and Eunice Walters; Charles Brocker and Victoria Jones; Eugene L Deason and Jennie Suggs.

DEATHS
White: Julius Bernstein, 51; T M Jones, 30; W D Pury, 56; Mary Radford, 21; Mrs. Hariett N Coffee, 77; Mrs. Martha B Sutten, 62.
Black: General Kilbert, 58; Peter Bryant, 42; Calvin Atkins, 25; William Bell, 29; A Hamilton, 35; Ellis Boston, 30; George Powell, 47; Richard Butler, 69; Mary Pamperton, 32; Mamie Derere, 26; Lula Barnes, 30; Corinne Craft, 40; Tinie McDavid, 24.

Issue of Mar 30, 1913:

Board of Health Statistics ending Mar. 29, 1913

MARRIAGES (No race shown)
John Clemino and Dora Rappolo; William H Goodman and Carrie Abshier; Alvin Mayes and Cornelia Moldon; Austin McDaniel and Mattie Adger.

DEATHS
White: L E Wagner, 84; T H Frechde, 84; Katie McKasle, 35; Mary Mayes, 64; Freda Converse, 17.
Black: Alberta Perkins, 23; Lillian Harris, 5; William Tiggs, 49; Charlie Sanders, 80; Hy Jackson, 60; Charles Jones, 30.

Issue of Apr. 6, 1913:

Board of Health Statistics ending Apr. 5, 1913

MARRIAGES (No race shown)
Bain McLemore and Lillie Washington; Joe Slattery and Margaret A Dartois; Aubrey Angel and Mary Thomas.

DEATHS
White: Mrs. L W Logan, 54; Laura S Ratcliff, 56; Mrs. U L LaPal, 35; Mrs. C R George, 27; Henry Guth, 56; W J Young, 82.
Black: Hayward Jackson, 83; W Battle, 6; W Jones, 26; Miller Haire, 25; George Kiser, 54; Jerry Springs, 80; C Woodruff, 45; Will Jennings, 38; Johnny Green 28; Lewis Taylor, 37; Berry Jelks, 68; Add Phelps, 52; Rachel Jones, 30; Mary Desota, 32; Patsy Farmer, 45; Margaret Williams, 66; Sudie Williams, 32.

Issue of Apr. 13, 1913:

Board of Health Statistics ending Apr. 12, 1913

MARRIAGES (No race shown)
A Roatcap and Ruth F Lindsay; Roy Bennett and Estelle Louise Braunig; George M Leach and Blanche Jeffries; D C Scarborough and Margaret Bell Whited; E M Hinkle and Nancy Bird Bateman; Rufus Johnson and Maud E Mercer.

DEATHS

<u>White</u>: William Herman, 35; A R Ross, 46; J W Gilmore, 78; P Cavanaugh, 87; Mrs. Myrtle Cox Bounds, 18; Christian Dunn, 69; Mrs. Foster Shelton, 26.

<u>Black</u>: Robert Green, 25; Dave Johnson, 31; Arthur Barns, 24; R Sibley, 18; George Bendow, 30; Morris Hayes, 39; Joe Meyers, 23; Alph Randolph, 56; Charlie Tisby, 55; L Davidson, 16; Nellie Dicks, 22.

Issue of Apr. 27, 1913:

Board of Health Statistics ending Apr. 26, 1913

MARRIAGES (No race shown)

W M Giles and Marah Thomas; Ernest White and Ollie Jackson; Thomas Jones and Lizzie Morris; Anderson Wilson and Carrie Spencer; Gus Dickson and Annie Miles; Samuel Baker and Beatrice L Chancery; R E Rountree and Evaline Dupuy.

DEATHS

<u>White</u>: William Kempt, 58; R D Anderson, 33; W D Howard, 35; F F Jones, 52; J F Haskell, 61; C R Lochamer, 74; Maggie Quinn, 70; Mrs. Ann J Rouch, 92.

<u>Black</u>: Columbers Easters, 25; B Lewis, 20; Eli Grosby, 47; Leon White, 24; Rose Lee Thomas, 26; Hattie Adams, 38.

Issue of May 4, 1913:

Board of Health Statistics ending May 3, 1913

MARRIAGES (No race shown)

A L Martin and Rosetta Bradford; Preston L Howard and Nellie Voelcker; James L Sims and Frances Bown; Percy Washington and Lillie L Smith; Jim Coleman and Pinky Decatur; Early Maywether and Alice Bird; William White and Ethel Donehew; Charles Easley Jr and Jimmie S Harris; Dan Thomas and Gertrude Hattoway.

DEATHS

White: Charles Kanely, 54; John L Rucker, 77; James C Duke, 30; Mrs. R F Malone, 21; Mrs. H J Bolts, 56.
Black: Mingo Edwards, 70; Joe Neely, 38; Bob Robinson, 54; Charlie Howard, 50; Roscoe Vickers, 30; James Haynes, 25; Ester Wilson, 30; Hariett Hearne, 65; Edena Moore, 6; Daisy Richmond, 17; Lucille Powdrill, 12; Mattie G Wilson, 32; Susie Southall, 30.

Issue of May 18,1913:

Board of Health Statistics ending May 17, 1913

MARRIAGES (No race shown)

Grant M Scott and Inez Colts; Elbert Taylor and Lugenia Duncan; Jules Jacobs and Mary Franklin.

DEATHS

White: T E Lambert, 22; Frank Preston, 40; H N King, 33; Paul Lowenthal, 62; Mrs. Nannie Palmer, 46; R P Motley, 23; Mrs. Margaret Smitt, 68; Mrs. H L Haberson, 38; Mrs. Mary Hudson, 70; Mrs. W R Collins, 37; Mrs. Julia Heise, 43; Mrs. Laura Coke, 68; Conde Researo, 55.
Black: W H Mays, 1; Glenn Ferro, 20; Jim Muslin, 22; Aaron Johnson, 23; Jim Nash, 20; Alex Hall, 70; Tempsy Harris, 30; Lelia Blake, 18; A Vogel, 21; Anna Gooch, 59; Adeline Johnson, 18.

Issue of May 25,1913:

Died May 24, George M Gillespie, a veteran of the Confederacy. He was born January 18, 1847. He leaves his wife, whom he married June 12, 1872, four sons, R V Gillespie, St. Louis, Mo., W H, P B, and E A of this city, and a daughter, Minnie May Gillespie. Burial was in Greenwood Cemetery.

Issue of May 28, 1913:

Board of Health Statistics ending May 27, 1913

MARRIAGES (No race shown)

Edward B Frawley and Gladys P Long; W A Argo and Alice Thompson; Johnnie Hall and K Kemp; J K Smith and Mateline D'Appliget; J E Golden Jr and B E Lunsford; Will Thompson and Mary Granaberry; Grover Atkinson and Mrs. Sarah Corry; George Anderson and Virgie Tucker; Zach Oliphant and Cecile Evans; Isaac Abner and Martha Woodruff; B R Robinson and Lilly Thomas.

DEATHS

White: J E Brenon, 42; H B Williams, 35; Mrs. W E Kirklin, 24; W W Westehover, 30.
Black: Jonnie Hill, 19; Niel Jetson, 21; Richard Herndon, 31; Ike King, 65; Green Bell, 63; Sallie Woods, 20; Fannie Haynes, 19; Lit Simmons, 18; Kate Bayliss, 75; Daisy Adair, 9.

Issue of June 1, 1913:

Board of Health Statistics ending May 31, 1913

MARRIAGES (No race shown)

Ernest Johnson and Carrie Woolford; Eugene Wooten and Henrietta Williams; Root Mitchell and Anna Williams; Joe Owens and Eliza Ens.

DEATHS

White: Rainey C Munier, 26; George M Gillespie, 66; B P Parker, 76.

Black: J Smith, 17; Thelma Franklin, 4; Charley Mason, 30; Paris Fangell, 75; Freddie Thomas, 2; Louis Dawson, 21.

Issue of June 8, 1913:

Board of Health Statistics ending June 7, 1913

MARRIAGES (No race shown)

Pinckney E Barnett and Geneva L Mills; Edward Kelland and Myrtle Blackman; Andrew Hymel and Leila Blanchard; William Boyston and Mariah Jones; George A Bauer and Myrtle Gillett; Robert M Bailey and Gertrude Boney; Samuel Hanheim and Rena Leah Josey; George M Mehas and Despina A Coureas; C N Christansen and Mabel Clair Baxter; Lee Holcomb and Lina Thomason.

DEATHS

White: Milo Booher, 81; Ruel Lacy Anderson, 1; John Brooks, 45; Joe E Platt, 9; L L Crow, 55; John Wright, 63; Mrs J R Collins, 28.

Black: Frank Young 62; Dan Williams, 35; Willis Gooden, 39; George Moore, 45; Bale Payne, 43; Adeline White, 22; Sarah Jane Taylor, 19.

Issue of June 15,1913:

Board of Health Statistics ending June 14, 1913

MARRIAGES (No race shown)

M O Simpson and Augustus E Block; William W Lyon and Mrs. Mabel A Norwood; William H McMichael and Allie T Roach; M E Pike and Allie M Newman; William Harvey and

Inita Hopkins; Walter McCoy and Mattie Hudson; T J Ostendorf and Myrtle E Levy; Virge Johnson and Joe Joseph.

DEATHS
White: J B Dixon, 53; F L Eyre, 52; W J Hutchinson, 80; Porter Windham, 30; William F Adair, 31; Hazel Abramson, 8; Euginia Travis, 3; Agnes P Harp, 70.
Black: Ike Barnette, 42; Martin Johnson, 39; Ben Luster, 27; Ben Flowers, 45; Ella Davis 25; Charlotte Alexander, 25; Susan Brockett, 48.

Issue of June 21, 1913:

Board of Health Statistics ending June 20, 1913

MARRIAGES (No race shown)
Moses L Johnson and Myra Dawson; Ed Deady and Lillian Teach; Fred Landrum and Rosa May Brown; Tom L Hudson and Slise Cleveland; R H Gibson and Corinne Pearce; C C Crenshaw and Luella D Foster; J A Alch and Esther Schwartzberg; Conrad Lubber and Marie Louise Walker; Pink L Butler and Mary Rochelle; W L Garland and Eva Maben.

DEATHS
White: A D Roberts, 25; George Weeks, 57; Alfred Granath, 70; Vincent Palmer, 5; Percy Palmer, 2; James Keeney, 58; Mary L Rogers, 62.
Black: Robert Mitchell, 17; Bertha Palmer, 22; Jake Dray, 19; U Williams, 5; Rebecca Ford, 35; Gladys Bowens, 3; Nancy Powell, 15; Mineola Waterman, 18; Callie Hutchinson, 24; Mahley Hillman, 23.

Issue of June 29, 1913:

Board of Health Statistics ending June 28, 1913

MARRIAGES (No race shown)
William L Behan and Georgia V Strongfellow; James E Whittington and Jennie Holm; R H McLean and Pansy Holler; Pope Woden and Pearl Dillon; Hervey S Little and Anna Boyd Newson; Joseph Node and Mary Walker; Henry Reviers and Eliza Butler; James L White and Mary L Flores; Elijah Helton and Edna Breefired; George F Buckley and Ruth Eakin; A D Keeney and Annie M Kelly; Robert H Her and Essie Gauthreaux.

DEATHS
White: Charles Roerety, 56; William Moro, 78; Ira May Wood, 2; Dora A Stone, 1.
Black: John Dunkin, 30; Jesse Shambre, 26; Ed Brown, 44; Hattie Clayton, 23; Liza Smith, 42; Mary Etta Thompson, 42; Oda Clarkson, 39; Pearlie Ivey, 32; Rubie Bingham, 11; Betty Hopkins, 28; Clarence Tomplin 20.

Issue of July 6, 1913:

Board of Health Statistics ending July 5, 1913

MARRIAGES (No race shown)
Frank H Ford and Amanda Ford; F D Taylor and Gladdis Priggs; Wesley Johnson and Curtis Sibley; Alanzo V Stark and Margaret Meeker.

DEATHS
White: T N Pavey, 39; Antoune Fredien, 42; Landrie Causton, 2; Tom Hendricks, 39; S W Matthews, 52; Charles Roarety, 56; William Moro, 78; Mrs. C H Blish, 27; Elvie Evans, 24.

Black: Robert Taylor, 46; Early Johnson, 12; Mike Edmond, 42; Ernest Royal, 20; Sam Anderson, 31; C Tomplin, 20; L Richardson, 15; Sarah A Moore, 34; Lena Warren, 27; Effie James, 24.

Issue of July 13, 1913:

Board of Health Statistics ending July 12, 1913

MARRIAGES (No race shown)

Charles Seymour and Annie Lee Davis; Frank Jackson and Mamie Lewis; Pete Molant and Angeline Summerdon; Voice Perry and Eva Code; Marks Jackson and Mary Davidson; Wesly King and Bessie Bonner.

DEATHS

White: P B Barlow, 73; N B Willoby, 45; S C Huey, 75; C M Walke, 55; C Smith, 49; Dr. T G Ford, 64; D T Hallbrook, 54; D M Durkin, 1; Donie Everett, 18; Joice Moore, 9 months; Mrs. Mary Caple, 69; Mrs. E Payne, 74; Mrs. George M Hearne, 46.

Black: B H Anderson, 6; L Jordan, 36; P Christmas, 21; Amos Dawson, 50; Annie Thompson, 28; Mary Owens, 23; Alice Washington, 20.

Issue of July 20, 1913:

Board of Health Statistics ending July 19, 1913

MARRIAGES (No race shown)

Sam Grubbs and Annie King; Harold Armstrong and Wynona Burnell; Gus Robinson and Jessie White; L A Sims and Belle L Johnson; Robert J Hall and Ruth Oaks; Will Simpson and Berthards Moton; W F Hitchet and Myrtle I Sempe.

DEATHS

White: Frank Wright, 55; William Hudnall, 33; John Gossioa, 35; E Evans, 46.

Black: Elva Vinzant, 37; A Scott, 3; M Gravens, 16; J Fields, 39; Willie B Calloway, 24; Inez Metcalf, 45; Jennie Mitchell, 30; Alice Moore, 28; Annis Parker, 28; Fannie Duma, 50; Sara Miles, 40; Mary Petis, 32; F Davis, 33; Carrie Williams, 29; Luese Carter, 1.

Issue of July 27, 1913:

Board of Health Statistics ending July 26, 1913

MARRIAGES (No race shown)

Mat Fulwood and Bertha Smith; A F Sales and Mrs. Ethel Griffin; A Cheatham and Savannah Henderson; Chales F Mercer and Winnie Davis Butler; Moses Karpoll and Lula Lewis; Dr. A P Crain and Annie L Lawhon; George G Dimick and Bashie English.

DEATHS

White: W M Leyton, 42; Tony Parlenchio, 23; E A Prothro, 63; L F Schooler, 74; Addie Smith, 5; M E Redding, 38; Lucy Gillis, 46.

Black: A Ross, 37; Ben Hall, 42; Wilkam Brown, 36; H Debos, 39; James Wilson, 29; Fred Parker, 21; George Jackson, 21; Mary Brooks, 24; Marie Starks, 10; Mandy Jackson, 85; Mollie Green, 36; Ella Lewis, 35; Fannie Car, 23; Martha Manning, 35.

Issue of Aug. 3, 1913:

Board of Health Statistics ending Aug. 2, 1913

MARRIAGES (No race shown)

Blanche Lambkins and Maggie L Jones; Charles Atkins and Sarah Stackman; Andrew G Shabay and Beulah May Meek.

DEATHS

White: H G Glass, 38; N B Leopard, 30; J C Sewell, 60; L S Keuger, 60.

Black: L Washington, 25; Lee Sholden, 6; Watson Fox, 66; Charley Crewer, 32; Mabel Phillips, 10; C Thompson, 42; Callie Watson, 41; Mollie Gibbs, 45.

Issue of Aug. 24,1913:

Board of Health Statistics ending Aug. 23, 1913

MARRIAGES (No race shown)

John Gary and Martha Robinson; Charles Peterson and Clara Garett; Thomas Hall and Ethel Mayo; W M Spence and Beulah Neighbors; Duncan McDonald and Mrs. Julia Brodin; Henry Cockrell and Susie Nelson; Lee Brown and Carrie Thomas; E H Norton and Mrs. Ida Brown; H L Andrews and Julia C Atkins; M M Harris and Josephine Josey; B L Adcocks and Elizabeth Wimberly; Will Morgan and Evelyn Bryant.

DEATHS

White: Laura A Wells, 77; J L Gilliland, 44; Josephine Spurta, 34.

Black: Mary Hart, 50; Mary Thomas, 50; Mary Scott, 22; Emma Samuels, 59; V Flynn, 23; Walter Lemon, 20.

Issue of Aug. 31,1913:

Board of Health Statistics ending Aug. 30, 1913

MARRIAGES (No race shown)

Sam Byas and Nonie Holt; A L Stevens and Sue Ella Givens; Henry Clifton and Jenny Buvens; John Bailley and Maggie Windham.

DEATHS
<u>White</u>: J J McClean, 24; J W Sikes, 35; W W Paylor, 57; Mandy Blanton, 57; Isabella Hayes, 52; William Gideon, 64; N Chambers, 40; Mattie Pickett, 26; Sadie Harrison, 20.

Issue of Sept. 7, 1913:

Board of Health Statistics ending Sept. 6, 1913

MARRIAGES (No race shown)
A E Suggs and Gladys E Hutchens; Walter Williams and Leola Kennedy; Jake Cook and Nancy Johnson; Antonio Guerro and Rosa Valchez; John Jackson and Mary Harris; A E Barnett and Emma Harvey; Vito Viola and Guisippena Aliuse; Ernest Gaskin and Hazel Williams; Robert Clay and Jareshan Barlowe; Vincenzo Matason and Mary Liberto.

DEATHS
<u>White</u>: S L Greenblatt, 38; J M Leeds, 16; John Higginbotham, 23; Mrs. W R Simmons, 34.
<u>Black</u>: W Carter, 25; Jim Meek, 27; G L Abner, 6; Lonnie Williams, 9; J Cody, 59; Willie King, 22; Tom Snell, 49; Latha Lowery, 26; Emma May, 28.

Issue of Sept. 21, 1913:

Board of Health Statistics ending Sept. 20, 1913

MARRIAGES (No race shown)
Harry T Keith and Lena Scott; M Moranty and Dashie Staton; Richard M Deer and Lula Bennett; J F Clemner and

Mrs. Janie P Scott; Frank Crowboy and Lina Moore Dowdell; C W Atkinson and M L Pollard; E J Ogle and Nellie Greer.

DEATHS
White: Fred Jordan, 20; Augusta Pincus, 78; Jessie May Riddle, 18; Cora Franklin, 33.
Black: John White, 80; Joseph Gibson, 20; Richard Moore, 67; Thelmer Armstrong, 7.

Issue of Oct. 11, 1913:

Board of Health Statistics ending Oct. 10, 1913

MARRIAGES (No race shown)
Walter Wilson and Delia Johnson; James Collins and Creno Kendall; Elijah C Vinson Jr and Elizabeth Thomas; Allen Hall and Irene Thomas; Frank Bell and Roxy Smith; John Terry and Elizabeth Hall; Fannie Price and Mary Starky; M D Harris and Vada Atkins.

DEATHS
White: J K Boone, 64; Ed Boles, 55; Van D Whittle, 35; Mrs. H D Watson, 58; Mrs. Louise Lawrence, 68.
Black: Vance Docky, 21; Alice Taylor, 13; Ellen Parks, 36.

Issue of Nov. 9, 1913:

Board of Health Statistics ending Nov. 8, 1913

MARRIAGES (No race shown)
Claude Jones and Oma Williams; J B Hollowell and Mrs. Mearl Matthews; Claiborne Brown and Rosalie Rambo; E M Denkins and Gussie L Jones; Clarence M White and Florence Smith.

DEATHS
White: J L Summerlin, 40; Elvin Kemp, 12.
Black: Jim Belts, 53; Nathan Hill, 55; Frank Snowden, 45; A Watson, 23; A Parker, 6.

Issue of Nov. 16, 1913:

Board of Health Statistics ending Nov. 15, 1913

MARRIAGES (No race shown)
Benjamin Ollie Page and Josie Lee Moss; Feley Searles and Katie Williams; Charles W Adair and Bessie L Hartman; T L Blalock and Mary Young; H Hunsicker Jr and Carrie K Fox; Root Brown and Ruby Ashman; Henry Brown and Bella Jones.

DEATHS
White: S O Admas, 66; W J Stallings, 1; David Carter, 6; Lee Ross Beard, 8; D H B Stone, 67; J N Skidmore, 28; Mary Shirley, 64; Mrs. M E Gothier, 78.
Black: Robert Smith, 22; Henry Williams, 55; Henry Duke, 45; Manie Fields, 25; Rilla Phelps, 22; Luesia Parker, 50.

Issue of Nov. 23, 1913:

Board of Health Statistics ending Nov. 22, 1913

MARRIAGES (No race shown)
John Gray and Edna Davis; Walter Saxton and Annette Hughes; Fisher Hopkins and Inez Dupre; A L Currie and Geneva Cansup; L T Rogers and Rebecca Sewell; R J Barry and Mrs. Leota Maxwell; Dave Oneill and Nannie Thomas; J H Cunningham and Sadye Daniell; Wade Berry and Essie Crutchfield; Aubert S Simmons and Mary P Saunders.

DEATHS
White: Carl S Dare, 4; Hattie Hodges, 58; C E Anderson, 61; C D McCaa, 62; J J Van Cleave, 34; W D Maddry, 35; Belton Doby, 68; J H Stewart, 57; E R Dougherty, 58.
Black: Gill Mason, 50; Tena Swan, 80; Martha Jones, 49; Carlee Rose, 30.

Issue of Nov. 30, 1913:

Board of Health Statistics ending Nov. 29, 1913

MARRIAGES (No race shown)
Ben Nevins and Josephine Davis; John C Reynolds and Minnie Lee Melton; E O Payne and Norma Higgins; Fred McKenzie and Ethel Holmes; Chris O'Brien and Loraine Ludolph.

DEATHS
White: Stella E Rutherford, 8; Floyd J Ross, 25.
Black: Dewitt Williams, 25; Stella Williams, 36; William C Porter, 42; Peter Hart, 68; Elizabeth Williams, 19; Christine Sly, 21; Lash Harold, 30; William Dodd, 76.

Died December 1, Howard F Doll. He was born in Adams County, Pa., November 8, 1847. Survived by wife and children, daughters, Mrs. W C Belcher, Mrs. J T Broghan, Mrs. Lewell C Butler, sons, E T John, Charles Doll, and daughter, Loretta Doll, brothers, James Hall, Riverton, Wyo., George Doll, Marion, Ind., and Marion Doll, Germantown, Indiana. Burial in St. Joseph's Catholic Cemetery.

Issue of Dec. 7, 1913:

Board of Health Statistics ending Dec. 6, 1913

MARRIAGES (No race shown)
Robert Davis and Josephine Harris; Walter Ivy and Rosalie Estes; James A Marmouget and Lillie Elizabeth McGrath; Jimmie Riggs and Charlie B Johnson; Britton Wilkinson and Leslie Murphy; Frank Minor and Alice Maus; J Lindsay and Mrs. Nellie Land; Daniel Floyd and Eldoza Fuller; Roy James and Ruby Ruth Dees; J E Purtell and Rosa Durden; W F Crawford and Eva Franklin.

DEATHS
White: H F Doll, 66; Tom Barber, 19; Mrs. M A Belcher, 63; Stella Carnegie, 19.
Black: Irvian Meyers, 75; Willie Whitehead, 1; M Hilard, 37.

Issue of Dec. 14, 1913:

Board of Health Statistics ending Dec. 13, 1913

MARRIAGES (No race shown)
Fred Carter and Mamie Ishmael; Harrison Robinson and Geneva Green; John Patterson and Lillie Walker; Charley Jones and Emily Love; S F McMackin and Andrey Marren; Dave Martin and Rosette Shidicet; I D Rose and Henrietta Unbehagan.

DEATHS
White: Thomas Fleming, 35.
Black: George Conway, 33; Sims Williams, 23; James Noll, 49; Eli Green, 50; Annie Butler, 14; Alice Brooker, 36.

INDEX

AARON, Edward 142
ABBOTT, H M 32 J W 80 Mariah 52
ABBY, C 131
ABEL, Henry 21 Pollie 53
ABNER, G L 158 Isaac 151
ABRAHAM, J 4 82
ABRAHAMSON, August 16
ABRAMS, Gussie 19
ABRAMSON, Hazel 153
ABRANTES, Joe 43
ABSHIER, Carrie 147
ACENCIA, Calcida 83
ADAIR, Charles W 160 Daisy 151 Juna 88 William F 153
ADAMS, Annie 124 Charles H 47 E 81 E M 70 Ella 127 G L 40 G W 97 George 3 Hattie 149 J M 79 Josie 73 Lizzie 120 Matie 107 Minnie 127 Ola 39 Rosa 59 Ruth 90 Sam 103 William 47
ADCOCKS, B L 157
ADDE, Joe 2
ADDINGTON, Davey 30
ADGER, E M 24 Mattie 147
ADKINS, John 147 Mary 119
ADMAS, S O 160
AIKEN, Will 60
ALBERT, M V 123 Prince 85 131
ALCH, J A 36 153 Zetta 124
ALCOCKE, Julia W 83
ALDRICH, M G 91
ALEXANDER, Charlotte 153 E 70 E B 66 Mrs. E J 127 Mrs. E S 3 Esther 70 Floyd 128 Jennie 108 Kathleen 143 R C 112 S A 32 S Y 32
ALFORD, Evanston 1 Susie 131 W M 129
ALIUSE, Guisippena 158
ALLEN, Arthur L 127 C 141 Cora 125 Edmonia 94 Frances 0 69 Frank 19 Henry 144 Hiram J 67 J F 4 Jeff 139 John C 138 Joseph 105 L L 21 Martha A 88 Martha E 108 Maude M 76 Minnie 114 Mollie 63 Richard 111 S 34 W F 119 Walthie 18 Wash 124
ALLEY, Charles E 63
ALLIOSO, Francis 3
ALLISON, Sallie M 95
ALLMAN, C V 24 Edyth 78 Mrs. Van Simon 132
ALSTON, C A 103 Lilly 20 Willis 96
AMISS, C L 50
AMOND, Dollie 128

AMOS, Joe 24
ANDERSON, Allie 7 B H 155 Booker T 73 C 95 C E 161 Dudley B 137 Elizabeth 142 Evelyn L 35 George 151 Harriett 3 Harris 111 Henry 8 23 J B 91 James 22 Jennie 84 Jester 86 John 89 Julia 61 Mrs. M J 19 Mandy 64 Mary 38 Mary F 7 Ora 120 R D 149 R L 145 Richard 8 Roberta 36 Ruel Lacy 152 S A 33 Sam 83 155 Seany 129 Susie 30 Topsy 125 Will 145 Wilson 92
ANDREOLA, William 109
ANDREW, M 81
ANDREWS, A 41 Alma 19 Arthur 138 Australia 29 C H 139 H L 157 H 111 Jenie 143 Sallie 120
ANDRIEU, E 2
ANGEL, Aubrey 148
ANKRON, Mathew 104
ANLIN, Y 37
ANSLEY, Mary C 49
ARCHIBALD, John Z 5
ARDIS, Bryan 120 133 C H 52 Mary Lou 52
ARGO, W A 151
ARKANSAS, Caroline 86
ARMSTEAD, Dave 38 Prudence 44

ARMSTRONG, Angeline 61 Annie 53 Charity 60 Harold 155 Martha 142 Nora 127 Pollie 142 Ruth 79 Thelmer 159 W M 74
ARNOLD, A H 5 Maru L 5
ARTHUR, James 124
ASEUNES, Sara 94
ASHBORN, J L 10
ASHLAND, Jennie 77
ASHLEY, Charley 33
ASHLY, Eveline 108
ASHMAN, Ruby 160
ASKEN, Eugene 118
ATKINS, Alice 50 Calvin 147 Charles 157 Julia C 157 Robert 38 Rufus 49 Tom 38 Vada 159 Will 117
ATKINSON, Bulah 46 C W 159 Grover 151
ATTAWAY, D 63 Mrs. Douglas 102 Gussie 132 Wayne 84
AUBREY, Roberta V 144
AUCHOR, John 20
AUHELZE, Mat 43
AULD, Clarrence 30
AUSTEN, Frances X 34
AUSTIN, R E 73
AUTHOR, Anderson 105
AVERY, C L 29 Leonard 61 Ophelia 73 William 20
AVINGER, Charles D 1
AVIS, E 69

BABERS, David 121
BACKARD, Mary 73
BACKUS, J C 95
BACON, Florie 78
BAGLEY, Ella G 73 Mrs. J
 M 40 Kattie L 120
BAIFIELD, J S 92
BAILEY, Bill 146 C T 15 F
 110 Harriett 2 Harry 117
 Mrs. J A 144 James A 74
 Nanie 38 Robert M 152
 West 69 112
BAILLEY, John 158
BAILY, Dell 104 Jim 102
BAIN, Ida 60
BAINER, Edith M 52
BAINS, A C 107
BAIRD, Effie 34 Justice 88
 Zidia 9
BAISCH, E 90
BAKEFIELD, Alfred 124
BAKER, Alice 118 119 E
 107 Henry 66 Julia 123
 M 126 Samuel 149
BALARK, Nettie 145
BALCOM, Harry 81
BALDEN, John 147
BALDING, Carl 79
BALLAUF, F W 4 Mamie 4
 Scharl R 4
BANKS, Alf 71 Andrew 107
 Clara 111 Elias 109
 Ennis 86 Irma 123 James
 35 Jim 94 Leta 137
 Maggie 103 Orilla 105

BANNETT, Mezekiah 7
BANNON, T E 38
BARBER, John 52 Omey 36
 Susie B 53 Tom 162
BARETT, Alex 142
BARFIELD, C C 138
BARIE, Nellie 67
BARLOW, Joseph F 137 P
 B 155
BARLOWE, Jareshan 158
BARNARD, S F M 108
BARNCASTLE, H 33
BARNES, Charles A 74
 Mrs. E D 3 Henry 34
 John 75 Johnnie Moore
 105 Lula 147 Wes 145
BARNETT, A E 158 Albert
 86 F 89 Martha 142
 Pinckney E 152
BARNETTE, Ike 153
BARNS, Arthur 149
BARNWELL, T M 54
BARRET, A 7
BARRETT, Josephine 80
BARRON, Lizzie 130
 Virginia 30
BARRY, R J 160
BARTLETT, Will 24
BARTON, Lucy 115
BASCH, John 17
BASKE, John 8
BASS, Aleck 84 Charles 33
 Leola 75
BASSET, Ella 31
BATCHELLOR, Minnie 29

BATEMAN, Nancy Bird
    148
BATES, Mrs. A 6 Albert
    145 Eva C 146 G N 109
    J F 109 Lucile 6 Pearly
    143
BATOM, Judge 78
BATSCH, John 17
BATTLE, A 6 Abner 107
    Maggie 49 Sallie 68
    Vallie 116 W 148
BAUER, E R 91 George A
    152
BAUMAN, Susie 108
BAXTER, Mabel Clair 152
BAYLISS, Kate 151
BEACH, Julia 67 Lavelle 46
BEAIRD, Grace 89
BEANS, Maria 85
BEARD, E 30 E G 1 Lee
    Ross 160 Victoria 88
BEARDON, George 83
BEASLEY, A 6 Dessie 94 J
    C 93 Nellie 72 Will 103
    143
BEATTY, Fred E 139
BEATY, A J 49 Joe Ela 23
    Leo 104
BEAVER, Rebecca 83
BEAZEALE, Willie 92
BEAZLEY, W 106
BECK, George 94
BECKWITH, Samuel 138
BEDARD, Mrs. P A 138
BEDFORD, Annie 6

BEEFE, John 95
BEESON, T 128
BEHAN, William L 154
BELCHER, M A 30 Mrs. M
    A 162 Mrs. W C 161
BELDON, Irene 113
BELL, Arthur 72 Carrie 40
    Charley 139 Eugene 89 F
    W 42 Fannie 129 Frank
    159 G F Jr 110 Green
    151 Harrel 8 J A 103
    Julia 70 Lelia 109
    Marietta 39 Mary 66
    Mary J 52 Rosanna 73
    Mrs. T F 101 W F 43
    William 147 Willie 53
BELLAH, M T 67
BELTON, N J 118
BELTS, Jim 160
BENDOW, George 149
BENJAMIN, Albert 130 Joe
    87 Lena 87 88 Louis 87
BENNETT, Charles 55
    Fannie E 115 Frank B
    125 John 15 Josephine 7
    Lula 158 Mable 126 Roy
    148
BENNICE, Claude 123
BENNINGS, Emanuel 96
BENSON, Yetta 36
BENTFIELD, Theado 6
BENTLEY, Emerson 98
BERLIN, Gertrude 4
BERNSTEIN, Caroline 80
    Jacob 80 Julius 147

BERRET, Newton F 139
BERRY, Alma 139 B F 95
    Grant 121 Lucindy 115
    Pessiro 106 Pierce 1
    Wade 160
BERTELS, Father 17 32
BERTRAND, Florence 109
BESSET, Julius 49
BEST, William C 126
BETHLEY, Lula 6
BETTY, J O 5
BIAS, Ida 33
BICKHAM, Donnie 36 Julia
    F 115 Myra 104
BICKNELL, Frank 128
BIES, Mollie 35
BIGGERS, Jim 127
BILES, Willie 109
BILLIU, D H 7
BIMMERY, Henry 1
BIND, Edith 128
BINGHAM, Rubie 154
    Sallie 44
BINGSTON, John 38
BIRD, Alice 149 E D 128
    Hasker 145 Ivey 128
    Rochelle 111 Sarah 105
    T E 119
BIRGE, Rebecca 24
BIRIL, Willie A 88
BISHOP, Effie 85
BLACHINS, Sopha 109
BLACK, Allie M 8 Dela 126
    Goodin 65 May 84
BLACKBURN, Jimmie 116

BLACKER, Rosa 117
BLACKMAN, Babe 2 Birdie
    53 Foster 113 Myrtle 152
    Virginia 112
BLACKMER, Maude 36
BLACKSHEAR, Joe 88
BLACKSHIRE, Willie 96
BLACKWOOD, Helen 60
BLAIR, E P 120
BLAKE, Arthur 73 Lelia 150
    R W 124
BLALOCK, T L 160
BLANCHARD, Floyd 143 L
    C 55 Leila 152
BLANE, Josephine 143
BLANKENSHIP,
    Richardson 43
BLANTON, J J 59 J R 7
    Mandy 158
BLARKMAN, Robert 143
BLATTMAN, John 77
    Pauline 36
BLEDSAL, M I 16
BLISH, Mrs. C H 154
BLOCK, Augustus E 152
    Isadore 143
BLOCKER, A B Jr 85 Frank
    110
BLOOM, Margaret 51
BLOR, A L 10
BLOUNT, Ed 29
BLUE, Sarah 45 Willie F
    106
BLUESTEIN, Harry 69
    Isadore 87

BLUM, E 38
BLUMBERG, Rosa 53
BLUNSEN, Dan 108
BLUNT, Mrs. L P 116
BLUSTEIN, Mrs. M 87
BLYTHE, J P 7
BOARDMAN, Charles 107
BOATCAP, E 85
BODENHEIMER, Mrs. Henry 90
BOETON, Anderson 120
BOGEL, Julie W 81
BOGGS, Rev. 15
BOISSEAU, Exzena 33
BOLES, Ed 159
BOLIN, W H 3
BOLLINGER, Isa 81
BOLTS, Mrs. H J 150
BOND, G H 70 Joe S 69
BONDEY, Chief 82
BONEY, Dick 133 Gaston 133 Gertrude 133 152 Jack 133 Lela 74 Wimberk 133
BONNEGENT, Mrs. M A 64
BONNER, Ben 85 Bessie 155 John 131 Oliver 71 Roy E 117
BONNETTE, E 110
BONNEY, Elsie 64
BOOHER, L Z 84 Milo 152
BOOKER, Albert 42 Fidelia 34 Henry 118
BOOKOUT, Blanche 17

BOOMS, Laura 86
BOON, Anna 67 Inez 47
BOONE, Ada 40 Effie 103 Harriett 112 J K 159 Jim 53 M 35
BOONS, Mack 89
BOORES, Robert 3
BOOTH, Carrie L 98 John 145
BORING, Mack 138
BORKLAND, W T 70
BORLING, Pearl 78
BOSLEY, M J 22
BOSS, Annie 16
BOSTON, Ellis 147
BOSWELL, Lucindy 64
BOUNDS, Alva 142 Budie 142 F B 142 Ida B 142 143 Myrtle Cox 149 Thomas R 109 Una 118
BOURDETTE, Frank 37
BOURGEOIS, Mrs. Etienne 144
BOURQUIN, Albert M 98 Maggie 102
BOWENS, Gladys 153
BOWER Jr, Andrew 117
BOWERS, Caroline 109 Mrs. Lloyd 100 Mattie 113
BOWN, Frances 149
BOXLEY, Ben 125
BOYD, Clara 113 James 77 Lummi 138 Tug 105 Will E 110 Mrs. William

99
BOYETT, Della 90
BOYKIN, J F 45 L 67 Mary 19 138 Pattie 18
BOYLES, H 62
BOYLSTON, _____ 39
BOYNTON, Mattie B 39
BOYSTON, Bertha 143 William 152
BOZEMAN, C 1
BOZIE, A R 44
BRACK, Jacob 96
BRADEN, Fran 105 Louis 111
BRADFORD, Ben 15 Corine 24 Frank 92 Mellow 59 Rosetta 149 Thomas 16 W T 125
BRADLEY, J B 130 Lea 63
BRADY, C 143 J P 38 Marcella E 143 Mildred 131 William 127
BRANDENBURG, Marie 119
BRANIN, F H 54
BRANNON, Anna Bell 118
BRANTE, Rosie 52
BRANTES, Elizabeth A 66
BRASSILL, Maude E 51
BRASWELL, Jesse W 110
BRAUER, J H 115
BRAUNIG, Estelle Louise 148 Pauline 145 S J 92
BRAVELLE, Bessie 120
BRAY, Robert 97

BRAZELLE, Bernard 126
BRAZIER, Lizzie 127
BREARD, D A 38
BRECKENRIDGE, Wallace 96
BREDA, J E 144
BREEFIRED, Edna 154
BREEMIN, Mandy 73
BREFFIEH, John 95
BRELFORD, D M 48
BREMAN, Milton 39
BREMEN, Howard 64
BRENON, J E 151
BREWER, E 84
BREWSTER, Mrs. J M 105
BRICE, Marie 124 Susan 120
BRIDGER, Estella 98
BRIDGES, Myrtle 107 W R 120
BRIDGMAN, Emma L 7
BRILY, Flora 2
BRIMMER, Litta 37
BRINGER, Roy 138
BRITE, Rex 131
BRITT, W F 22
BROCK, Anna 22 John 38
BROCKER, Charles 147
BROCKETT, Susan 153
BRODIE, Myrtle 29
BRODIN, Julia 157
BROGHAN, Mrs. J T 161
BROOKE, Joseph 92
BROOKER, Alice 162
BROOKS, Ann 19 Bert 114

Cleveland H 137 Frank
89 Henry 49 John 152
Martha 19 Mary 156
Parthena 139
BROSINGTON, Lydia 137
BROWN, Aaron 65
  Alexander 35 Allen 31
  Almer 113 Ananias 103
  Annie 86 Arthur 76 Bert
  107 Bessie 126 Carrie 60
  101 Charles 104 Charley
  H 19 Claiborne 159
  Columbus 141 D C 130
  Ed 63 154 Eddie 34
  Edith 7 Ellen 126 Elmora
  96 Eva 75 F A 125
  George 19 126 Hattie 4
  Henry 74 160 Hy 59 Ida
  83 157 Isy 74 J D S 110 J
  W 34 John 130 Laurence
  21 Leather 22 Lee 157
  Lettie 37 Lillie S 110
  Lizzie 40 Louisa 119
  Luke B 76 Mallie 30
  Malliso 33 Mandy 104
  Margaret 124 Mary J 37
  Mason 73 May 36
  Melissa 31 Minnie 31
  Mirah 67 72 Nettie 7 Phil
  118 Reace Lee 94 Rhoda
  5 Richard 119 Robert 53
  Root 160 Rosa 142 Rosa
  May 153 Sadie 128
  Sarah 132 Sauie 8 T M
  44 Tom 53 W H 68

  Wilkam 156 Willie 106
  Yale 132
BROWNING, J B 69 Mrs. R
  A 3
BROWNLEE, Mrs. L 114
BRUMFIELD, Bob 143
BRYAM, C 76
BRYAN, Beni 87 Effie May
  36 Mrs. R M 48
BRYANT, B 50 Calvin 120
  E C 116 Evelyn 157
  Fannie 20 Jerry 141 Julia
  121 Lucille 70 Maud E
  21 Mazie 142 Patsy 90
  Peter 147 Walter 119
  Willie 92
BRYSON, Agnes 132
  Martha 132 R A 132
  Mrs. S 132 W A 120
BUCKELEW, Andrew 101
  Fred 101 Nettie Wood
  101 Newton 101 Wilbur
  F 101 Will 101
BUCKELLS, J C 30
BUCKLEY, George F 154
BUDDERBROCK, E O 117
BUDROW, John 75
BULL, Alfred 91
BULLESON, Lou Ellen 41
BULLOCK, E 119
BULLOK, T J 5
BUNKIN, Julia 34
BUNSTON, Howard 79
BURCH, Jonie 130
BURDOCK, Christopher

BURK, Lula 77
BURKE, Virgie 126
BURKETT, J R 73
BURKS, Elener E 137 Henry C 137
BURNELL, Wynona 155
BURNES, Ed 7
BURNHAM, Charles 91 W H 19 114
BURNS, Charles 35 Ella 79 Fanny 108 Mattie 70
BURNSIDE, J R 61 James W 61 James A 61 Poland Belmont 61 R F 37
BUROUGH, H 73
BURR, Amos 67
BURRELL, William 63
BURRIO, Cladys 76
BURRIS, J A 108
BURROUGHS, T 86
BURROW, Evangeline 92
BURRS, Nettie 54
BURSON, T W 118
BURT, Ed 99 Jim 99 William Miles 99
BUSBY, J L 4 Mrs. J L 4 Tweáttie 4
BUSCOM, E 6
BUSE, Harrison 147
BUSH, E S 37
BUTLER, Alice 62 Annie 162 Bertha 118 Carrie 4 Eliza 154 Frank R 145 H 127 J W 24 Jessie M 128 Jo 21 L C 132 Mrs. Lewell C 161 Pawnee 99 Pierce 99 Pink L 153 Richard 147 Roy 146 Ruth 109 Winnie Davis 156
BUTTLER, E 111
BUVENS, Jenny 158
BYAS, May 42 Nathaniel 95 Sam 158
BYNAKE, Tony 49
BYRD, Joe 81 John Adlin 114 Mary 109
CADE, Eleanor 88
CAFEE, Mable 19
CAFFA, Louisa 84
CAFFRAY, Carrie 50
CAGE, Eastman 113
CAIN, C C 35 Mrs. E J 124 Emma L 10 John R 18
CAINS, Tosy 81
CALDWELL, John W 117 Maud 55 T 1
CALEY, John 130
CALHOUN, A 114 Amanda 81 Robert 139 Warren 50
CALKINS, A M 36
CALLAHAN, Ed 17 Pat 138
CALLAY, Georgiana 107
CALLEY, Jim 141
CALLOWAY, Archie 24 Jackson 68 Will 115 Willie B 156
CALMEZ, Rose 49
CAMERON, Lillie 102 Will

52
CAMP, Maggie 141 Mary Ellen 22
CAMPBELL, Belle 53 Clint 92 Duncan L 103 Eugene 146 L L 32 Lamar 32 Mandy 67 Nellie M 120 Willie 18
CANCETTA, Dannice 19
CANGLIALOSI, Henry 146
CANNON, G E 132 J G 54 Sam 62
CANSUP, Geneva 160
CAPERS, L C 145
CAPERTON, Mat 74
CAPITAN, John A 1
CAPLE, Mary 155
CAPLIS, Charles 131
CAR, Fannie 156
CARDARO, Antonio 115
CAREY, Lewis 39 Pat 2
CARGILE, Euna 95
CARGILL, Clara N 128
CARL, Pearl 66
CARLEY, Bernice 71
CARLTON, Annie 102 W U 127
CARNAHAN, Fannie 6
CARNEGIE, Stella 162
CARNES, Manny 50
CARNS, Fannie 129
CARPENTER, Frank 119 H 118 Lottie 24 Victor 127
CARR, A 130 Sidney 114 Willis Rosson 2

CARRIGAN, Joseph 124
CARROLL, Mary 33 R C 86
CARTER, Bert F 98 Charley 47 David 160 Elijah 107 Emma 73 Foster 124 Fred 162 Henry 66 Horace 101 James 91 Julia 41 98 Lucy 73 116 Luese 156 Mary 88 Mattie 34 R E 38 Robert 131 W 158 Walter 31 Willie 91
CARTHAN, Dan 80
CARTWRIGHT, Clyde 43
CARY, Annie 107
CASCIO, V 124
CASEY, Ella 1
CASH, Pouncey 115 Uncle Jack 8
CASHORE, Mrs. John 83
CASON, Henry 78
CASSIER, Dallas 105
CASTLE, S J 10
CASTOR, H 30
CATES, Jim 24
CATHEY, D H 55
CATHROM, D C 9
CATO, Anderson 111
CAUSLEY, J A 124
CAUSTON, Landrie 154
CAVANAUGH, P 149
CAYCE, E S 111
CEGAR, Cyrus V 127
CHAMBERS, A 123 Francis 119 Jimmie 73 N 158

Penny 24
CHAMPION, Lucindy 112
  Miss Sallis 44
CHANCERY, Beatrice L
  149
CHANDLER, Birtie 138
  Charles 112 Esther 77
  John P 144 Minnie V 50
CHAPMAN, E A 119
  Elizabeth 79 Ida Lee 108
  Matthew 24 Rosa 139
CHARLES, Erwin 96
CHASE, Estella 68 William
  Jr 109
CHATAIN, Sofa 86
CHATMAN, Mandy 141
CHEATHAM, A 156 Ella 74
CHEESMAN, Walter L 89
CHELSON, Mose 92
CHERRY, Ned 70
CHESTER, Amile 128 Sallie
  55
CHESTNUT, Bertha 67
CHEW, Carrie 18 Eloise H
  137 Nathan 105
CHILDERS, Zella 103
CHIPS, Lizzie 62
CHOLKER, F 145
CHOTLIN, Maggie 108
CHRISTANSEN, C N 152
CHRISTIAN, Bertha 63
  Mrs. C M 63 Charles 63
  Ethel 67 83 Grace 63
  Lena 127 Lettie 83 Ruth
  91

CHRISTMAN, Robert 111
CHRISTMAS, P 155
CHRISTOPHER, J B 61
CHUMLEY, Ora 118
CHURCH, George W 86
CHURCHILL, Rachel 127
CILLULON, J 142
CIMER, Dick 72
CLAIRBORNE, Cora 118
CLANCY, C Edwin 78 Mrs.
  D A 78
CLANEGAN, N 113
CLANTON, George F 138 R
  A 52 Rosalie 102
CLARK, Benton 51 Mrs. C
  115 Cecila B 8 Della 38
  Helen 125 Henry 61 John
  72 Julia 107 Rosa 94 124
  Sumie 74 Welborn N 141
  Will 118 Willie 119
CLARKSON, Oda 154
CLAUSON, Lally C 132
CLAWSON, Ida 60
CLAY, Charles 81 Robert
  158
CLAYTON, Hattie 154
  Mary 128 N C 10
  Roberta 94
CLEMENTS, J D 121
CLEMER, Willie 59
CLEMINO, John 147
CLEMNER, J F 158
CLEVELAND, Slise 153
CLIFTON, Henry 70 158
CLOCISO, Joe 98

CLOS, Alie 145
CLOUD, J W 22 Mable 104
CLYDE, Rosa Lee 143
COATS, Clab 24
COBB, George 97
COBEL, Fred 52
COBURN, Mrs. E C 92
COCKRELL, Henry 157
CODE, Eva 155
CODY, J 158
COEL, Tony 48
COFFEE, Hariett N 147
COFFER, Lum 53
COFFIND, _____ 69
COGGIN, Jannie K 78
COHEN, J E 16 William H 3
COHN, Mary 109
COKE, Laura 150
COKER, Prudie 35
COLBERT, W C 1 Will 33
COLE, James S 118 Melvin
   40 Tomey 104 Viola 88
   W P 84
COLEMAN, Duglass 126
   Frank 62 George 129
   Harriett 40 Jim 149 M
   117 Manerva 119 Mary
   106 Mattie 94 Olive 112
   S L 84 Willie 85
COLLIER, Ida 99 John 22
COLLINS, Andrew 93
   Caroline 90 Clyde A 78
   Dora 8 Emma W 111
   Fred D 97 Genevieve R
   50 H 55 105 Henry 145
   Hugh 129 Mrs. J D 47
   Mrs. J R 152 James 159
   Joe 2 John 7 Laura 29
   Leala 105 Lena 76 Mrs.
   M A 23 Odell 87 R G 90
   Rebecca 70 Robert 109
   Virginia 31 Mrs. W R
   150 Yancy 113
COLOME, Mary J 74
COLQUITT, L C 40 Pennie
   34
COLTER, J M 87
COLTS, Inez 150
COMEAU, Pearl 30
COMMELIAS, Jones 38
COMPTON, Emma 72
CONADA, F 86
CONADO, Silas 55
CONDON, W E 95
CONELL, Maggie 121
CONNEL, Sango 121
CONNELL, Elias A 77
CONNOR, Edgar 103
CONSTANTIA, Bessie 65
CONVERSE, Freda 148
CONWAY, Adeline 3 C G 3
   E A Jr 121 Eugene 119
   Frank 145 George 162
   Josie Leonard 3 Julia 82
   Maggie 123
COOK, Alice 107 Blanche
   10 Charlie 123 E 53 Eva
   138 J 29 J A 68 J B 143 J
   M 30 Jake 158 Joanna 54
   Mose 44 Ola 91

COOKE, Allana 103
COOKSON, Charlie R 74
COOLIDGE, A S 18
COONEY, J 2
COOPER, A 1 C C 53 Clara 78 Eva 70 Henry 53 Ira 64 Ora Lee 70 Walter 81 Willie 142
CORBETT, John 20
CORCETT, Maria 119
CORNELIUS, D L 144
CORNERS, L B 121
CORNWALL, J H 81
CORON, Victoria 114
CORRY, Sarah 151
COSTANSA, Rosa 35
COSTON, Bunkly 111
COSTROVE, B J 15
COTTON, Lucindy 66
COTTONREADER, Emma 35
COTY, Mary J 131 P H 53 Richard M 81
COULSON, James 81
COULTER, Hazel 2
COUREAS, Despina A 152
COURETS, E 29
COURTNEY, Gladis 19 Mrs. J W 143-144 Marshall 126
COUSTON, Perl 2
COX, Effie 77 J F 39 Rebecca 68 William B 96
COY, John 73
COYTEN, William 48
CRADDOCK, A N 71
CRAFT, Annie 108 Corinne 147 J C 75
CRAIG, Grace 37
CRAIGHEAD, Ruth 125
CRAIN, A P 156
CRANDALL, B C 107 Mrs. B C 64
CRAWFORD, Julia 59 Mrs. M T 51 S B 6 W F 162
CREET, Eliza S 6
CRENSHAW, C C 153 Mattie 121 Willie 83
CRETON, A 110
CREW, Maude 63
CREWER, Charley 157
CREWS, Mrs. B T 146 K T 36 Nan 105
CRIMMEAL, John 95
CRIPPER, Ethel 138
CRIS, Annie 86
CRISP, George B 109 Jim 115 L N 44 Mrs. L N 44 Minnie Lou 44 45
CRISS, Charley 88
CRITTENDEN, Carrie 74
CROCH, Viola 61
CROCKNELL, John 39
CROOKS, C C 19 George W 123
CROSS, Kittie 113
CROSSMAN, Anna 144
CROTCHETT, Tina 35
CROW, Eliza R 6 G T 117 L

L 152 Lucy 54
CROWBOY, Frank 159
CROWDE, Walter J 33
CROWDER, A B 33 Ben 34
    Clara 42 Jennie 40 Lina
    107 Mary 24 W J 35
CROWELL, James 1
CROWLEY, D J 96
CROWNRICH, J R 106
CRUNK, S H 85
CRUSE, Gregory 88
CRUTCHFIELD, Essie 160
CUFF, J C 123
CULLINEY, John 85
CULLINS, George 127
CULPEPPER, Allen 38 Nina 39
CULVERSON, Mamie I 46
CUNNINGHAM, J H 160 J P 42
CURN, John 88
CURREY, W S 30
CURRIE, A L 160 Mabel M 62
CURRUTH, Charles 71
CURRY, A L 24 Alen 104
    Alfred 35 Logan 40
CURTIS, Aubrey 129
    Isabella 79 J J 129 Louis
    129 Marie 42 May 129 R
    L 7 W J 129 William 129
CUSTER, John 75 L B 75
CUTLIFF, A 73 Augustus 121
DABINSKI, Therressa 3

DAGGS, Arthur 50
DAGL, Martha 130
DALE, Alice G 63
DALIA, Estella 40
DALTON, Mrs. Kate 93
DALY, A C 124
DALZELL, Estelle Logan 99
    W G 99 Mrs. W G 144
    W T D 99
DANCE, Maggie B 124
DANDOLDS, A 41
DANIELL, Sadye 160
DANIELS, Caroline G 115
    Eliza 79 J C 41 James
    104 Julia 49 Mariah 96
    Minnie 86 Raymond 52
DANSBY, Binum 86 Mary 46
D'APPLIGET, Mateline 151
DARE, Carl S 161
DARK, Monroe 54
DARROW, Nancy 143
DARTOIS, Margaret A 148
DAUGHTREY, Rosa Lee 22
DAVANIE, Mary 80
DAVENPORT, James 53
    Polly 47 Sam 115
DAVIDSON, Fred 110 H
    137 L 149 Mary 155
    Wilson 70
DAVIS, A G 21 A R 104
    Alfred 132 141 Annie
    Lee 155 Bettie 118
    Carrie 93 Coltis 93
    Dinkey 130 Edna 160

Eliza 19 Ella 153 F 156
Francis 8 George 39 Ike
93 J 94 Jane 85 Jeff 66
Jesse 128 Jim 139 Jim C
21 Josephine 161 L Edith
4 Linda 114 Mack 83
Mamie 19 Mary 70
Mattie 121 Nancy 64 R I
19 Rafe 121 Robert 162
T H 105 Tom 106 Will
73 William A 88 Willie
113
DAWSON, Amos 155 Jarrett
76 Lizzie 75 Louis 152
Myra 153
DAY, Sallie 124 Tomye 117
DEADY, Ed 153
DEAN, Henry 31 Maud 121
Sallie 104
DEARBORN, F 126
DEAS, Elizabeth 107
DEASON, Eugene L 147
DEBARGO, Sam 143
DEBO, Jesse 115
DEBOS, H 156
DECATUR, Pinky 149
DECK, Mrs. L E 121
DECKER, C F 121
DEELEY, Patrick 17
DEER, Richard M 158
DEES, Mary 130 Ruby Ruth
162
DEGAN, Rafin 113
DE GRAFFENREID,
Christopher 66

DEGRAFFENREID, Emilie
118
DELKEE, Julia 76
DENEKE, G 22
DENKINS, E M 159
DENLER, Dora 124
DENMAN, Dan 70
DENNIS, Adkins 113 Edith
131 Madison J 119 Mary
123
DEPREE, Julia 84
DERBAN, Frank 33
DERERE, Mamie 147
DESIMER, Ed 50
DESOTA, Mary 148
DESOTO, J L 52
DEVENESS, J A 82
DEVIT, E R 124
DEWITT, Lizzie 93 W S 45-
46
DIAL, J C 22
DICKERSON, Noma 113
DICKINSON, Emma C 123
Julia 123
DICKLEBERRY, D F 44
DICKS, Nellie 149
DICKSON, Brown 43
Cordell 10 Daniel 92
Florence 34 George S
112 Gus 149 Joe 45 Otis
36 Perlina 120 Robert
129 Roy 117 S A 113 W
L 44
DILLARD, Addie 95
DILLINGBERGER, Mrs.

Philip 114
DILLINGER, Lizzie 69
DILLINGHAM, B 113
 Joseph 107
DILLMAN, J J 36
DILLON, Captain 18 Pearl
 154 Rachel 18
DIMICK, George G 156
DINGLE, L 124
DIVENS, Mary 138
DIXON, Grafton 73 J B 153
 Mary 107 Zola 71
DOAD, Rev. 133
DOAK, Rev. 18
DOBY, Belton 161
DOCKMAN, Charles 5
DOCKWELL, Lavina 65
DOCKY, Vance 159
DODD, Ed 8 William 161
DOLAN, William 16
DOLL, Charles 161 George
 161 H F 132 162 Howard
 F 161 Loretta 161
 Marion 161 Mary Lou
 132
DONAHUE, Eliza 114
DONDY, Peggy 60
DONEHEW, Ethel 150
DONEHUE, Emma 138
DONNER, Bertha 41
DONOHUE, John 92
DONOVAN, Daniel 138
DORA, Garrett, 93
DORCH, Earl S 95
DORDEN, Myra 117

DORIAN, B F 98 E R 76
DORINE, Loire 25
DORIS, Phebe 64
DORSER, E S 109
DORSEY, John 144
 Marcello 137 Robert 129
DORTCH, F W 59
DOTY, J E 9
DOUGHERTY, E R 161
 James 102
DOUGHTY, J 10
DOUGLAS, Abie 44 G 121
 H 68
DOUGLASS, Andrew 86
 Julia 71
DOUGLESS, Anthony 127
DOWDELL, Lina Moore
 159
DOWDEN, Mira 61 Willie
 May 48
DOWLING, Mrs. M H 35
DOZIER, John 50
DRAGON, Barina 103
DRAIN, Bessie 55
DRAKE, F L 71 Will 97
DRAUGHN, John 144
DRAY, Jake 153
DREW, Ernest 89
DREYER, Sarah 81
DREYFUS, C 16
DREYFUSS, H 110 Mrs. H
 93 Jules 79
DRISCOLL, John 75
DUBOIS, Mrs. M 97
DUBOLES, Julia 48

DUDLEY, Catherine 142
    Richard 142
DUFFY, Pat 79
DUGGARS, J W 45
DUKE, Daisy 43 Henry 160
    James C 150
DUMA, Fannie 156
DUMONT, Paralee 126
DUNAWAY, John 94
DUNBRAM, Eva 6
DUNCAN, J L 2 Lugenia
    150 W P 121
DUNDAS, R W 7
DUNDO, Leola 92
DUNK, Isaac 21
DUNKIN, John 154 W S 90
DUNLAP, Charity 72 Judith
    E 112
DUNMIRE, Nathan 108
DUNN, Christian 149 Cora
    81 Fanny 143 J A 24
DUNSMIRE, Susie 99
DUPRE, Inez 160 Levi 114
DUPREE, Annie 97 Francis
    110 L B 46
DUPUY, Evaline 149
DURDEN, Rosa 162
DURIO, R A 125
DURKEE, William B 125
DURKIN, D M 155
DURR, Emaline 23
DURRUM, Bessie 6
DWYER, Z T 24
DYAR, Elean 128
DYER, William J 78

EAKIN, Ruth 154
EALY, Clarence 45 Ida B 39
EARLS, Carlia 94
EARLY, Charles 2
EARP, W E 59
EASLEY, Charles Jr 150
    Alice 51 Ardath 145
EASTERS, Columbers 149
EBERT, E W 68
EDDINS, William H 138
EDGAR, Alfred 146
EDISON, Willie 121
EDLY, Willis 15
EDMOND, Mike 155
EDMONDS, Elizabeth 101
    Susie 110
EDWARD, Emma 41
EDWARDS, Ben 138 Cacey
    128 Effie 72 Gus 112
    Harry 84 Howard 83
    Ictavia 83 J 5 James 19
    Jesse 53 John 138
    Josephine 139 Lena 67
    Leo 130 Lizzie 48 Lula
    111 Mattie 121 Mingo
    150 Nannie 121 Newt
    141 Pearl 59 Rhoda 81
    Sally 117 T J 105
    Winston 128
EFFINGER, Nettie B 71
EGAN, J C 120 Lavina H
    120 W L 102
EILBOTT, G G 119
EISTNER, Alma 30
ELAM, Mrs. Charles 48

ELDORS, Nancy 124
ELENS, George E 16
ELESON, Maude 104
ELHIHES, Edgar 126
ELIAS, Ella 21 Lake 30
ELLINS, Sam 93
ELLIOTT, J P 46 Julian 130
　　Robert 61
ELLIS, Charles 124 Joe 30
　　139 Lloyd 125 Steve 90
ELLISON, Estelle 125
ELLMORE, Frank 139
　　Robert 107
ELSTNER, Hayden 100
　　Jennie R 100 Lee 100
　　Monroe 100 Richard 100
ELY, Louis 24
EMBERS, Rachel 39
EMERSON, Eliza 5
EMERY, Ora 18 Sam 72 83
EMLEY, Hilton 84
EMMETT, Lee 108
ENGLISH, Bashie 156
　　George 5 R E 47
ENRIGHT, John T 95
ENS, Eliza 151
ERICKSON, Ella 123
ERTZ, Marie 111
ESKRIDGE, Hilliard 30
ESTES, Rosalie 162
ETHRIDGE, Richard 138
ETON, R W 10
EVAN, A 8
EVANS, A 116 Andrew J Jr
　　128 Cecile 151 Ella 19
　　Elvie 154 Fanny 130 G
　　V 1 J 118 J R 115 L L 8
　　Margaret 139 Susan 30
　　W C 144
EVE, Mother 115
EVERETT, Donie 155
EVERHARD, J E 63
EYRE, F L 153
FAGANS, Dora 112
FAHAN, B 76
FAIRTH, Philena 59
FAIT, Will 124
FALKNER, Albert 111
FANGELL, Paris 152
FARLEY, Ben 96 J C 117
FARLY, A 95
FARMER, Evie 68 J M 16
　　Nathaniel 139 Patsy 148
　　T W 45
FARNELL, Mack 130
FARNIER, Beatrice 130
FATE, Joe 117
FAUNTLEROY, Gussie 45
　　T A 45
FAUSS, Allen 81
FAZIO, D 70 Domica 36
　　Samuel Jr 30
FEARAL, B 127
FEDUCIA, Entonia 36 Ida
　　85
FEENEY, C D 142
FELDHAUS, Mary 22
FELLOWS, E M 102
FELSCHKER, John J 124
FELTON, C M 33

FENCH, John 38
FERGUSON, Annie 19
   Annie E 143 Ida 130
   Peter 85
FERREL, Obedia B 108
FERRO, Glenn 150
FETZER, Addie M 3
FEUTIESS, Fred 102
FIDUCIO, M 70
FIELD, Mollie 109
FIELDS, Adrian 115
   Alberteen 83 Alexander
   87 Charlotte 77 F 30 J
   156 M 6 Manie 160
   Willie 147
FIGGINS, Jim 53
FILES, Charlotte 117
FILHIOL, Alfred E 60
FILMORE, George 145
FINCH, H 1
FINCHER, Nettie 114
FINDAY, Mary 106
FINDLEY, Irene 76
FINDLY, M 91
FINESTEIN, Shaag 63
FINK, Mattie May 17
FINNEGAN, J S 7 Nettie E 42
FISH, Helen 83
FISHER, Annie 96 Bessie 63
   Charles 4 D 110 Delinda
   102 Elizabeth 102 H H
   29 Hy 60 Jessie H 137 L
   H 102 Mack 8 Mollie 95
   Pearl 33

FITZPATRICK, Mary 18
FIXARY, L J 52
FLANAGAN, Jane 137
   Lucy 109
FLANAGER, Rosetta 60-61
FLAPION, Main E 29
FLEMING, Marthy 71
   Thomas 162
FLEMMING, George 105
FLETCHER, Chester L 137
   Dick 6
FLICK, A G 7 Lewis 19
FLIMMINS, Rila 61
FLINT, Henry 62 May 81
FLOOD, E R 69
FLORES, Lillie 146 Mary L
   154 R E 83 S J 62
FLORSHEIM, Blanch H 7
   Clara 141 Ida 59
FLOURNOY, Mrs. J P 3 J
   W 24 Margaret 132 Mary
   B 126 T E 64
FLOWER, Cecile 83
FLOWERS, Ben 153
   Charles 102
FLOYD, Daniel 162 Melvin
   35 Robert F 50 Willie
   145
FLYNN, Janie 21 Rapp 64 V
   157
FOGLE Jr, William R 85
FONTENETTE, August 37
FORAN, J F 35
FORD, Ada 79 Ada P 118
   Allie Gae 118 Amanda

154 Archie M 118 B F
119 Bertha 85 Mrs. Clark
116 Dora 144 Essie 75
Frank H 154 Harry 5
Herbert G 118 J W 10
Jim 33 John 48 Mrs. L T
  118 Lennie 74 Lettie 114
  Louise 113 Lucius L 118
  Oscar 42 Rebecca 153
  Richard 91 Robert 42
  Sam 24 T G 73 155
  Thomas 73 Thomas W Jr
  62 W C 68 Walter 70
  Wesley 35 William D
  118 Mrs. Zachary 118
  Zachary Taylor 118 Zack
  A 118
FOREST, Jim 131
FORKER, Albert 31
FORSHEE, Willie 39
FORSMAN, Oscar 24
FORSYTHE, Thomas 18
  107
FOSTER, Ed 86 Elsie 104
  Mrs. J C 73 James
  Martin 99 Jim 99 Luella
  D 153 Mary 2 Nellie
  Long 99 T Olive 4 W L
  99
FOUTS, Earl 65
FOWLER, Scott 45 W M 45
FOX, Carrie K 160 Mrs.
  Simon 101 S C 69 Simon
  Patrick 68 Watson 157
FRAENKEL, Palmyre 63

FRALEY, A M 119
FRAMES, Cora C 55
FRANEY, Mary A 17
FRANK, H 88 Henry 6
FRANKEL, Herbert 69
FRANKLIN, Arthur 16 Cora
  159 Curtis 130 Eva 162
  Leonard 107 Mary 62
  150 N B 97 Nancy 112
  Ruby M 107 Thelma 152
FRANKS, W J 139
FRANTZ, Dolph G 90
FRASURE, Maggie 119
FRATER, John 88
FRAWLEY, Edward B 151
FRAY, Mrs. J W 6
FRAZIER, D V 46
  Florintine 105 George 21
  Josephine 115 Kid 146
  Nellie 31
FRECHDE, T H 148
FREDIEN, Antoune 154
FREDRICK, Albert 24
FREEDMAN, Levi 47
FREEMAN, Annie 41
  Arthur 132 F G 50
  George 65 102 John 43 L
  52 Lewellin 143 Robert
  94 Willie 121
FRENCHE, George H 74
FRENCHIES, Isiah 34
FRENEBER, Sue 83
FRETTA, Joe 60
FRICK, Emma S 110
FRIE, Roberta 64

FRIEND, Hallie 88
FRIERSON, Mrs. Caro B 65
 Lucy 107
FRINCHELL, Matildy 112
FRISBIE, Hattie C 22
FRITTS, Mrs. C 5
FROIB, Pete 108
FRONER, Isa 92
FROST, Roy 62
FUCHS, John 67
FULCHER, D 107
FULCO, Annie 98 Ida 60
 108
FULLER, Eldoza 162 John
 139 Lige 108 Wesley 96
FULLILOVE, Eddra 2
 Florence N 113 S C 15
 Mrs. S C 113
FULSO, Joe 145
FULTON, Robert 115
FULWOOD, Mat 156
FURGERSON, Harry 77
FURK, J 49
FURLOW, W R 103
FURMAN, F S 93 Frank 93
 Ingersoll 8 Mary 93
 Mattie 93 Mrs. N M 93
GAGE, Vincent 16
GAHAGAN, Louis 38
GAINES, Mattie 30
GAINS, Richard 114
GALES, Phil 105
GALLAGHER, Mary 147
GALOWAY, Betsy 139
 Lillie 115 Oscar T 79
 Ruby 116
GAMBLE, Rosa 145
GAMBLIN, Vivian E 1
GAMLIN, John T 68
GANT, John 74 Lucius 137
GANVIAL, Julia 92
GARBOROUGH, Leila 103
GARCIA, C 93
GARCULIS, Bertha 16
GARDEN, Lizzie 104
GARDENER, H 98
GARDNER, Collie L 143
 Ernest 68 Maple 108
 Robert 132
GARETT, Clara 157
GARITY, Ann 54
GARLAND, W L 153
GARMONY, George M 98
GARNER, C H 37 E 121
GARRETT, Clara 144
 Clifford 112 George B
 52 Julia 44 L E 79 Leona
 29
GARY, John 157
GASKIN, Eliza 124 Ernest
 158
GASKINS, E Z 145 Kate 2
GASTON, Aline 23
GATES, Clara 110 J N 36
 Mary 68
GATLIN, Pearl 111
GAUDIN, J W 102
GAULDEN, Thelma 105
GAULDER, D 77
GAUTHREAUX, Essie 154

GAY, Fannie 69 Nanie 51
GAYLE, John Head 25 John L 25
GEAGLER, May 67
GEER, Ed 130
GEISE, Clara 50
GENTRY, Paul 141
GEORGE, Amanda 21 Mrs. C R 148 Charlie 143 James 49 James L 138 L R 90 Pearly 23 W 116 Willie 31 Willie C 47
GERMAIN, Clopha St. 40
GERMAN, C C 120
GESTINE, Jane 90
GIBBS, J C 89 Mary 60 Mollie 157
GIBSON, Bob 139 D 95 Ed 16 Gus 37 Hattie 24 J 34 John L 68 Joseph 159 Murphy 46 R H 153 Silas 20 W T 22
GIDEON, Hattie 138 Primous 45 William 158
GIDION, Cli 146
GIESEN, Marian 87
GIFFEN, Camille 3
GILBERT, Mrs. A L 120 A W 8 Ella 106 George 51 May P 78 R L 95
GILES, J G 21 James R 125 W M 149
GILFORD, R 37
GILLAN, Tom 69
GILLEN, Lillian 85 Nina 110
GILLEPSI, Pearl 41
GILLESPIE, E A 151 George M 150 152 Minnie May 151 P B 151 R M 9 R V 151 W H 151
GILLETT, Myrtle 152
GILLIAM, Orange 125
GILLIAN, Mrs. J E 16 Walter 39
GILLILAND, J B 8 J H 39 110 J L 157
GILLIS, Lucy 156
GILLS, Della 30 Hallie 126
GILMER, Susan 138
GILMORE, Birtha 23 J W 149 Robert 69 Rose 43
GINABIRTH, Florence 96
GINS, Bella 84
GIPSON, A P 35 Aline 33
GIVENS, Sue Ella 158
GLAPPION, A A 37
GLASPER, Pennie 98
GLASS, H G 157 Irvin 46
GLASSCO, Noma 109
GLASSELL, Alfred C 128 Mrs. John 128 Mary A 121
GLASSPOOL, C W 146
GLEBERMAN, Ida 143
GLEMMONS, Edith 119
GLEN, Albert 35
GLOSTER, Myrtle 144
GLOVER, Van 143
GOCH, Robert 24

GODER, M 93
GODFREY, Adella 21 Mrs. M E 18
GOETSCHEL, Evelyn 121 Hattie 119
GOFF, Joe 83
GOIN, Mattie 70
GOLBERG, Sam 20
GOLD, Lena 143
GOLDEN Jr, J E 151
GOLDENBURG, A 70
GOLDMAN, Florence 71
GOLDSBERRY, Hugh 23
GOLDSTEIN, Bertha 111
GOLSTEN, Mary 142
GONZALEZ, Corsoro 110
GOOCH, Anna 150 Orlando 21
GOOCHE, Henry 62
GOODEN, W D 145 Willis 152
GOODENOW, George I 145
GOODMAN, William H 147
GOODRICH, Ben 95 Harriett 106
GOODWIN, Gus 146 Wesley 128
GOOLEY, Mollie 103
GORDON, H C 39 Mary 33 Riley 64
GORDORF, Ellen 10
GOSHER, S 49
GOSS, Lucy 34 Pearl 21
GOSSIOA, John 156
GOTHIER, Mrs. M E 160

GRACE, Emmett 138
GRAHAM, _____ 43 Bob 129 G W 41 Gladys 5 M 39 Mary 24 Monroe 42
GRAN, H 33
GRANABERRY, Mary 151
GRANATH, Alfred 153
GRANT, Harold 92 Lewis 137 Lissie 145 Richard 91 Willie 83
GRANTHAM, Isaiah 95
GRAVENS, M 156
GRAVES, Edna 70 V C 117
GRAY, Delia 131 Elizabeth 129 Ema 8 Jessie 53 Jim 93 John 160 Klay 20 S 112 Susie 69
GRAYHAM, Bertie 115
GRAYS, Sadie 59
GRAYSON, Mina 71 W P 111
GRAZA, S P 3
GREELIE, C 40
GREEN, Ada 144 Alice 53 Alma 47 Annie B 18 Bartee 48 Carrie 102 China 98 Cleo T 131 Cozie 142 Dave 92 Ed 38 Eli 162 Emery 66 Geneva 162 Handy 87 Henry 38 74 123 J B 76 137 John 52 Johnny 148 Katie 61 71 Laura V 5 Lewis 107 Mallie 64

Margaret 68 Mary 30 47
Mollie 156 Noah 91
Noble 43 Peter 77 Robert
  149 Sarah 123
GREENBLATT, S L 158
GREENHILL, William 117
GREENING, Mrs. E A 38
GREENWOOD, Cora 116
GREER, Eddie 112 Nellie
  159
GRENIEUX, A L 38
GREY, T C 95
GRIFFIN, Cornelia 3 Ethel
  156 J A 62 James M 43
  Mattie 111
GRIFFITHS, Agnes 145
GRIGGS, C 40
GRIMES, C A 7 Thomas
  109
GRIMSTEAD, Cloteal 120
GROSBY, Eli 149
GROSJEAN, Mattie 54 V 63
  Mrs. V 63
GROSS, Thomas M 128
GROVER, Lizzie B 139
GRUBBS, Sam 155
GRUNDGONK, Anton 127
GUERRO, Antonio 158
GUETTER, E J 37
GUICE, N M 130
GUILLILAND, Ben F 46
GUNNING, Leo 16
GUNTHIER, F L 38
GUSE, Maude D 125
GUSTINE, Richard 107

GUSTUS, Ella 67
GUTH, Henry 148
GUTLER, M E 70
GUTTING, O J 22
GUY, Fannie 48 J E 49 Lily
  48 Tom T 22
GUYSLER, Martin 48
GWIN, Tobe 29
GYSPI, C M 37
HABERSON, Mrs. H L 150
HACKBACK, Willie 121
HAGAN, Wes 63
HAGEN, E M 8 Hazel Dell
  139 U B 118 W B 119
HAGER, S 6
HAINES, M 30
HAIRE, Miller 148
HALE, B 38 Charles 112
  Minnie 43
HALL, Adam 15 Add 102
  Alex 150 Allen 159
  Annie 123 Ben 115 156
  Effie 33 Elizabeth 159
  Ethel 16 Eva 116 George
  42 125 Grover 91 James
  161 James C 107 Jim 89
  John 66 Johnnie 151
  Laura 79 Lem 71 Lillian
  29 Louis 107 M 114
  Marie 86 Matt 76 May E
  31 Prymus 78 R H 68
  Richard 67 Robert J 155
  Thomas 157 W G 79
HALLBROOK, D T 155
HALSTEAD, Thomas 106

HAMANS, Eldridge H 119
HAMAS, Levina 19
HAMEL, J P 30
HAMIL, Mrs. V A 51
HAMILTON, A 2 147 Ada 59 Amanda 129 Charles 97 Ella 145 Freddie 124 L B 142 Margaret 98 Mrs. T H 6 Will 73 William 29
HAMMELL, Mrs. Charles 63 Mrs. J P 63
HAMMER, Susan 31
HAMPSON, Estelle L 121
HAMPTON, Hester 18 Jeff 86 Robert L 89 Tom 116
HANADAY, Albert 113
HANCHEY, Theodore 65
HANCOCK, Mrs. I 6
HANDY, C P 76 George 125 Nellie 119 Sam 52
HANHEIM, Samuel 152
HANKINS, Floyd 29 Lloyd 132
HANKS, David 139 John 29
HANLEY, Cora M 50-51 Green 47 M 108
HANNA, Bertha 127 Mark 141
HANNAN, J 37
HANSFORD, Julia 7
HANSON, F 98 George 48
HARBER, Savanah 137
HARBESON, W H 114
HARDEN, Wiley 127

HARDIA, Sam 86
HARDING, D F 108 E A 16 Rosemary 66
HARDMAN, C C 36
HARDWICK, C L 7 H V 128
HARDY, Horace 67 Hosey 126 Ollie 128 Quilla 76 Walker 75
HARGIS, Alice 45 Jennie 44 Q A 121
HARGSON, A 115
HARIS, J B 110 Pink 146
HARKEY, Mary 102
HARKRIDER, J C 76
HARMAN, Bertha 44 Mrs. J S 113
HARMON, Jim 115
HARNBILL, Silas 128
HAROLD, Lash 161
HARP, Agnes P 153 Bertha W 41
HARPER, Albert 125 Caterine 111 Willie 96
HARRELL, Charles 106 John 88
HARRIE, Ollie 75
HARRIS, Albert 84 Amanda 10 Aron 5 Mrs. C D 124 Carrie 24 Charles 77 Charles D 79 Charlie 105 Clarra 1 Cleo 130 Don 144 Dona 85 Emile 126 Essee 106 F N 125 Frank 98 144 Georgie 131

Henrietta 106 Jesse 126
Jessie 72 Jimmie S 150
Joe 37 John 40 119
Josephine 162 L C 118
Laura 114 Lee 70
Leonard 131 Lillian 148
M D 159 M M 157
Mamie 29 Mary 158
Mary J 111 Mattie 130
Mittie 18 P 138 Pearl 36
Simon 83 Tempsy 150 W
H 30 Willie 8 Willon 8
HARRISON, Hobson 46
Julia 103 Lillie W 89
Margaret F 50 Sadie 158
HART, Cora 32 Cora J 32
Johnnie 143 Mary 157
Peter 161 Trelie 120
HARTMAN, Bessie L 160
Trebie 52
HARTON, Fannie 22
HARTS, Mary 131
HARTSFIELD, Edna 108
HARVEY, Claudia 43
Emma 158 Henry 70 L L
79 Mary 146 Roberta 50
Will 8 William 152
HASKELL, J F 149
HASKET, Laura 118
HASSON, Albert 142
HATCHER, L B 68 Mamie
Bell 139
HATIE, W C 110
HATLER, Alice 91
HATTON, Silas 78

HATTOWAY, Gertrude 150
HAUGHTON, Ruby 52
HAURN, George 60
HAUSER, Martha 95
HAUTON, Lizzie 75
HAVELL, C E 61 Ethel 44
HAVEN, Lee 142
HAVRELL, Lillian 71
HAWKINS, Ada 139 Edwin
146 Eva 127 Evyline 85
Joana 22 Joe 5 Sal 2
HAWLEY, P 84
HAYDEN, Buford R 120
Elizabeth 24 R 6
HAYDON, M A 92
HAYES, Anthony F 85
Blanche M 139 H 29
Isabella 158 Jim 30
Maggie 37 Morris 149 R
H 3 Sam B 24 Thomas
126
HAYMES, Roberta 131
HAYNES, Alfred 78
Clarence 128-129 E P
115 Fannie 151 George
Jr 65 James 150 L 53
Mittie 17
HAYS, Blanche 138 R H 3
HAZEL, George 85
HEAD, W J 42
HEADWICK, Hartley 42
HEARD, Jim 138 Snyder 49
HEARN, Ben 68 F 36 H B
32 Mary 32 Wesley 29
HEARNE, Mrs. George M

155 Hariett 150 Mary E 83
HEART, W 6
HEARTMAN, Irene J 105
HEASY, Albert 8
HEAVES, Watson 143
HEBERT, C B 79 H 44 John R 18
HEBLER, Joe 76
HEELMERS, H 111
HEFFTE, Sam 43
HEIDINGSFIELD, J L 10
HEILPERIN, Mrs. H L 87
HEINE, Samuel H 138
HEINEMAN, Charles 124
HEISE, Julia 150
HEITER, L 51
HEITZMAN, Sue 73
HELPMAN, I I 52
HELTON, Elijah 154
HENDERSON, Alberta 138 Amanda 128 Ben 62 Caroline 1 Dinah 130 Eliza 142 George 8 H 71 Jennie 112 John S 139 Julia M 66 K 35 Kate 142 Mandy 137 Mary 105 106 112 Mollie 74 Sallie 21 Savannah 156 V A 115 Veva 90 Willie 22 31 145 Z 30
HENDRICK, A O 15 John 15 Mary 138
HENDRICKS, Tom 154 W 147
HENDRICKSON, Andrew 29
HENNERTY, James E 48
HENRY, Anderson 69 Ida 36 Josephine 91
HENSHAW, J M 124
HENSHOW, Ben 119
HENSON, F T 49 James 126
HENTON, Burt 79
HER, Robert H 154
HERBERT, John 128
HERMAN, William 149
HERNDON, D R 18 Daniel 18 J E 16 Richard 151
HEROLD, A A 125 Arthur 60 Flora 60 Henrietta 60 Joseph K 60 Lech 60 Sallie 60 Sidney H 60 Simon 60 Tom 24
HERON, Lizt 130
HERRETT, Fannie 86
HERSEY, Jessie 112
HERSON, Iona 33
HESTER, Annie 85
HETTLER, E E 43
HEWEY, Leah 130
HEWITT, Hary 102 J 41 Pearl 102
HICKMAN, John 98
HICKS, A W O 38 Alex 119 Annie Leigh 118 Bennie 84 Cal D 40 Fannie 51 Jane 139 John N 86 Mary Leta 45 Mazie 97 Rocksie 137 S H 59 S J

119 Winnie 138 Wyley 36
HICKSON, Mira 107
HIDGE, Miss E 8
HIGGINBOTHAM, John 158
HIGGINS, Hat 95 Norma 161
HIGH, Angline 141 Minnie L 34 Odessa 71
HILARD, M 162
HILBURN, Eddye 69
HILL, A 110 Annie 1 37 Ellen 44 Felix 73 George 143 Grover 88 Isom 98 Jonnie 151 Nathan 160 Owen 90 R M 72 Robert A 146 Rufus 121 T H 145 Walter 35 Willie 40 105 Zoe 75
HILLIARDS, A 29
HILLMAN, Mahley 153
HINCKLEY, Mattie 65
HINDS, L E 39
HINES, John 92 Susie 44
HINKLE, Annie 34 E M 148
HINSEY, Grace 111
HITCHCOX, I N 51
HITCHET, W F 155
HOBBY, Mrs. A E 85
HOBSON, John 88
HOCKBERGER, S 19
HODGE, A G 90 Mrs. Arthur 65 Arthur G 65 91 B L 91 Carrie Dudley 91 F 41 Ione 113 Isabelle Williamson 65
HODGES, Ben 47 H S 126 Hattie 161 Thomas F 83
HOFFHEIMER, Nettie Herold 60
HOGG, Cary 23
HOKE, D R 34
HOLBERT, Maggie P 55
HOLCOMB, Lee 152
HOLDEN, C 82 J M 107
HOLLAND, Bertie 67 Crawford 68
HOLLER, Pansy 154
HOLLIDAY, Minor 76
HOLLINER, Frances 105
HOLLIS, Clint 138 Jim 103
HOLLOWAY, B 112
HOLLOWELL, J B 159
HOLLY, Mrs. B F 142 Temple 131
HOLM, Jennie 154
HOLMAN, Charles 118 Ella 40
HOLMES, Ethel 161 Evans 62 Floyd 23 Martha 112 May 106 Sandy 89
HOLSINGER, Alice 74
HOLSTED, Vera M 77
HOLT, L 10 Nonie 158
HOOD, Julia B 85
HOOKER, John 90 Lula A 104
HOOVER, C D 33 C E 18 James 23

HOPKINS, Betty 154 C D
41 Fisher 160 Inita 153 J
Craig 36 Joseph 16
Peggy 38
HORACE, C 77
HORD, Annie 83
HORN, Jeff 7 Nora 127
Robert 84
HORREGUE, P 104
HOSS, T F 8
HOULIHAN, G H 1
HOUSE, J L 118 Mary 51
HOUSTON, Ella 60
Henrietta 78 J E 20 J R
60 Mrs. L A 36 Mertil E
125 Minta 23
HOVER, Ernest 110
HOWARD, Ambers 108 C
83 Mrs. C 7 Charlie 150
Clint 125 Edna May 24
George 23 94 Hattie M
146 Henry 31 Jake 19
Joana W 21 L H 39
Preston L 149 Ralph 53
Susie 33 Susie A 130 T
C 6 W D 149 Walter 120
Willie 30
HOWE, Annie 1
HOWELL, Amanda 113
Dena 117 Fannie 1 John
L 88 Sallie L 112 W G 3
Zack 113
HOYER, Robert 111
HUBBARD, Mack 71 Mary
Helen 137

HUBERT, Emma 131
HUCHENS, F 10
HUCHER, E O 102
HUCKINS, Mrs. Leon 144
HUDGINS, James M 130
HUDNALL, J H 139
William 156
HUDSON, B 110 F O 7 Mrs.
F O 132 Leonard 7 Mary
150 Mattie 153 Miriam
108 Rosanna 7 Tom L
153
HUEY, Ella 41 S C 155
HUFFINE, Mattie 39
HUFFMAN, Sam 104
HUGHENS, E 111 V H 81
HUGHES, Abbie C 126
Annette 160 Annie E 119
Julia A 40 L 6 Leola C
137 Leonard 36 Mary E
86
HUGHS, Sam 55
HUKI, S 47
HULDEN, Florence 118
HULER, Vink 123
HULMAN, W E 146
HULOND, John 121
HULSEMAN, F 6
HUMEAR, Howard 21
HUMPHREY, Hattie 43
HUMPHY, F J 34
HUNHANALLEN, W A 46
HUNSICKER, Carrie 101 H
17 H Jr 160 Henry 68
101 Susie 69 Susie

Elizabeth 68
HUNT, Mary V 77 Mary D
  112 Mollie 85 T M 61
  Walter 16
HUNTER, Blanche W 30
  Derry 128 Ed 70 121
  Edward 129 Harry 17
  Hazel M 69
HUNTLY, Francis 118
HURST, W J 142
HURT, Nora 21
HUSON, R T 78
HUSTON, W C 143
HUT, C L 92
HUTCHENS, C W 37
  Gladys E 158
HUTCHINS, G W 142
HUTCHINSON, Callie 153
  Robert 30 T S 10
  Theodore 68 W J 153 W
  M 85
HUTTON, Annie R 9 T H 9
HYAMS, Ella 44 Preston 4
HYDE, W H 92
HYMEL, Andrew 152
HYMES, Nelson 31
HYNES, Cleveland 126
  Nelson 68 S 80
ICE, Illmond 33
ICHER, F M 115
IDENS, A D 1
IDON, Olie 66
ILER, R L 7
ILKE, Richard 7
IMBROGULIO, J 126

INGERSOLL, Mrs. A J 99
  Andrew J 145
INGRAM, Emma L 120
  Rachel 127
IOSAS, Angiline 54
IRION, Mrs. C H 120
IRVEN, Harriett R 62
IRVINE, Mary 23
IRWIN, James 69
ISAACS, Barney 128 Mary
  127
ISHMAEL, Mamie 162
IVEY, Pearlie 154
IVORY, Perry 41
IVY, Lee 9 Sallie 86 Walter
  162
JACK, Elizabeth 138
JACKSON, A 62 Alice 111
  Allen 29 Amanda 16
  Andrew 33 87 127 Ann
  107 Annie 15 Aron 88
  Arthur 67 Bettie 90
  Charles 105 144 Charley
  124 Charlie 77 Della 74
  Dock 142 E W 77
  Elizater 126 Ella 76
  Emma 84 Eugene 77
  Fannie 78 Florence 42
  Francis 112 Frank 155
  Gabe 70 George 97 156
  Gus 146 Hannah 116
  Hattie 8 Hayward 148
  Henry 90 147 Howard 77
  Hugh 77 Hy 148 Idona
  76 J E 87 J I 69 John 3

18 137 158 Josephine 97
Leah Prudhomme 105
Lena 38 Louis 44 62 127
Mandy 156 Marks 155
Martha 118 Mary Ann
138 Mattie 51 144 Ollie
149 Paul 146 Rebecca 77
Richard 107 Robert 38
Rosa 126 Sallie Belle 77
Sally 5 Sam 9 131 Stella
34 Susie H 22 Vera 77
Viola 10 Virginia 47
Will 63 William 85
JACOB, Hattie 6
JACOBS, Alberta 71 Annie
F 32 Florence 32 Francis
Otelia 119 Henry 36
James 51 Joseph 37 Jules
150 June 108 Maggie
130 Moses P 45 Oma 83
Walter B 32
JACOBSON, Ernestine 105
M M 38 M P 60 Moses
87
JACQUET, Emile 51 85
JAMERSON, Alex 130
JAMES, B G 47 Carrie Lee
106 E B 7 Effie 155
Lavinia 109 Louis 46
Roy 162 W C 48
JAMIONS, Charlotte 129
JAMISON, Gertrude 93
Sarah 131
JANERSON, Alva 73
JARRETT, B K 86

JAY, Dallas 130
JEFFERSON, Amy 23
Carrie 68 Margret 90
Wesley 21
JEFFRIES, Blanche 148
Hester 91 James J 82
JELKS, Amanda 16 Berry
148 Mary 97
JEMEE, Mollie 78
JENKINS, Lela 105 Martha
A 117 Oscar 75 Silas 81
Sy 71
JENNINGS, Will 148
JERNIGAN, Pearl 69
JESTER, Birdie 103
JETERS, J W 16
JETSON, Niel 151
JEWITT, Ansie 52
JILES, Lizzie 39
JOHN, E T 161 Shalboy 35
JOHNIKIN, Hattie 49
JOHNS, Leon 121
JOHNSE, J W 54
JOHNSON, A J 64 A L 9
Aaron 150 Ada 126
Adam 129 Adeline 150
Al 94 Albert 36 130 Alex
92 130 Alice 1 67 94
Alice H 132 Andrew 65
Angeline 66 Angie 96
Ann 82 B 34 Banister
137 Belle 35 Belle L 155
Bennie 41 Bettie M 76
Burrus 118 C 138 C B 90
Callie 68 Camille 85

Carrie 59 113 Charles 33
47 84 96 145 Charley 69
Charlie B 162 Clara 7 85
Clober 127 Cora 54 D W
77 Dan 86 Dave 149
Delia 159 Dora 97 Mrs.
E K 132 Early 155 Eddie
131 Edith 121 Effie 119
Elen 93 Elnora 31
Elonzo 40 Emanuel 68
Emma 6 Emma L 21
Ernest 151 Esther 118 F
47 Fannie 114 Fisher 39
Frank 129 G M 123
George 69 Georgie 118
Gertrude 83 Harry 63
Hattie 24 Hattie B 59
Henrietta 3 92 Henry 15
18 139 J H 54 J T 54 141
Jane 10 Jerry 77 Jessie
64 Joe 120 John 113 114
Jonnie 127 Julius 131
King 8 Laura 61-62 66
Lee 78 Leonard 68
Loveley 36 Lula 91 105
M 21 39 40 Miss M E 16
M V 84 Mack 37 Martha
125 Martin 153 Mary
114 Mathews 40 Mattie 2
16 22 May Bell 39 Mittie
129 Mollie 131 Mose 53
Moses L 153 Nancy 158
Nathan 72 Peter 16 R 41
Rena 38 Robert 9 38
Roda 96 Rosa 88 Rufus
148 S 110 S A 105 Sam
21 60 72 84 Sarah 4 128
Susie 143 Sybe 105 T
106 T C 17 Tim 10 Tom
44 121 Vinie 127 Virge
153 Virginia 21 81-82
Wash 39 Wesley 154
Will 59 103 William 110
145 Willie 146 Winfred
89

JOHNSTONE, Dallas 92
JOINER, Tom 146
JOLLY, A 117 Alice M 118
JONAS, Annie 68
JONES, A M 46 Addie 24
Albert 19 42 Albert H 84
Andrew 147 Aron 102
Arthur 93 B W 86 Bella
160 Bessie 145 Bethusel
89 C 98 C L 2 99 Carrie
5 Charles 15 73 148
Charles J 70 Charley 162
Claude 143 159 Claude
A 3 Dixie 80 Dolly 37
Effie 82 Eliza 3 Etta 110
F F 149 F G 85 Frances
112 Frank 33 Frankie
108 Fred 62 George 85
Gussie L 159 Hattie 7
Henry 30 33 125 Henry
L 129 Ike 72 Isaiah 37 J J
113 J M 118 J P 53 J R
36 Jane 117 Jessie 55
John 85 Jospehine 1 50
Julius 33 K 42 Kathleen

E 30 Kirby S 94 Lillian 92 Liza 113 Lizzie 18 Lula 5 Mrs. Lyle 9 M 31 Mrs. M C 10 Maggie 72 Maggie L 157 Mai 92 Manury 114 Mariah 152 Marrietta 127 Martha 161 Mary 82 112 Mary Lee 72 Mattie 31 Nancy 89 Nellie 79 Ophelia 121 Parthenia 40 Paula 114 Pearl 55 Peter 130 Posey 22 Rachel 148 Rebecca 137 Robert 38 Rosa 92 Ruline 30 S B 96 Sam 32 Sam L 129 Samuel 24 Sarah 93 Sidney T 42 Singleton 90 T L 6 T M 147 Thomas 89 130 149 Victoria 84 147 Vink 138 Virginia 4 6 W 148 Walter 106 Will 84 129 William 18 129 Willie 31
JORDAN, A C 124 Ella 89 Fred 159 Julius 139 L 155 Mrs. M C 145 Mrs. T J 33 S 41 T C 85 U B 94
JOSEPH, Ameline 74 Edward 129 Emiline 75 Joe 153 Millard 137 Miller 74 Waddy 81
JOSEY, Florey 143 Josephine 157 Rena Leah 152

JOSIAH, Frank 53
JOURNET, V 124
JOVETT, J B 10
JOWELL, C R 2
JUDKINS, W D 109
KAHN, Arthur 114 Carrie Lee 10
KANE, Tom 8
KANELY, Charles 150
KARAM, Henry 70
KARPOLL, Moses 156
KATZ, A 138
KAUFMAN, Mrs. A M 87 I S 71 Sophie 60
KBOURZ, L 117
KEENE Y, A D 154 James 153
KEER, Leadie 124
KEESE, C P 83
KEISER, C W 112
KEITH, Mrs. G 7 Harry T 158 Mary W 76 Susie M 77 Mrs. W A 147
KEITH-CARLSON, Josephine 131
KELLAN, Elizabeth 16
KELLAND, Edward 152
KELLEY, Mary 146 Thomas H 142
KELLY, Anna H 52 Annie 142 Annie L 7 Annie M 154 B F 118 Emeline 64 Ernest 62 Hank 142 Joe 142 John 39 85 Leo 62 M 42 Monroe 48 Nelly

142 Paul 142 Thomas
142 Thomas H 142
Thomas J 74 W C 75
Will 142
KELSO, Ray 10
KEMP, Elvin 160 George 21
K 151 Martha 33
KEMPER, Zazli 1
KEMPT, William 149
KENDALL, Anna 101
Creno 159 Gib 138
Hattie 121 Henry 101 J
W 2
KENDRICK, A D 123 Annie
May 106 Floyd 79 R G
45
KENNEDY, Arthur 30
Dalzell 29 Dorlean 60
Estelle L 119 Ethel 81
James 70 Leola 158 Lula
119 Walter F 103
KENYON, Claude R 139 M
E 89
KERLEY, Louisie 88 Neva
111
KERRY, Emma 35
KERVIN, Agnes 32
Anthony 32 Edward 32
Nannie 32
KETTER, C E 43 P E 44
KEUGER, L S 157
KEY, Leslie 47
KEZERLE, Tony 141
KEZIAH, John 9
KILBERT, General 147

KILLINGER, Elva 95
KIMBLE, Matilda 69
KIMBROUGH, T L 54
KING, Annie 155 Carrie 78
Clarence W 83 Elizabeth
109 Grandison 50 H N
150 Hampton 20 Ike 151
J R 44 Lawrence 147
Virginia 132 Wesly 155
Willie 158
KINKLEY, W P 19
KINNEY, Annie 50 Annie C
90 Bressau 50 Francis 50
Leonard 50 Paul 50
William 50 51
KIRBY, Eunice F 110
KIRK, Mrs. E L 132 Jessie
51 N I 132
KIRKLAND, Rachel 10
KIRKLIN, Mrs. W E 151
KIRKPATRICK, C W 137
KIRN, B G 146
KIRSCH, Abe 45
KIRVIN, E S 37
KISER, George 148
KISM, Hannah 117
KITCHENS, Louisa 121
KLETHEY, Mrs. J C 147
KLINE, John J 94 M 84
Susie 102
KNIGHTON, John M 90
KNOBLE, Mrs. E 40
KNOTT, Elra 6
KNOX, Ettie 10 Lula 63
Molly 75

KOA, Manda 34
KORNEGAY, C G 104
KOSAKOFSKY, Joseph 59
   Mollie 116
KRAFT, Carl 52
KRALDICH, John J 51
KRAMER, Antone 59
KRAMEROSKI, W J 113
KREE, H C 42
KRESSE, O E 144
KROLL, Ida 68
KRUHEN, A K 41
KUCKLER, Hamp 121
KYE, Belle 29
KYTRNIKE, Stef 94
LACASH, Ben 128
LACONN, Theo 121
LACY, Frances 111
LAENGER, Charles 108
LAFALL, Lawrence 82
LAFIN, Beckie 127
LAFITTE, William 22
LAFTIN, Anna B 103
LAJAMES, Robert 138
LAKE, Jim 131
LAMBERT, Bruner 102
   Eleanor Frances 17
   Elmira 21 George 64
   Lizzie 77 T E 150
LAMBETH, D 10
LAMBKINS, Blanche 157
LAMOTHE, Albert 9
LAMPLAIN, Dora 62
LAND, Annie Burt 99 Nellie 162 Thomas L 99

LANDMAN, Ben 97
LANDRUM, Fred 153 Kate 133 N 124 Nancy 85
LANE, Charles 128 Fannie Elvie 128
LANGSTER, Will 79
LANIER, Annie 110
LAPAL, Mrs. U L 148
LARANT, D 119
LARKIN, Donovan N 143
LARNUM, Owen 138
LASHWISH, Theodore 127
LASWAH, Theodora 23
LATHAM, George W 47
LATTER, F J 68
LAVELL, Rose 96
LAW, Wallie 130 Rainie 84
LAWHON, Annie L 156
LAWLEY, W H 85 86
LAWRASON, G B 101
   Marie Benus 101 Zelia 101
LAWRENCE, Emma 103 John 115 Louise 159 Sallie 69
LAWSON, Fanny 96 N 117 R F 45
LAYSOME, H 81
LE PARD, Caroline 145
LEACH, George M 148
LEARY, Mrs. A M 31 Leslie 15
LEATON, Ruby E 126
LEAYER, Ruth 124
LECALLE, Josephine 2

LECALS, H J 2
LECK, Marie T 120
LEDDENHAM, Lydia 66
LEE, Adam 145 Caro 125
    Effie 30 Henrietta 46 Ima
    38 L 44 Leman 67 Leon
    89 T M 68 W H 93
    Willie 88
LEEDS, J M 158
LEES, Willie 130
LEGARDY, F S 97 Mary
    103
LEGG, Pauline 68
LEGGIN, J 40
LEGGIO, S 81
LEGRONE, Leon 126
LEHMAN, Carrie M 31
LEJOY, J W 106
LEMELL, H 2
LEMLE, Caroline 60 L 81
    Rosa B 81
LEMOINE, Irene L 129
    Louis P 129
LEMON, John 35 Walter
    157
LEONARD, Adeline 7 Will
    16
LEOPARD, Mary 21 N B
    157
LESEUR, Pearl 30
LESLIE, Robert 125
LETSON, Lillie 50
LEVASSER, Hilda 55
LEVISTONE, Willie 77
LEVY, E 41 Ella J 55 Jake G
    70 John 16 Marian 124
    Myrtle E 153
LEWAY, Joseph 18
LEWIS, A 42 142 Mrs. A 4
    Adline 38 Allen 16 Anna
    105 Athlene 146 B 149
    Bill 54 Charles 105
    Donnie Z 117 Ella 156
    Emily 127 Emma 103
    Ernest 85 Estelle 125 F J
    15 Felicia 47 Fred 121
    James 95 Jefferson 103
    Jerry 119 Jim 145 Joe 18
    111 John 62 Levi 112
    Lillian P 39 Lula 156
    Lula A 130 Mabel L 103
    Mamie 155 Marceline 19
    Marie A 19 May 41
    Miles 128 Nettie 124
    Sallie 106 W S 124 Will
    29 130 Willie May 108
LEYTON, W M 156
LIAS, Penny 6
LIBERTO, Mary 158
LICHIA, Katherine 34
LICHNER, May 67
LIETO, L 66
LIGINIS, Emas 37
LINCH, Lane 5
LINDLEY, Henrietta 142
LINDSAY, J 162 Ruth F 148
    W H 89
LINMAN, Herman 103
LINSON, Bill 84
LINXWILER, Jennie 10

LITTLE, Ed 53 Hervey S 154 Letta 53 Mary T 113
LIVENGOOD, C 20
LLOYD, Elsie Jacobs 81
LOCHAMER, C R 149
LOCKE, A V 19
LOCKETS, Jim 121
LOCKETT, Annie 138 Leroy 127
LOCKHART, Alice 37
LOE, Mrs. E E 91
LOEAB, Mrs. Leon 106
LOEB, Eda 106 125 Flora 19 Herbert 106 Herman 106 Mrs. Herman 106 Leon B 19 Matilda 106 Sol 106 Tillie 106
LOGAN, Gus 78 Mrs. L W 148 Nancy 147
LOMNEPIE, Edward 79
LONEY, John 32
LONG, George 47 Gladys P 151 Keno 88
LONGSDON, Mrs. J 2
LOONEY, F J 7
LOPER, E H 34
LOPEZ, Bessie 144
LORENZ, Henry 146
LORETTA, Sister 127
LOSSON, Notts 23
LOTT, Mary 29
LOTTIMORE, Jobe R 141
LOUIS, F N 55
LOVE, Augustus 75 Eddie 118 Emily 162 Henry 111 Johnie 124 Laura 126 Prince 94 Susanna 111
LOW, Lucy 92
LOWE, Albert 143 Hamilton 120 R 35
LOWENTHAL, Paul 150
LOWERY, Latha 158
LOWRY, Kate 118 W F 23
LOYD, Brinnie 24 Luke 109
LUBBER, Conrad 153
LUCAS, C H 125 Emma 143 John 76 N 117 Virginia 105
LUCHLIA, Lucy 22
LUCIEN, Henry P 124
LUCK, William 88
LUDLOM, Drew T 1
LUDOLPH, Loraine 161
LUKE, E 112
LUMAS, William 41
LUNDSFORD, O A 70
LUNSFORD, B E 151 Lena 82
LUSTER, Ben 153
LYMER, E A 54
LYNCH, Ed 93 Mrs. W S 43
LYNN, Thomas 77
LYON, William W 152
LYONS, Johnie 118
LYSLE, Kate 1
MAAS, Josephine 109
MABEN, Eva 153
MACEN, John 24
MACINTOSH, Mabel 77

MACK, Charlie 115 F 34
MACKLIN, J S 33
MACKROY, Rebecca 138
MADDRY, W D 161
MAHAN, John 6
MAHON, Nellie 6
MAIDEN, Abram 125 Isiah 108 Katie 46
MALEKOWSKE, Paul 8
MALLARD, Sallie 130
MALLORY, Gordon 1
MALONE, Mrs. R F 150
MALONEY, Joe 23 Mike 36
MALOY, Mabel 125
MALTBY, C E 76 Marion 96
MANDEL Jr, A 120
MANKHAM, Martha 50
MANLEY, Mrs. M F 6
MANN, Mary 40
MANNING, Martha 156
MANON, Mollie 132
MANUEL, Henry 121 George Jackson 127 Thomas P 111
MAPLES, Mrs. Addie C 123 Hy 6 W E 86
MARCUS, Abe 131
MARGROVE, John B 103
MARINA, Henry 139
MARINZ Jr, E P 128
MARION, George 47
MARIONEOUX, Joseph W 144
MARIONNEAUX, F L 66
Hortense 89
MARISELLI, Edgar 138
MARKHAM, Ella 15
MARKS, Allen 38 Sara 87 Stephen 24 William 84
MARMOUGET, James A 162
MARONEY, Nora 97
MARREN, Andrey 162
MARSDEN, F M 117 Mabel 46
MARSHALL, Dora 89 Ella 59 Evy 146 Fanny 124 Foster 114 Hattie 29 Henry M 93 John 29 59 John J 124 John James Sr 124 Lillian 74 Lizzie 76 Mary 124 Mattie 106 Phillip 1 Rosa 121 W C 124 W H 61
MARTELE, John 75
MARTIN, A L 149 Alice Guenemer 123 Arnold 94 Cora 7 Dave 162 Esther 116 George T 123 J M 10 James L 123 Jerry 127 Joe 78 126 Loula Boyd 61 Marguerite 123 Mary 40 N 72 Percilla 36
MARTINEZ, Fabio 68
MARVILLE, Laura A 90
MASHAW, Lucile 41
MASON, Adeline 128 Charley 152 Eliza 33 Gill 161 Joseph 91 L 123

Minnie 118 Mitchell 118 Sarah 3
MASSEY, Lee 96 Oliver C 64
MAT, Joe 62
MATASON, Vincenzo 158
MATHEWS, Dave 121 Eliza 88 George 98 Harrison 46 Mabie 32 Willie 119
MATOVICH, Carry M 105
MATRANY, Josephine 31
MATSON, Lillie 33
MATTHEWS, Allene 132 Edward E 130 Emiline 125 Mrs. Mearl 159 S W 154 T J 82
MAUS, Alice 162
MAXEY, Hessie 37
MAXIE, Alex 121
MAXING, Johnnie C 146
MAXWELL, Leota 160 P A 104 Virginia 33
MAY, Emma 158 Sallie 24
MAYBORN, Mrs. S J 4
MAYBRIGHT, M L 95
MAYER, Annie 74 August 65 Julia 94
MAYER, J D 16
MAYES, Alvin 147 Mary 148
MAYHEM, A L 119
MAYO, Bessie 102 Ethel 157 W H Jr 94
MAYOR, L 110
MAYS, A H 19 Adam 129 Charlotte 127 Sadie 141 W H 150
MAYWETHER, Early 149
MCADAMS, Emma 131 G H 67 J E 15 W F 145 William 84
MCAFEE, Mrs. Edward 31 Mrs. J M 18 Katherine 18 Katie 19 Lucile C 24
MCANALLAN, Allie 23
MCANN, Robert 83
MCBRADY, Pauline 96
MCBRIDE, Dan 35
MCCAA, C D 161
MCCABE, Alice 127 Dora 77 Laura 8 May 43 81
MCCAIN, George 131 Henry 97 Mack 49 Maddie 107
MCCALISH, Moss 112
MCCALL, Allen 105
MCCALLY, George 102
MCCANN, James 99 T E 99 Thomas E 118
MCCARTNEY, Nellie P 43
MCCAULEY, R 50
MCCLAIN, J R 72 King 84
MCCLANEY, Maude 76
MCCLARY, Ed 5
MCCLEAN, J J 158 T L 102
MCCLELLAND, J W 95
MCCLEMORE, Wilson 139
MCCLOUD, Pearl B 68
MCCLUE, Nancy 46
MCCLURE, Mrs. E 18

MCCONNELL, Rosa 43 S C 102
MCCOOL, L J 54
MCCORD, F P 41
MCCOY, Carl 76 Constant 90 Estella 79 Frank 77 Jesse 55 Lily 120 Lindsy 130 Lulla O 5 Maggie 85 Nathaniel 21 R C 84 Walter 153
MCCRACKEN, Mildred 31
MCCRAY, Mose 96
MCCUTCHEN, A M 73 Amelia Ford 73 Bessie 73 S B 73 Sam B 73
MCDADE, Broadie 89 James D 89 Nona 108
MCDANGEAL, Ora 145
MCDANIEL, Austin 147 L 107 Volney 143
MCDAVID, Tinie 147
MCDERMOTT, J M 85 James J 127
MCDONALD, Adline 88 Alma 2 Belle 94 Duncan 157 Fannie 35 Mrs. I 80 J A 111 Lee 147 Martin L 104 Robert 96 117 Ruby 87 W R 96
MCDUFF, Oscar M 128
MCDUFFIE, Henry 47
MCDUFFY, Viney 127
MCELVEEN, Fred 108
MCFARLAND, Jackson 54 John 127

MCGEE, Ella 39
MCGELLERY, Jessie 46
MCGILL, Mrs. _____ 49 Hugh W 85
MCGILLIS, Peter 18
MCGLOKEN, Mamie 69
MCGOWN, L D 19
MCGRADY, James 20
MCGRATH, Annie 128 Lillie Elizabeth 162
MCGRORY, Patrick 65
MCGRUENE, Jack 117
MCINTYRE, Stella 129 Thomas J 127
MCKASLE, Katie 148
MCKEE, L L 46
MCKEEL, F S 131
MCKENNEY, Julia 102
MCKENZIE, Fred 161
MCKIE, Chatham 138 Grace 138
MCKINEY, Beatrice 92
MCKINNEY, Banks 15 Carl 104 Joe 41 90 John 39
MCKITTREL, Anna 117
MCLAIN, H M 128
MCLAUGHLIN, Lenora 124
MCLAURIN, Felix 4
MCLEAN, Ann 96 Beatrice 71 R H 154
MCLEMO, Harriet 89
MCLEMON, John 125
MCLEMORE, Annie 96 Bain 148 R J 105
MCMACKIN, S F 162

MCMAHAN, Dennis J 107
MCMAHON, Annie M 55
    Mike 145
MCMICHAEL, William H 152
MCMILLAN, Mrs. Benton 99 Floyd 108
MCNEIL, Henry M 40 J A 139
MCPHEE, George N 42
MCPHERSON, Bertha 83 Cassie 42 E 91 Roy 59 Virginia 51
MCRAY, Albemonia 67
MCSHOW, Caroline 88
MCVEE, James 52
MCWILLIE, Felix 4
MEADE, R D 63
MEANS, Mrs. Paul 93
MEEK, Beulah May 157 Jim 158
MEEKER, Margaret 154
MEHAS, George M 152
MEIX, Josephine 21
MELADY, Andrew 64
MELTON, Minnie 101 Minnie Lee 161 Willie 146 Willie M 119
MELTSON, Freadia 18
MELZER, John 55
MERCER, Chales F 156 Emma 44 Maud E 148
MEREDITH, A E 21 Hanna 5
MEREER, M 130
MERLDON, L 120
MERRELL, Joe 36
MERRITT, Ada 69
MESSENGER, C M 126
METCALF, Inez 156 Mary Etta 15 Sadie 81 Sarah 6 V W 15
METHWIN, C 121
MEYER, Gabe 106 Mrs. Gabe 106 P B 106 Percy 106
MEYERS, Irvian 162 Joe 149 Sam J 74 Viola 124
MIDGETT, R E 67
MILES, Annie 92 Annie 54 149 Bulah 101 Della 42 Ella 31 F 7 Glen 90 J 59 J W 9 James 40 Mattie B 98 Sara 156 Tom 131 Willie 84
MILHEAM, J D 45
MILLER, Anna 69 Annie L 127 C M 40 E 110 E D 111 Elizabeth 9 Emma M 128 Frances 130 Henry 33 52 64 J A 21 Julius 60 Lillian 18 Mrs. M P 3 Maggie 128 Magnolia 5 Marion A 76 Maud 55 Robert 86 Rosa 92 Rosalee 126 Rosalie 139 Sam 33 Temmie 52 V I 66 W B 77
MILLIF, J T 119
MILLS, Ardis 82 Geneva L

152 George Hardwick
133 Pennie Ardis 120
133
MILTON, Crese 146 Durand
F 129 Lula 88
MIM, Fred 43
Mims, C R 126 Hattie 53
Sam 23 Willie 114
MINDEN, C 83 John 43
MINER, Gertrude 72
MINGE JR, C H 10
MINOR, Andrew 18
Beatrice 120 D A 5
Frank 162 Jenny 95
MITCHELL, Addie 103
Antennette 9 Bob 93
Charlie 93 Della 96
Henry 33 J 2 Jennie 156
Robert 16 153 Rock A
111 Root 151 Strother 66
MIXON, George 46
MIZE, Martha A 10
MOBLEY, Zeta M 107
MOCK, M D 24
MODKIN, James 5
MOFFIN, W G 88
MOGAN, E A 55
MOHOOFFEY, Lee 64
MOINES, E 83
MOLANT, Pete 155
MOLDON, Cornelia 147
MOLINE, A 52
MONCRIEF, Mrs. K 110
MONGOGNA, Maude 60
MONIS, Sam 111

MONROE, Ann 117 J M 92
MONSOUR, Barbara 115
Mary 145
MONTGOMERY, A C 139
F E 116 Nina 106 R M
128
MOODY, P 95
MOORE, Alice 156 Alvie
146 Bertha 34 Binnie E
114 E T 111 Edena 150
Edgar 118 Edith 120
Emma 105 George 152 J
S 24 John 83 Joice 155
Kattie 66 Mandy 65
Marie 128 Mary 90 115
Mary Belle 15 Oscar 131
142 Richard 159 Sarah
103 Sarah A 155 Susie E
112 T J 61 Mrs. Willie
143
MOOREHEAD, Florence
May 74
MORAN, Jackson 110
MORANTO, Joe 83
MORANTY, M 158
MORENT, William 109
MORGAN, Addie T 127 H 5
Inez 105 Mary 54 Robert
130 Stephen 36 W C 107
W H 45 Will 157
MORIN, William 88
MORIZAT, Charles 67
MORIZOT, Julian 103 Louis
A 130
MORLEY, Jennie 104

MORO, Margret 121
   William 154
MORRIE, E C 108
MORRIS, Bertha 19
   Ebenezer 111 H A 124 J
   C 61 Joe 29 John 90
   Lizzie 149 M 119 Mose
   71 Noah 22 W C 104
   Will 102
MORRISON, George 65 L
   81
MORTEN, J G 48
MORTON, Mrs. S E 125 W
   H 31
MOSE, Katie 105
MOSELEY, Abe 60 Adeline
   74 Major 107 P 3
MOSELY, J B 147
MOSER, H 102
MOSIQUE, Mary Ann 59
MOSLEY, Ras 89
MOSS, D E 52 E Colbert
   126 Eliza 118 119
   Florence 55 Jessie 16
   Josie Lee 160 Robert B
   137 Willie 142
MOTHER Eve 115
MOTLEY, R P 150
MOTON, Berthards 155
MOUNTFORD, Emma 115
MOYBREM, Alma 83
MOZELY, Sadie 44
MOZIQUE, Io 33
MOZUQUE, Dan 124
MUELLER, Catherine 84

MULFORD, L M 68
MULLEN, Katie 141
MULLIGAN, T R 71
MULLINS, Katie 44 O W 84
   Thomas 144
MUNIER, Rainey C 152
MUPINGTON, T T 6
MURDOCK, Will 39
MURPHY, Ed 138 Golden 6
   Hettie 87 Leslie 162
   Willie 38
MURRAY, Burt 103 Eleese
   48 Lillie 130 Ora Irene
   146 Susie 141
MURRELL, Henry 16
MURRY, Georgie 123 Sallie
   46 Will 86
MUSLIN, Jim 150
MUSTACHIA, A 83
MUTCHINSON, Joseph 104
MYER, Nathan 48
NALIN, Mrs. J J 129
NAPOLEON, Lucinda 53
NAPOLIAN, Nancy 70
NASH, Jim 150 Sadie 123
   W K 59
NEAL, J H 70 Jackson 63
   John 145 Maggie 42
   Ruby L 91 Vashti 1
   Wash 69
NEALLY, Robert 29
NEELY, Joe 150
NEIGHBORS, Beulah 157
   Charlie 113
NEILL, F W 131

NELSON, Mrs. Barton 32
  Dena 124 E D 132 E F
  145 E J 41 Emma 33
  Florence 138 George 49
  John 51 85 Lula 89
  Northe 55 Richard 88
  Sallie 41 Sarah 48 Susie
  157 Willie 22 Winnie 15
  Zola 81
NESON, Charles N 29
NETTLES, Armstead 46
  Ella 109
NEUCENT, L 35
NEVELL, Randolph 59
NEVINS, Ben 161
NEW, Amelia 37
NEWMAN, A N 123 Allie
  M 152 F 127 J F 46 M 6
NEWSON, Anna Boyd 154
NEWTON, Adline 6 Mattie
  36 Robert 2 Will 138
NICHOLS, Jake 50 John 20
NICHOLSON, Clio 104
  Mrs. D E 32 Mamie 33
NICKERSON, Casey 112
  George 24
NICKOLAS, Julie 125
NIXON, Effie May 7
NIXSON, Hellen 44
NOBLE, Agnus 88
NOBLES, Rosetta 86
NODE, Joseph 154
NOEL, J S 128
NOLAN, Lee 77
NOLES, John G 108

NOLL, James 162
NORMAN, Adline 131 Alex
  31 Edithe 64 G 47 J D
  144 James A 49 Jessie 89
NORRINGTON, Eliza 67
NORRIS, Jennie 89
NORSWORTHY, Walter 38
NORTH, William 60 91
NORTHERN, Mrs. J A 23
NORTON, E H 157 J W 51
  Mrs. J W 132 Juliett R
  51 Mrs. M E 6
NORVINSKY, Phillips 84
NORWOOD, Mabel A 152
NOTARIO, Dora 23
NOTINI, John 64 P 92
NOYD, Sallie 20
NUETT, Annie M 50
NUNERY, Nat 48
OAKS, Ruth 155
OARS, George 107
OATS, Charles 44 Dennis 20
  Floriada 17 Nannie 75
O'BRIEN, Amelia 146 Chris
  161
ODELL, Sarah J 143
ODEM, Rosa 109
ODEN, E V 1 Ethel 64 Evie
  1 Julius 55 Mary 29
  Palsey 43
ODUM, Mrs. _____ 34
O'DWYER, Frances 52
OGDEN, Jenette 130
OGILVIE, C E 70 Sam 104
OGLE, E J 159 W L 123

OGLESBY, Ella 76
OGLIVIE, Frank 44
OKEITH, Laura 5
OLDA, George 29
OLDS, Papia F 5
O'LEARY, Mrs. Frank 129
OLEARY, F C 79
OLINS, J H 7
OLIPHANT, Zach 151
OLIVER, Adam 36 B 129
    Charity 46 Josephine 126
    Leana 90 Necie 113 Sam
    Jr 120 Wilber I 139
OMLAS, Jim 54
ONEAL, A O 70 Eta 93
    Harry 50 J H 90 Joseph
    B 123 Willie 105
O'NEIL, Carrie B 144
ONEILL, Dave 160
ORANGE, Melvin 117
ORR, Dora 54 J C 64 Nellie
    131 W S 53
OSBORN, C W 10
OSBORNE, E C 116
OSTENDORF, T J 153
OUSLEY, E T 53
OUTERSIDE, Annie 62
OVERTURE, J W 75
OWEN, Columbus 147
OWENS, Della 139 Joe 151
    Mary 155 W A 139
    William 138
PACE, A 6 Martha 119
PACKLECK, Francis 93
PAGE, Benjamin Ollie 160

    Emmett 115 John 144
    Lou 91 Margret 36 Marie
    55 Thomas 34 V N 66
PALACIO, Jesua 68
PALMER, Bertha 153 C E
    83 Easter 30 Leola 53
    Mary 138 Nannie 150
    Percy 153 S 35 Vincent
    153
PAMPERTON, Mary 147
PANDER, D C 142
PARDER, Will Ann 43
PARHAM, A E 86 A J 46
    Adell 76
PARISH, Percy 81 Perry 52
    Shurley J 111
PARKER, A 160 Annis 156
    B P 152 Blake 90 C B
    138 Charles 120 Della 8
    Ella 64 Fred 156 Horace
    65 J W 44 Julia Saxton
    141 L E 130 Linda 51
    Luesia 160 M B 51 52
    Marke 138 Peter 82 S A
    45 Wash 64 Wilten 88
PARKHAM, F T 31
PARKS, Ellen 159 Jane 69
    Viola 96
PARLAVECIO, Toney 108
PARLENCHIO, Tony 156
PARNELL, Fannie 62 James
    59 Luke 146 Sallie 125
PARRY, Cora V 78
PARSONS, Bettie 2 F L 120
    Florence 37 John 55

PATE, Mamie L 7 W M 54
PATTEN, Alfred 20
PATTERSON, Alonza 138
    Amanda 45 Clara 77
    Dennis 107 Elsey 45
    Elsie 44 J R 7 Jim 4 John
    162 Louisa 139 Maggie
    129 Pickins 93 R B 17
    Sella 92
PATTON, E W 52 John J Jr
    1 Lelia M 68 Susan 36
PATZMAN, John 35 John H
    35 129
PAUL, Mrs. Otto 3
PAVEY, T N 154
PAXTON, G 6
PAYLOR, W W 158
PAYNE, Bale 152 Mrs. E
    155 E O 161 Martha 20 P
    83
PEACE, Millie 65
PEARCE, Corinne 153
    Sarah Woods 106
PEARSON, Fannie 145
PEATROSS, F E 111
PECK, G B 103
PECOR, W E 107
PEDDY, Leha 65
PEDRO, Joseph 83
PEEBLES, D E 35
PEFFER, Annie 74
PEGUES, Mary Z 102
    Willie Gray 117
PELLARS, Selma 55
PEMBERTON, Randell 104

PEMERTON, Mary 81
PENICK, Nathan T 1 Mrs.
    Nathan T 51 W S 42
PENIFF, D C 103 Dave E R
    118
PENN, J B 64
PENNINGTON, Sue M 47
PENNYWELL, Allen 35
    Alvie 6 Arnie L 87 T P
    46
PENTECOST, Mary L 71
PEPPLER, Edgar 83
PERCELL, Henry 60
PERKINS, Aaron 108
    Alberta 148 Elenora 1
    Thornton 71
PERRIN, Hattie 110 Leona
    24
PERRITT, J 123
PERRONCEL, E 6
PERRY, Anny 143
    Holcombe 74 Jack 83 L
    P 45 Pauline 31 Polly 42
    Robert 102 Voice 155
PETERMAN, Albert W 144
PETERS, Henry 36
    Hylander 19
PETERSON, A T 124
    Annette 103 Charles 157
    Lina 52 Ralph 108 Rosie
    121
PETIS, Mary 156
PETRAS, Mary B 8
PETTIC, Bettie 96
PETTIWAY, Dan 146

PEYTON, William 101
PHELPS, Add 148 Ben A 16
　Rilla 160 Ruben L 143
PHILIBERT, W P 96
PHILLIPS, Albert 69 C C
　104 Cora 66 George 41
　126 Goldie 42 Mabel 157
　R J 40
PHILSON, D V 91
PICKARD, N T 7
PICKENS, Mrs. J D 48
PICKETT, Evie 112 James
　24 Lewis 74 Mattie 158
PIERCE, Annie Jetta 60
　Clara M 18 Dock 67 Eva
　R 69
PIERSON, Sarah 44
PIKE, M E 152
PILIOT, Walter 36
PILLIPS, Rena 76
PILLOWS, Cornelius 61
PINCHERA, J A 77
PINCUS, Augusta 159
PINKNEY, Jacob 52
PIPKIN, L 103
PIPKINS, James 91
PIRARO, S 19
PLATT, Joe E 152 W H 59
　W J 131
PLAYER, Rebecca 108
PLEISANCE, J M 10
POINDEXTER, Vic 114
POLEMAN, George 92 H A
　36 Herman 109
POLITSKI, I 141

POLLARD, M L 159
POLLY, Amanda 107 John
　52
PONDER, J T 97 Rila 62 T
　S 97
POOLE, H D 62 W T 88
PORATH, Ida 102 William
　F 137
PORE, Willie 108
PORTER, Allison 45 Eddie
　Lee 41 Eliza 107 L 37
　Lillie 120 S R 62 Susie
　63 W B 125 William 78
　William C 161
POSEY, O M 121
POSTON, H 113
POTENZA, Margaret 39
POTTER, Inez M 119
POUNCY, Rosa 23
POWDRILL, Lucille 150
POWELL, Chester 144
　George 147 H P 124 J E
　95 J M 42 Jack 141 May
　L 39 Nancy 153 Tom 40
POWER, Carrie 62
PRATT, Helen 144
PRAYTOR, Francis 76
PREDO, Emaline 23
PRESCOTT, Maimie 114
　Nicie 107 Mrs. Walter
　116
PRESLAR, Flossie 29
PRESLEY, Lucy 124
PRESO, Emily 47
PRESTON, Edwin S 127

Ernest 70 Frank 150
PRESTRIDGE, Floyd 71
PRETZ, Ethel 59
PRICE, Crystal 33 F J 44
    Fannie 159 J D 71 W C
    81
PRICHARD, Cora Lee 84
PRIGGS, Gladdis 154
PRIKLE, H L 38
PRIMER, Frances 35
PRINCE, J R 119 Julius 41
PRINGLE, Bettie 107
PRINT, Mary Ann 116
PRIOR, Margaret 43
PRIRNA, B 37
PRITCHARD, Lucy 126
PROTHRO, E A 156
PROVENZA, May 83
PROVEZA, Maria 64
PRUDE, Cora 85
PRUDHOMME, A J 133
    Caro 133 Henry 77
    Jennie 109 John E 117
    Mary L 45 R L 144
PRUITT, Alice 19 R F 19
    Roy 132 Ruth 108
PRUNTY, Will 83
PRYMANS, James 43
PRYOR, Eliza 37
PUCH, Dennie L 125
PUGH, Ivie 97 J M 98
    Lillian G 5 Minnie 47
    Root 21 Virginia 107
PUNCH, Sam 23
PURNELL, Charles 106

PURSER, H M 123
PURTELL, J E 162
PURY, W D 147
PUTTEYMAN, Leala 123
QUARLES, Mary 35
QUARRIER, D W 54
QUIGLER, Murray G 126
QUINN, Emma H 92
    Maggie 149 Pink 38
RABB, Christiana 29 W M
    Jr 120
RABON, Arnett 52
RABURN, J T 67
RACALE, Dasha 22
RACCICH, Peter 104
RACHAL, Paul M 4
RADFORD, Mary 147
RAFE, J 105 Joe 47 Johnnie
    1
RAFFOLO, S 126
RAGAN, J A 65
RAGLES, Bubble 69
RAGSDATE, Frank 41
RAINEY, J W 75
RAMANGE, C S 47
RAMBO, Rosalie 159
RAMBRIS, Lula 138
RAMINGE, J E 34
RAMSAY, George D 130
RAMSEY, Maggie 107
RANDALL, John 146 Laura
    113
RANDOLPH, Alph 149
    Arthur 121 Della 124 E
    H 82 Leonard 127 Robert

90 Tom 20
RANEY, Hattie 10
RANGER, Lizzie 69
RANSON, Will 117
RAPPOLO, Dora 147 Mary 71
RASCOE, Hattie 75
RATCLIFF, Carey 110 J C 144 Laura S 148
RATZBURG, Frederick 138
RAUNCHE, Tillie 29
RAVIANA, Margia F 37
RAVINIA, Harry 36
RAWLS, M L 50
RAY, Amelia 5 Mrs. C F 145 George H 79 James 121 Martile 117 Mathew 74
RAYFORD, Sims 104
REACE, Dave 30
REAGAN, Charles 92
RECHER, Jennie 92
REDDEN, Susie W 66
REDDING, M E 156
REDWINE, D M 37 Ophelia 66
REECE, Hattie 49
REED, Ada 87 Andrew 65 Dock 79 Emerline 103 George 3 68 Janie 47 Jimmie 82 Ollie 143 Randall 82 Rebecca 88 Richard L 141 Thomas 84 Willie 84
REEDE, Octavia 93
REESE, F 6 Paul 121
REEVES, A S 87 Claudia 115 Lucy 115 Oren 19
REGGIO, Rosa Lee 144
REICE, Edith 22
REID, Clarence 101 S H 10
RELAND, W M 55
RENCHIL, Kate 118
RENDALL, Mrs. Allen 144
RENEAU, Jennie 138
RENEFRAE, Alice Y 142
RENFRO, W 3
RENON, Will 121
RESEARO, Conde 150
RETTIG, Dinah 67
REVES, Eugene 118
REVIERS, Henry 154
REVLIN, Benny 125
REYNOLDS, George 108 John C 161
RHINES, Ben 102
RHODES, T 9
RICE, Annie 125 Rufus 104
RICHARD, M M 36
RICHARDS, Fannie 69 George 127 Harriett 78 Rube 81
RICHARDSON, Ada 145 Archie 106 Celest 48 Charity 40 D C Jr 127 J M 70 John 103 L 155 L H 9 Larry 20 Mack 141 Oscar 110 Pearl 113 R D 48
RICHMOND, Daisy 150 Z

90
RICKS, Mattie 93
RIDDER, J W 82
RIDDLE, Jessie May 159
RIDENBOCH, Chloe 99
RIDER, Green 107
RIDLEY, Annie L 38
    Minnie J 40 Willie M
    129
RIFE, C G 95
RIGDON, Howard 66
    Robert 53
RIGGS, Jimmie 162
RIGSBY, Jeff 105
RIJOE, Charles 52
RILEY, Emma 16 Lilla 29
    Salina 81
RILLAR, Will 7
RIMES, George C 96
RINES, Lizzie C 50
RINGGOLD, Annie 91
RIVES, Tom 145
RIX, Louis 95
RIZER, H N 21
RIZZO, Vincenzo 97
ROACH, Allie T 152 E C 44
    Ord 120 William 127
    Willie 19
ROACHE, W M 55
ROAHITY, Mrs. S M 137
ROANS, V A 55
ROARETY, Charles 154
ROATCAP, A 148
ROBARDS, Julia White 2
ROBERSON, Belle 36 Dora
    84 Emma 51 G 142
    George 103 John 23
    Leon 114 142 Louisa 84
    Luelia 120 Nancy 139
    Ollie May 19 Racel 37
    Roberta 131 W C 59
ROBERT, Luin 7
ROBERTS, A D 153 C D
    142 Callie E 116 Codilia
    104 Rose L 77 Thomas
    G Jr 107
ROBERTSON, Alfred T 18
    Bessie 116 Gazelle 126
    H B 61 Lizzie 107 Mary
    72 Mattie 73 Oscar 69 P
    A 141 Pearl 41 R 69 R E
    40 Viola 82 Will 39
    William 62
ROBIE, Margaret D 139
ROBINSON, Adelina 138
    Ann 34 Annie 79 B 90 B
    R 151 Ben 54 Bob 150
    Carnelia 29 Caroline 44
    Carrie 95 Etta 115
    Francis 127 George 46
    Gus 155 Harrison 162
    Harry 16 118 Hattie 72
    74 Mrs. Howell 70 Ivena
    4 J R 53 Jim 81 John 86
    John P 117 Josephine 6
    95 Lena 82 Lena Ann 94
    Lizzie 127 Lula 29
    Martha 88 157 Mary A
    128 Nina 106 W 95 W H
    126

ROBSON, Ella 115
ROCHELLE, Prudie 35 Mary 153 Simmie 79
ROCKMORE, Marian 96
ROERETY, Charles 154
ROGER, Charles A 111
ROGERS, Bob 10 Charles 110 I B 143 John 101 L T 160 Mary L 153 Nathanel 24 Sara 81 W 81 Will 146
ROHMAN, H A 55
ROLAND, W J 61
ROLLEIGH, George 88
ROLLIN, Francis 93
ROLLINS, Peter 36
ROLSTON, Cevil 116 Mary L 93
ROOPE, James 23
ROQUEMORE, El 34
ROSCOE, Mrs. A F 98
ROSE, C W 41 Carlee 161 Ella 91 George Thomas 137 I D 162 Louise 29 Mariah 60 Roberta 40 Will 117
ROSELL, Memphis 113
ROSEN, Jake 127
ROSENBERG, Hilda 93
ROSS, A 156 A R 149 Alex 97 Black R 5 Corine 84 David 20 F C 5 Floyd J 161 Halie 146 Robert L 8 Tom 104 Viola 71
ROSWELL, Tom 119-120

ROTSENBERGER, A 130
ROTTSEBAL, Alvina 107
ROUCH, Ann J 149
ROUGET, Clara 94
ROUNTREE, R E 149
ROUX, Harry 83
ROWDER, L 83
ROWDY, Ed 109
ROWE, W E 22
ROWLING, Hortense 97
ROYAL, Ernest 155
ROYNOR, Ellis 143
ROYSTON, Frank 59
RUBE, Madison 115
RUBY, F 96 Watson 120
RUCKER, John L 150
RUDDER, Ben J 124
RUDY, C 113 Isah Jerome 138 L M 89 Mrs. S M 22
RUFF, Eliza 47
RUFUS, Sallie 9
RUITER, Lizzie 95
RUMKIN, Amanda 74
RUNNELS, H C 141
RUPELL, Estelle 103
RUSHDON, A D 125
RUSHING, J W 55 Tracy 4
RUSS, Octavia 39
RUSSELL, B A 46 Carrie 68 Don 116 George 116 George Jr 114 George H 116 J F 118 Janie S 23 Leon 116 Mannie 105 Susie 103 T 123
RUTHERFORD, H M 95

Mrs. S A 3 Stella E 161
RUTLEDGE, Nathan 142
SACTION, Jim 40-41
SALES, A F 156
SALMONSON, A S 81
SAMPLE, Arthur 48 Guy 48
　Fannie Guy 49 Mary
　Frances 48 O H 48
SAMUELS, Alice 95 Allen
　Jr 59 Emma 157 Miles
　22 William 86
SANDELL, E 86
SANDERS, Charles 62
　Charlie 148 Cornelius 64
　Frank 124 J Y 127 James
　W 112 Jessie Lee 31
　Mary 88
SANDORA, John 97
SANFORD, Jerrimia 111
SARGENT, Ophelia 117
SARITINA, Mary 112
SARTIN, Henry 142
SARTINI, H 92
SARTINO, Joe 44
SAUNDERS, Mary P 160
SAWYER, Corrie 146
SAXTON, Walter 160
SCANLON, Susan 81
SCARBOROUGH, D C 148
SCHAEFFER, Charles 25
　Kate 25
SCHENDLE, Joe H 145
SCHERMERHORN, T E 17
SCHILLING, J F 91
SCHILLS, J 138

SCHLIEPAK, Oscar 98
SCHOOLER, L F 156
SCHULER, Ernest 41
SCHULTZ, Mrs. Lester 145
SCHUMEPT, John I 132
SCHUTZ, Sallie 108
SCHWARTZBERG, Esther
　85 153 Henry 107 J B
　143
SCHWARTZBURG, P 110
SCOTT, A 156 Adeline 141
　Barbara 1 Bessie 101
　Betty 79 C 112 Calvin
　138 Caroline 83 Corrie
　147 Mrs. Field 82
　Geneva 61 Georgie 92
　Grant M 150 H 34 Hiser
　121 J J 54 Janie P 159
　John 78 John J 53 Mrs. L
　A 32 L L 113 Lena 158
　Martha 69 Mary 157
　Matt 96 Ollie 118 Rachel
　110 Russell 44 Zell 67
SCOVELL, M L 18 Noah 18
SCRIBER, A C 39 L L 18
　Mary L 1
SCROGINS, Jim 72
SEACER, Sam 29
SEALES, Oscar 131
SEARIS, Fannie 129
SEARLES, Feley 160
SEASTEAD, A L 18
SEAY, G D 105 Nina 10 W
　E 146
SEBASTIAN, Mary E 130

Sarah 102
SEBASTION, W M 77
SEGUE, Taylor 31
SEIBERTHALE, F 124
SELF, Ellie 68
SELGER, F 104
SELIG, S C 19
SELL, Susie 123
SELLERS, F A 91
SEMANS, Sarah 30
SEMPE, Myrtle I 155
SENORD, Eugene E 102
SERVERE, R S 18
SESSIONS, Pleas 59
SEWELL, J C 157 John 4
   Mattie 102 Mildred 4
   Rebecca 160
SEXTON, E P 102
SEYMOUR, Charles 155
SHABAY, Andrew G 157
SHACKLEFORD, Moses 106
SHAFNER, Mrs. J F 86
SHAHAN, Addie 74 J F 44
SHAMBRE, Jesse 154
SHAN, May 40
SHANDLE, Sam 36
SHANNON, George 9
   Louisa 131
SHARPE, Hamilton E 32
   Herbert 129
SHAW, D E 95 Jeff 95 Lola 143
SHEAMAN, Harry J 141
SHELAN, Mrs. Jack 116

SHELBY, Mary 139
SHELDON, Ella 61
SHELTON, Abe 15 Mrs.
   Foster 149 J L 43 John 131 Lizzie 131 Rachel 75
SHEPARD, B 90
SHEPHERD, Dick 115 J H 59 James 53
SHEPPARD, C F 7 Estelle
   Rumply 7 Julia 116
SHEPSHIRE, W M 37
SHERMAN, Henry 20
SHIDICET, Rosette 162
SHIRLEY, Mary 160 Vera May 105
SHIRRELLE, W W 64
SHIVEN, Luther 141
SHIVERS, Annie 86 Helen 45 Nathaniel 47
SHOLDEN, Lee 157
SHOUDS, Leo B 68
SHOUL, Marvin 116
SHOWERS, D J 105
SHOYD, A H 5
SHRE, Henry 62
SHREADGILL, S H 117
SHUCHLEY, H C 108
SHULTZ, August 81
SHYROCK, W L 29
SIBLEY, Annie 40 Bessie 68 Curtis 154 Mrs. J 128 R 149 R N 51
SIGHTLER, A H 52
   Gertrude 100
SIGNOR, Eli H 75

SIKES, J W 158
SILMAN, Ella 102
SILOT, Jim 21
SIMMONS, Aubert S 160
   Joe 89 95 John 48 Lena
   65 Lit 151 Mary 67
   Mattie 35 Ned 68 Oswell
   87 Rosa 60 W R 158
SIMMS, Eliza 84 F 6
SIMON, Emma 9 George 30
   Helen 60 Joseph 127
   Major 110 W J 70
SIMONS, Willie 60
SIMPSON, Annie 89 Annie
   L 29 C E 35 Gus 118
   John 22 M O 152 Mary
   113 T A 6 Will 155
SIMS, Alice 38 Everlina 97
   Fannie L 95 Florence
   107 Gus123 Hattie 59 I
   93 James L 149 John 98
   119 Julia 93 Mrs. L 37 L
   A 155 Luther 64 Mattie
   102 Miss Melvin 34
   Rosa 48 S J 24 Sallie 35
   William 103 146
SINCLAIR, Angeline 128
SINGLER, Elizzie 16
SINGLETON, William 108
SKANNAL, Neomie 52
SKIDEIT, Harry 145
SKIDMORE, Amandy 115 J
   N 160
SKINNER, Jim 103
SKOOG, Carl 101 Grover
   101
SLACK, William 36
SLAGLE, M S 99
SLATER, Eliza 129 Gus 41
SLATTERY, Ellen A 114
   Joe 148
SLOAN, Jack 5 Rosa 101
SLOANE, John 77 Julius 4
   Mary 111
SLY, Christine 161
SMALL, E H 92 Sims 116
SMIITH, Ethel 23
SMITH, A 5 41 Ada 116
   Addie 156 Alice 75
   Annie 66 125 107 Bell E
   9 Bertha 156 Burt 106 C
   155 Callie 51 Calvin 30
   Caroline 137 Carrie W 7
   Charles 4 121 Charlie 39
   Corry 115 Mrs. Dan 113
   E 70 Eddie Lee 97 Eliza
   78 Emile 91 Emma 47 91
   Ernest 110 Florence 159
   Frank 37 George 103
   Gracy 92 Gus 48 H 142
   H V 45 Hannah 16 Hardy
   137 Henrietta 127 Henry
   37 69 J 152 J B 71 J K
   151 Jasper K 98 Jerry 8
   Jim 96 Joe 49 John 5 48
   62 Joseph 123 Josephine
   46 Katey 5 L 30 34 82
   Largo 127 Laura 22
   Laurence 42 Lilie P 97
   Lillie 18 Lillie L 149

Littie 107 Little 48 Liza 154 Lizzie 92 M C 124 M E 90 Maggie 114 Margaret 70 Martha 144 Mary 123 Mary F 123 Mathilde 141 Millrage 128 Mira 61 O C 139 Patsy 142 Pheba 39 Phil 104 Phillip 22 Pressley W 100 R L 70 Richard 65 115 Robert 160 Robin L 70 Rose 41 Roxy 159 S C 54 Sarah 18 117 118 Sibel 72 Sidney 123 Silvia 131 Sophina 62 Tom 16 107 W 106 W H 82 Will 75 143 William H 113
SMITT, Margaret 150
SMOTHERS, Russell L 16
SMYRMOUDIS, F E 119
SNELL, Kate E 23 Tom 158 Walter 30
SNIDER, B F 75
SNOW, Henry 54
SNOWDEN, Frank 160
SNOWDER, Jimmie 34
SNYDER, Minnie 74
SOBER, Mary E 10
SOFIA, Frank 37
SOJOUMEN, J M 46
SOLITER, Anna 86 Felix Jr 128
SOLOME, Tom 75
SOLOMON, Archie 65

SONDEN, Precious 139
SORREL, John 131
SOUTHALL, Susie 150
SOUTHERN, Floyd 116
SPEARING, J H 3 32
SPEARMAN, Maude 68
SPEARS, John 65 Moses 78
SPECHT, Mainie O 98
SPELMAN, M 102
SPENCE, Mrs. James O 81 W M 157
SPENCER, Carrie 149
SPILKER, Media C 36
SPILLMAN, Lucinda 6
SPIVEY, Jim 130
SPRINGER, Zeb 143
SPRINGS, Jerry 148
SPROUL, George W 60
SPROUSE, William 107
SPURLINE, Blanchard 97
SPURLING, Charles 108
SPURTA, Josephine 157
SQUIRE, More 33
ST. CLAIR, Charles 72
STACKHOUSE, Lucindy 76
STACKMAN, Sarah 157
STALLINGS, W J 160
STAMM, Jennie 81
STANCE, Ira W 119
STANDEIRD, Lizzie 36
STANFORD, N 92
STANK, Joe 53
STANLEY, Jane 137 O W 124
STANTON, W A 69

STARK, Alanzo V 154
STARKS, Fannie 2 Lewis 24
    Marie 156
STARKY, Mary 159
STATON, Charlotte 60
    Dashie 158
STEERE, Grace E 78
STEERS, Lula 104 Mabel G
    76
STEIN, Annie 18
STEINS, H S 24
STEPHENS, David 112
    Edua L 137 Elizabeth
    119 Francis 9 George
    142 Georgia 117 Henry 1
    33 Ida 69 103 Joe A 130
    John W 121 W A 5
    Willie 109
STEPHENSON, A F 51 52
    Anne 1 Bow 108 D F 51
    Genevieve 146 George
    51
STERLE, Antonia 51
STERLING, Ben 9
STEVENS, A L 158 K T 67
    Marshall 118 Millie 117
    R L 17 T L 40
STEVENSON, Mary V 104
STEWARD, West 73
STEWART, Channy 125
    Clay 111 Elizabeth 66
    Ella 95 Emma 30 G 46 J
    H 161 John 37 130 L S
    70 M G 111 M I 29
    Mattie 8 Pearl 20 Robert
    74 Sam 142
STILES, Oliver A 142
STINSON, Sarah 102
STOAKS, Elgin 76
STOCKHEARD, R C 18
STOCKWELL, W H 93
STODDARD, J B 17
STOKES, H C 92 Harrison
    131 Inez 37 Mose 116
STONE, Annie 83 Charles D
    144 D H B 160 Dora A
    154
STONER, M 39 T J 81
STONEY, Hattie 137
STOREY, K C 10
STORRETT, Della 10
STOUTS, S M 144
STRATTON, Daisy 120
STRAUSS, Flora 74 M 90-
    91
STRICKLAND, J N 128
STRINGER, Henry 139
STRINGFELLOW, Miss A
    G 15 Georgia 69 Mrs.
    Levert 113
STRONG, Eliza 44 Julia 109
STRONGFELLOW, Georgia
    V 154
STROSNIDE, Mrs. H B 71
STROUD, Nancy 117
STUART, Hannah 143 John
    115
STUDEBAKER, Eugene L
    130
SUGGS, A E 158 Jennie 147

SULLIVAN, Ed 31 54 L 23 May 68 Pinky 106 Susie 61
SUMMERDON, Angeline 155
SUMMERHILL, J O 104
SUMMERLIN, J L 160
SUMRELL, H A 72 Hellen L 39 Henry Astor 121
SURRETT, Frank 133
SUSHNER, W 109
SUTHERLAND, George 95
SUTHERLIN, Mrs. Edgar 65 Mrs. W K 41
SUTLINGTON, J M 115
SUTTEN, Martha B 147
SWAN, Tena 161
SWANN, Charles 137
SWEARINGER, W H 110
SWIFT, Jim 138 P 121
SWITZER, B 112
TABER, David F 7
TABOR, Victor 37
TADD, Florence 66
TALIAFERRO, Edith 114
TALLEY, B P 146 Dixie 112
TALLY, Fanny 103
TALTON, Bert 114
TANANT, J F 69
TANNER, Mrs. B T 6 H N 145 Harriett Ruth A 72 James 74 Nellie 40 Tevey 102
TARKINGTON, Jane 21

TARLETON, W W 8
TARPLEY, J L 69
TARRANT, Lizzie 86
TATUM, R S 30
TATUN, Cilla 10
TATUNE, W O 146
TAYLOR, Alice 159 B S 110 Buck 19 Elbert 150 Ella 105 Elvira 102 Esther 119 F D 154 Frances 83 George 22 30 Gertrude 108 Hanna 141 Henry 67 Hilliard 83 J 145 James 126 138 Jessie 72 Leonard 19 Lewis 148 Mary 29 Minnie 78 Polly 95 Riley 67 Robert 155 Sarah Jane 152 Tyra 103 Vera L 59 Walter 31 Will 94 137 William 31 Zannie 95
TEACH, Lillian 153
TEAGUE, Sarah 49
TEKULSKI, Louis 37
TELL, P 21
TEMPLE, F W 116
TERRELL, James 8 Ranse 46
TERRY, Jim 67 John 159
THEBOLD, L C 124
THEO, Penny 62
THOMAS, Adelia 97 Albert 85 Alice 69 112 128 Andrew 94 143 145 Annie 48 Belle 63 Carrie

131 157 Charles 76 87
Charley 21 Clarnes 76
Clifford 103 Dan 150 Ed
44 Eliza 145 Elizabeth
159 Emma 30 F L 102
Freddie 152 George 81
141 Gus 79 Gussie 121
H J 51 H P 51 Harriett 50
Henry 22 107 114
Howard 147 Ida 117
Irene 159 Isiah 17 Janie
21 Joe 6 John 125 126
Josephine 143 Katie Bell
141 Katy 21 L H 34
Lavinia 111 Lilly 151
Lucil 121 Marah 149
Margret 29 Mary 148
157 Mike 15 Minnie 127
Mitchell 16 Mollie 77
Nannie 160 Nora 44
Ollie 52 Pearl 29 Robert
8 Rose Lee 149 Rube 85
Ruth 42 S 102 Sam 117
Savannah 110 Virginia
51 Will 110
THOMASON, Lina 152
THOMPKINS, Albin 59
THOMPSON, A P 50 Alice
    151 Annie 155 Ben F
    126 C 157 C E 42 Eliza
    104 Eula 143 F 126
    Fisher 70 Isaac 24 Jerry
    41 Katie Bell 19 Mary
    Etta 154 May 34 R L 45
    Robert 44 Salina 119

    Susie 141 Thomas 36
    Ula 59 Will 131 151
    William H 73
THOMS, H H 3
THOMSON, Robert 121
THORNE, R F 5
THORNTON, Ellen 125
    Mary L 46
THORP, Dr. 93 M D 119
THURMAN, Ella H 31
THURSTON, Julia 69
THWEATT, J R 84
TIDWELL, Sarah 66
TIERNEY, R A 114
TIFFEN, E S 111
TIFFIN, Blanche 50
TIGGS, William 148
TIGNER, L E 15 Malinda
    144
TIGNOR, Mrs. Leslie 51
TILLMAN, C 116 Mary 118
TIMBLER, Pearl 112
TIMMONS, Lula 131
    Melissa 72
TIPA, Lewis 110
TIPPS, Annie 77
TISBY, Charlie 149
TODD, Ella 29 Julia 64
TOLLIVER, V 111
TOMKIES, Llewellyn L 89
TOMPKINS, Ella 121
TOMPLIN, C 155 Clarence
    154
TONEY, Georgia 34 P 107
TONY, H A 38

TOOMBS, Arthur S 73
TOUBY, Ellen 16
TOWNSEND, W J 44
TRAPPIER, William 139
TRAVIS, Euginia 153 Joe 112
TREZEVANT, Peter J 78
TRICHEL, Clarence E 104 M C 29
TRIPLET, George 31
TRIPP, Cora E 48
TROEGEL, W A 146
TROSPER, Lena 121
TRUDEAN, Mamie 59
TRUSS, Frank 109
TUCKER, Alice 55 Charles 114 E D 80 J E 39 Jefferson 16 Mary 62 T H 6 Virgie 151
TURK, George 104
TURNER, A M 8 Annie 45 Cain 36 Carrie 91 Charles 59 Charles B 77 Ezra 139 Fannie 55 Hattie 91 114 J B 1 J Paul 143 Lou 30-31 Mary 29 64 Sarah 142 Sifana 76 Susie 146
TURNEY, Lois 144
TUTTLE, C R 144
TYLER, Augusten 46 East 144 Julia 34 M 30 Preston 107 Virginia 105
TYMAN, Emmett M 9
ULLUMS, Walter 146

UMBERHAGEN, E L 103
UNBEHAGAN, Henrietta 162
UNDERWOOD, _____ 30 Dolph 78 Hulda 102 Laura E 1
UPCHAW, Lillian 61
VACCARO, Frank 81 Marie 124
VALCHEZ, Rosa 158
VALENTINE, D N 10 J 44
VALERIN, H 92
VALLETT, E M 145
VAN CLEAVE, J J 161
VAN HOOK, Albert H 4
VAN HOOSE, Louise 75
VAN LEAR, Bille 31 John 31 Mrs. M 31 Matthew 31 Mrs. Matthew 31 Thomas 31 Will G 31
VANCE, Horwood K 144 Joe 89 John C 144 Theo 10 Mrs. W C 144
VANCLEVE, J J 124
VANDUSEN, A J 33
VANHOOSE, W A 114
VANN, Charles 77
VANSEN, Aaron 93
VANZANT, J 40
VARBLE, Gertrude 5
VARNER, Isam 43
VAUGHN, C L 131 Ed 69 Horace C 131
VEAL, Nellie E 144
VENELL, Nettie 142

VENSIN, Melvini 85
VENSON, Charles 42 T B 34
VICKERS, Roscoe 150 William 127
VICUS, S F 33
VINCENT, Ruth R 108
VINSON Jr, Elijah C 159
VINZANT, Elva 156
VIOLA, R 85 Vito 158
VISE, Girlsie 95
VLAHOYAMES, Mrs. N P 147
VOELCKER, Nellie 149
VOGEL, A 150
VOIGHT, Ida 2
VOIGT, Mrs. T L 142
VOISIN, Antionette 110 Lucile 96
VORTSEY, William 1
VOWELL, J C 47
WABERS, Clarke 98
WADE, Mrs. E A 20 Isaac 97 R H 85
WADLEY, Helene 15 Miss Severne 24 Mrs. W G 15
WAFER, Ola 42
WAGNER,_____ 30 August 54 C C 37 Charles 52 Joe 29 L E 148
WAIN, Maggie 46
WAISMAN, G W 41
WAIT, M R 62
WAITES, Luther 139 Sarah 62
WAITS, Lorita 23
WALDON, Mannie 67 Minnie 46
WALDROP, J L 103
WALDRUP, Florence 36
WALFORD, Lillian S 76
WALING, Earl 74
WALKE, C M 155
WALKER, Annie 114 Beatrice 91 Dan 73 Darkes 125 Ed 30 Emma 70 Fannie 126 Fritz 62 George 141 Georgie 90 James Sr 23 Joe L 97 Joe W 68 L G 19 L H 126 Lewis 24 Lillie 162 Marie Louise 153 Mary 154 Mattie 113 Mattie P 83 Minnie 142 Nathan 94 Nora 38 Robert 105 S 61 W J 89 Will 24 119
WALL, Edgar 67
WALLACE, D C 23 Frank 42 Harris 125 W E 105
WALLER, P L 16
WALLIS, Myrtle May 20
WALLS, Henry J 88 Julia 5 Lucy 29 S 30 Thomas 21
WALSEY, Albert 35
WALTER, A W 1
WALTERS, Eunice 147 R O 95
WALTON, Willie L 53
WANDELL, F J 64

WAPPLER, Ida 22
WARD, Edna 143 Ellen 38 Fletcher 91 G W 127 J R 6 John 114 Sallie 92 Sam 88
WARDER, Frank 81
WARE, Ben 79 Flora 50
WARING, Harriett Ruth Ann 72 W W 72
WARNER, Katie 16
WARREN, Ed 55 Lena 155 Mrs. T B 141 Thomas 82
WARRING, J 29
WART, Tom 108
WARTERS, Dollie 42
WASH, Fanny 143
WASHAM, Jessie 68
WASHINGTON, Adeline 79 Alice 155 Artella 36 Bab 116 Caroline 89 Cora 29 128 Cue 49 Daisy O 20 Ed 137 Elvira 54 G W 44 George 29 Georgie 137 Gilbert 64 H W 37 Henry 65 John 30 Kissie 75 L 157 Lavinia 84 92 Lillie 148 Maggie 94 Mandy 16 Martha 84 91 Mary 138 Matilda 35 Mollie 125 Morgan 103 Percy 149 Polly 129 Preston 29 144 Rose 42 Rozello 141 Ruby 64 Sam 89 Will 105 Zach 93
WASSINGER, H 131
WATERMAN, Mineola 153
WATKINS, Bill 146 Henry 34 Mrs. M A 3
WATSON, A 8 160 Annie E 9 B B 68 C M 50 Callie 157 Coleman 144 Dave 139 Ethel 49 Frank 109 Mrs. H D 98 159 Harry Douglas 98 J H 131 J W 47 John 109 L 84 Luda 8-9 Matthew 98 Nellie 1 Ralph 139 Sue Eleanor 98 W M 69 William 115 Willie 96
WATTS, Daisy D 115 J R 35 John 114 Lizzie 81 Lulia 105 Myrline 44 Osea 6 Rebecca 43 S S 90 Tyler 112
WAXWELL, Mary C 19
WAYMAN, Isabelle 59
WEATHERLY, G F 138
WEAVER, Elbert 54 Elda V 90 Mrs. Sam 5
WEBB, Isaac 139 J H 50 Mary 127 Mollie 147 Napoleon 52 R D 52
WEBER, H 69
WEEKS, Charley 145 George 153
WEHKE, Henry 1
WEHKIE, Maltilda 82
WEIL, Babette 90 Barbette 90 Charles 91 H M 91
WEILER, David 109

WEINSTOCK, Mrs. M 64
WEIR, Henry 71
WEISMAN, M 111
WELBORN, Fannie 45
WELCH, Bonnie B 71
WELLBORN, Sibella 60
WELLDON, Artie 45
WELLMAN, Lena 44
WELLS, Abe Jr 110 Bird M 127 Charles 83 Clarede 110 Daniel 142 Ellen 128 Frank C 106 Howard 62 Jim 19 Laura A 157 R D 78 Ruby 109 Ruby F 111 T J 69 Talbert 17 Virginia 103 Willie 40
WELSH, C 83
WENK, Victor H 102
WESLEY, Jo Anna 16 Lula 29 48 Rebecca 116 Willie 36
WEST, A B 44 Albert 131 Charles E 73 Henry 139 Julia 24 Marguerete 18
WESTCOTT, Albert C 138
WESTEHOVER, W W 151
WESTENBROKE, John W 113
WESTERN, Florence 86
WESTFALL, Henry 116
WESTMORELAND, John 138
WEVER, Bula V 15
WHALEY, John 86
WHARTON, Eugene S 9

Henry S 9 Henry Watson 9
WHEELER, C B 85 Nettie 5
WHELES, Wesley 76
WHILBY, W D 113
WHILTON, C 125
WHIPPS, Mary 126
WHIT, Mary J 7
WHITAKER, W 147
WHITE, A 29 63 Aaron 16 Ace 37 Adeline 152 Alex 3 Anna May 68 Arbella 55 Arthur 73 B 98 Bob 117 Bridgett M 21 Clarence M 159 Dr. 99 Eddie 16 Eli 114 Ellen 93 Ernest 149 Ernestine 94 Esah Allen 42 Filmore 138 Frank 52 George 66 J T 10 James L 154 Jessie 155 John 159 Leon 149 Luke 99 101 M 147 M M 75 Mary 146 Nina 112 P 35 Richard 113 Rosa 144 Sarah 95 Simon 127 Stella 110 V E 102 Violet 43 W M 67 Walter 84 William 149 Willie 87
WHITED, Margaret Bell 148 Nita 137
WHITEHEAD, E 10 Willie 162
WHITER, J G 5
WHITEWORTH, Julian E

41
WHITLATCH, C 45 John
117
WHITMAN, Myra 105
Myrtle 16
WHITMEYER, Catherine
112 W B 75
WHITTAKER, Homer 59
Joe 35 Sallie 127
WHITTED, Emanuel 72
WHITTEN, J T 82
WHITTINGTON, James E
154 Rube 47
WHITTLE, Van D 159
WICKERS, G 6
WIGGINS, Andrew 59
Charley 103 Dennis 130
Gussie 77 Leonia 59
Lizzie 88 Mary 118
WILCOX, J J 68 R J 119
WILDMAN, Arthur 6
WILER, Gilbert 115
WILEY, A 103 C 112 C H
18 George 106 Mary
May 9 Sarah 110
WILFONG, Julia 86-87
WILFORD, E H 7
WILKERSON, James 73
WILKINSON, Allie Mai 39
Britton 162 Father 129
132 J Murray 141
WILL, Comick 49
WILLEY, Fannie 116
WILLIAM, Clark 107
William J Jr 109

WILLIAMS, A 22 34 54 103
104 A J 33 Adeline 91
Alex 43 Allice 54
Anderson 141 Anna 151
Annie M 53 Arthur 143
B W 54 Bill 130 Bob 16
C B 83 Cally 115 Carrie
35 47 156 Charles 64
Claude 130 Clifton 55
Cora 46 Corine 97 125
Cy 95 Dan 152 Dave 49
Della 114 Dewitt 161
Dora 41 E D 105 Effie
106 Elijah 35 Elizabeth
161 Emma 137 Emma J
34 Eva 139 Mrs. Felix 99
Flora 35 107 Florence
111 Francis 92 Frank 24
George 44 Georgie 82 H
30 H B 151 Hallie 21
Harvey 18 Hazel 158
Henrietta 151 Henry 127
160 Horace 30 Howard
70 J 112 J B 90 131 J D
93 J M 98 James 65 71
104 120 121 125 James J
123 Jerry 115 Jim 101
113 John 81 82 John A
137 Josephine 105 Julia
55 Julius 143 Katie 160
L 117 Laura 76 Lillie
121 Lizzie 66 120 127
Lonnie 158 Louis 101
Luella 84 Lula 132 M 79
Mance 102 Mandy 93

128 Margaret 148 Mary
66 78 124 131 Mattie H
98 Mattie Lee 144
Maude 78 108 Mayfield
71 Millie 23 Minnie 41
138 Monroe 23 Myrtle
129 N B 126 Nellie 24
Newton 88 Nicholas 111
Olivar 83 Oma 159
Oscar 111 P 107 Paul
110 Peter 46 Pink 81 R N
111 Rachel 62 Rebecca
47 138 Robert K 103
Roland 124 Rose 30 78
Rufle 105 S G 8 Sam 91
96 Sarah 83 Sims 162
Stella 161 Sudie 148 U
153 Verna 33 118
Victoria 121 Virgie 127
W 6 W A 78 Walter 77
158 Will 22 Will T 118
William 87 Willie 114
Zenabia 101
WILLIAMSON, George 65
   91 Isabel Butler 91
   Isabelle Butler 65 Roland
   65
WILLIS, Edna 41 Florence
   130 James 29 Josephine
   5 Josie M 67 Mary 102
   Patsy 130
WILLOBY, N B 155
WILLOUGHBY, H L 10
WILMORE, Joe 108
WILSON, Anderson 149

Asief 141 Beatrice 130
Ben H 65 C A 43 Charles
116 Clara 121 105 E D
108 Effie L 143 Elvira
107 Emma 126 Ester 150
Exzena 33 George 59
Harvey 75 Hattie 98
Helen 79 I 112 Ida 6
Isaac 76 James 156
Jefferson C 4 Jerry 70
Joe 21 Joseph 143 L R 3
Lillie 52 Lucidy 107
Lula 29 Mattie G 150
Millie 117 Parthinia 125
Perry 92 R F 53 Robert
36 Rosetta 9 Mrs. S 4
Stella 35 Stephen 117
Susan 96 Virginia 66
Walter 159
WIMBERLY, Comfort 142
   Elizabeth 157
WIMBISH, Daisy 100
WINCHESTER, J A 21
WINDHAM, Maggie 158
   Maybelle 141 Porter 153
WINFIELD, W H 8
WINFRED, Albert 88
WINGATE, Barbara 54
   Margaret 67
WINHAM, L S 143
WINN, Annie 118 Effie 79 T
   G 41
WINSTEAD, F 102
WINSTON, Fanny 130
   Mahala 3

WINTER, Selnine 16 Stella 71
WISE, J Ben 121 Mrs. W H 33
WISEMAN, Ernest 89
WITHER, A S 22
WITHERSPOON, Thomas 40
WITT, Lurline 67
WODEN, Pope 154
WOLF, James 137
WOLFF, Mrs. E 10
WOLFRK, Addie 41
WOLZ, Eugenia 53
WOOD, Cary 106 Ira May 154 Lizzie 118 Octavia 15
WOODARD, Fannie 79 Georgie 103
WOODLARD, Hayellen 141
WOODLEY, Mattie 6
WOODRUFF, C 148 H C 21 Martha 151
WOODS, Albert 130 Annie 107 E N 4 George 85 H 112 Ida 19 Joe 113 Lelia 89 Mattie 85 Sallie 151 Thomas 71
WOODSON, Archie 127 Clara 142
WOODWARD, Dave 46 Minnie 119 William 79
WOODWORTH, Sallie 79
WOOLDRIDGE, Thomas H 66
WOOLFORD, Carrie 151
WOOTEN, Eugene 151 J E 120 S N 115
WORDS, Mary Lee 49
WORLEY, Carmelia 31
WORTMAN, Emilie 141 M E 121 Mary 92
WOUDS, Sara 61
WRIGHT, A W 8 C H 6 Earl 118 Frank 156 Fred 30 Henry 63 James 20 71 James R 79 Jeannett 105 John 88 152 Oliver 113 Sarah 22 Sherman 60 Wiley 121
WYATT, Alfred 47 Sydney 110
WYLIE, Marian D 127 R 126
WYNN, Frank 138 John 132
YARBROUGH, N 68 T M 6
YATES, T H 6
YEISER, Alphar 115 Mary A 131
YERGER, Annie 2
YERSER, James 79
YESBECK, Adalade 24
YORK, Eliza 8 Frances 141 Lucy Jane 1 Tommie 138
YOUNG, Alice 21 C 104 Celeste 78 Cole 82 D M 114 Daniel 72 Francis 30 Frank 152 Gus 101 Hy 109 Jeff 31 Lucy 77 Marian 90 Mary 160 P S

    31 Polly 38 Reed 21
    Rena 126 Sallie 137 W J
    148 Will 52
YOUREE, Henry 88
YOUST, Ada A 21
ZEFATO, Tony 71
ZEIGLER, Ethel 93 N 143
    Will 124
ZENO, Urma 3
ZIMMERMAN, Alma 110
    Girtie 86 Harry 54
ZORN, August 24

www.ingramcontent.com/pod-product-compliance
Lightning Source LLC
Chambersburg PA
CBHW070735160426
43192CB00009B/1449